W9-AXK-053

SUMNER PUBLIC LIBRARY
206 N. Railroad St.
Sumner, IA 50674

WITHDRAWN

A Full Measure

Biographies of nine soldiers, sailors and marines
who fought in World War II

By Norman Rudi

Cheers! —
Norman Rudi —

McMillen Publishing Inc.
Ames Iowa | 2005

12/05 gift

Other books by Norman Rudi

SUMNER PUBLIC LIBRARY
206 N. Railroad St.

An Iowa Pilot Named Hap | 2001

A Neighborhood of Eagles | 2003

Lang - An American Guerrilla on Mindanao P.I. | 2003

© Copyright 2005 *McMillen Publishing*

All rights reserved. No part of this book may be reproduced or transmitted in any form or by any means, electronic or mechanical, including photo-copying, recording, or by any information storage and retrieval system, without permission in writing from the publisher.

Printed by:

McMillen Publishing.
A Sigler Company

Ames, Iowa 50010
www.mcmillenbooks.com

Library of Congress Control Number: 2005908067
ISBN: 1-888223-72-3

DEDICATION

This book is dedicated to the approximately 406,000 young American men and women who lost their lives preserving freedom in the world.

and to
Michelle, Brian, Paula and Chris

TABLE OF CONTENTS

PROLOGUE

Between sixteen and seventeen million young American men and women ultimately served during the international conflict called World War II. They left the cities, small towns and rural areas to enter a whole new world, performing tasks they would never have been exposed to had they continued to remain at home recovering from the severe economic depression. Not all who served were exposed to the frightening horrors of combat. Most performed in a variety of support activities to assure our ultimate victory.

This does not intend to downplay their many contributions. The totality of war includes training, manufacturing, distribution, supply, recovery, medical services, storage, records, logistics, assembly, warehousing, delivery, camp operations, transportation of personnel and supplies, and individual tasks too specific to mention. Soldiers who guarded warehouses, marines who raised the flags on naval bases world wide, women pilots who ferried airplanes across country and to England, members of the Coast Guard who patrolled our shores, planners who labored late hours at the Pentagon, all were a major part of the puzzle supporting the soldiers, sailors, and marines who ultimately stared the enemy face to face.

The young men who by chance were chosen to carry a Garand Rifle (M-1) or Browning Automatic Rifle (BAR) or a A-20 machine gun in an effort to kill, maim, or destroy the enemy would face an enemy with absolutely the same intentions. These young American men would crawl into aluminum flying machines, or steel containers with heavy steel treads to attack and attack again an enemy who had more battlefield experience, who had lived the horrors of war, yet still possessed great national pride fighting for their cause.

As children living through the depression, young Americans had experienced limited freedoms, lack of food, and occasionally, having to do without a number of what are now called necessities. But, they had never slept in foxholes, walked for days in the rain, hacked their way through a steaming jungle, or shivered through the night lying in a snow bank trying to avoid detection. Most of them had experienced outhouses with Sears and Roebuck catalogs for toilet paper, but they were not prepared for the slit trench and defecating in front of a hundred soldiers.

Too soon they learned that when steel and flesh meet, steel wins every time.

Perhaps the navy sailors had better living conditions, sleeping in a hammock and having hot coffee available at all hours. It was a better comfort index except when their ship took a torpedo, kamikaze plane, or a hit by artillery, and surviving in oily water thousands of miles from land was unfortunately an only option.

Maintenance crews of the Thirteenth (Jungle) Air Force spent three years literally in the jungle. Visited regularly by Japanese bombers, the men lived in tents and bunkers, faced jungle insects and disease, and devastating boredom. They occasionally met a few isolated island natives, but had no relief through visiting civilized communities or meeting other military personnel. For three years they kept planes flying while living in primitive isolated conditions. They were not unlike teams of six or eight weathermen placed on isolated islands in the Aleutian chain, given six months provisions and told to make do. The harsh landscape and intensely variable climate drove strong men to near madness.

For the men who faced the realities of war, the weather, the physical discomfort, knowing the next explosion was broadcasting chunks of whirling steel meant for them, there was no respite. They were on guard at all times to protect themselves and one another, hoping the ultimate fate had passed them by.

When Abraham Lincoln stood at the site of the Battle of Gettysburg, observing the carnage of war and violation of young men as the cemetery was being dedicated, his moving words summarized the great emotions of that event. In his address, Lincoln emphasized and extolled "…from these honored dead we take increased devotion to that cause for which they gave their last full measure of devotion…"

Fortunately for the men of World War II whose stories are here retold, it was not their "last", and they returned to continue their devotion to their families, their community and to their nation. The men whose stories are related here are but a few of the many thousand who gave "…a full measure."

BOOK 1

Ralph Corbin

Ralph Corbin.

US Navy
USS Arizona
BM/2

*"They keep sending Congressmen and Senators
over to see the Arizona Memorial,
but I've never been back!"*

~ Ralph Corbin

CORBIN • CHAPTER 1

The water in the harbor was calm. A light warm breeze had not yet rif fled the waters, and it was another beautiful Sunday morning as the three men ambled to a perch on a motor housing on the fantail of the big boat. Battlewagons in the harbor were starting to see some activity as marines in dress blues appeared and assembled to raise the flag. Band members in starched white uniforms started taking their positions as 7:30am approached. The three men pulled on cigarettes, topping off a big breakfast of eggs and bacon. They joked about the marines being "bellhops for the officers" and talked about plans for next Saturday when they would have their monthly twelve-hour leave.

Duty in Pearl was not that bad. The old battlewagon needed constant maintenance, and when they had first boarded her in Seattle, she seemed large but rundown. Constant cleaning, chipping paint and continual repainting helped conceal the deleterious effects of saltwater on steel. The ship had a certain majesty that inspired the young men from the plains. Firing the big guns in training exercises and answering the call to battle stations built pride in this aggregation of young sailors in being part of the team. It was the Navy way.

The big ship was divided into sections or divisions for organization of men and their activities. Division One was the prow of the big ship and Division Four the fantail aft of the vessel. The men would stand muster in their various areas, unless the full complement of the ship assembled forward, neatly arranged for a picture. The fifty-five officers and eight hundred sixty men all in dress whites lined up in formation made an impressive sight.

Today would be another typical Sunday attending to the mundane tasks that keep a big battlewagon tidy. Dressed in white shorts, skivvy shirts, and tennis deck shoes, the men finished their cigarettes, flipping them into the water. The three young men jumped to the deck to stand at attention as the flag ceremony was about to start. Three loud explosions erupted on Ford Island across the harbor.

Ralph Corbin, Boatswain, United States Navy, a twenty-three year old farm boy from Lucerne, Missouri, stood on the fantail of the USS Arizona and watched the first explosions on Ford Island on December 7th, 1941.

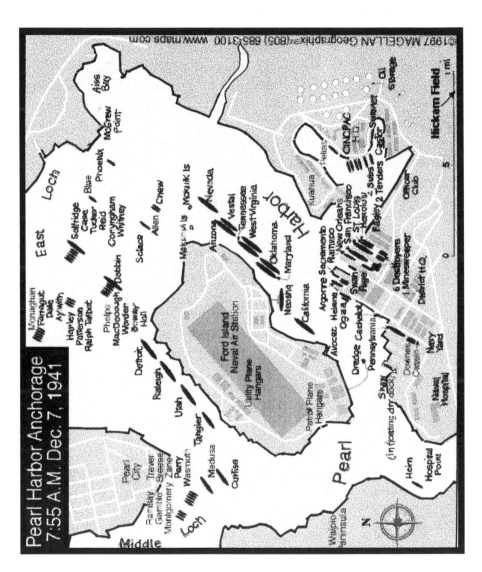

Ships in anchorage at Pearl Harbor on December 7th, 1941. The surprise attack inflicted severe damage to the Pacific fleet. Without follow-up attacks, most of the ships were repaired to see action in the south Pacific. (Map-Magellan Geographics.)

CORBIN • CHAPTER 2

Losing a farmstead during the depression was devastating to the human spirit. It happened far too often during the economic depression of the 1930's, leaving families destitute, without money, without hope, without futures. When Herman Alfred Corbin married Kitty Kay Kincade in the 1900's, there was an expansive feeling in America. During the 1920's, life was robust and good, and the farm outside Lucerne, Missouri, generated a good life and a large family. The marriage produced eleven children, first three girls, then three boys, all who kept their farmstead active and productive. Herman Corbin loved farming and made additional money shearing sheep for farmers in the area. He acquired a shearing machine that operated by turning a hand crank that caused the blades to slide. Ralph's older sisters accompanied his father on shearing jobs, taking turns cranking the machine until their arms were sore. Electric shears were new on the market, but most Missouri farms did not yet have electricity.

When the arid years of 1935 and 1936 produced no crops and payments to the bank could not be met, Herman Corbin lost his farm. He finally found work through President Roosevelt's Works Progress Administration (WPA) as a carpenter, and the one-dollar per day pay provided some food on their table, supplemented by what they could grow and shoot.

Ralph Corbin was the fifth child, the middle son of the three boys. Ralph was delivered in the farmhouse in Lucerne on November 9th, 1918. As a young child, he pulled cockleburs and picked potato bugs from the rows of potatoes in the family garden. He attended the one room school in rural Mt. Vernon and graduated from the ninth grade in 1933. In central Missouri, nine years of schooling was adequate to send young people into the work place to help pay their expenses. Ralph immediately started working as a farm hand for several adjoining farms. It was difficult finding work, as the large families in the area provided their own cheap labor.

After several years Ralph realized he was not making much progress, so in 1936 he volunteered to join the CCC, the Civilian Conservation Corps, a quasi-military organization that provided labor for many soil conservation projects in the Midwest. For his labors Ralph received thirty dollars per month, twenty-five of which was forwarded to his parents, and five dollars he kept for himself. His first job in the CCC was as a surveyor's assistant on the eastern border of Arkansas at St. Charles, along the White River, working on flood control. While working there, the area was inundated by a large flood and the surveyors spent time rescuing wild animals from the water, carrying them to safety on the dikes and levees. The work included deer, wild hogs and even bobcats, lassoing them in the water from a boat and pulling them to land where they were released. Later, CCC jobs included building farm ponds, and a road base near St. Joseph, Missouri. After one year in the CCC, Ralph returned to civilian life.

Ralph found work at a logging and sawmill operation in central Missouri, felling trees and cutting them to lengths for making pallets and other rough construction. His uncle wanted to start a coal mining operation in Missouri, so Ralph joined him as a partner in what proved to be a fruitless venture. Once again looking for work, he traveled to Kansas, where he found work delivering animal feed, coal and dairy products. While delivering milk in Wichita, Ralph discovered he was about to be let go (last man hired, first man fired!), so he visited a Navy recruiting office. They convinced him this was a good opportunity, and he signed up for a six-year enlistment.

Ralph boarded a train for the Great Lakes Naval Training Station outside Chicago, Illinois, where he took his physicals, received his shots and uniforms, and was sworn into service on October 11, 1940. Sixteen weeks later Corbin completed basic training as an ordinary seaman. His first assignment was to the Seattle (Washington) Navy Yard where the battleship USS Arizona was being refurbished in drydock.

The young lad from Lucerne was duly impressed. The Arizona was huge; 608 feet long. And impressive! It was built prior to the Great War (now called World War I) when Congress authorized its construction March 4, 1913. Anticipating the need to become a world power and requiring a Navy that reflected this importance, several large ships were approved for construction about that time. Arizona's keel was laid March 16, 1914, and launched June 19, 1915. It was finally dressed out and commissioned October 17, 1916.

The Arizona had a 97'-1" beam (widest point) that was later modified to 106'-2 _". During peacetime, it housed 915 officers and men, but during wartime, expanded to hold 1620 men. Most large ships are gauged in displaced tons and the Arizona originally displaced 31,400 tons, later modified to 32,600. Under full load it displaced 37,567 tons. The draught extended twenty-eight feet below the waterline. The big battlewagon carried 1,389,000 gallons of fuel for it's oil-fired boilers. The four propellers measuring 12'-7" in diameter were turbine-driven and the ship designed to knife through the water at 21 knots.

The USS Arizona as it appeared ready to leave Seattle mid year 1941. (Photo-US Navy)

Battleships are floating artillery bases, and in 1916 the Arizona was the finest America had to offer. It carried twelve 14" 45 caliber guns capable of firing armor-piercing shells over 18,000 yards or over ten miles. The faceplates protecting the turrets housing the big guns were all of 18" thick. In addition, the Arizona carried twenty-two 5" guns, four 3" guns and eighty .50 caliber machine guns. In Seattle, it was being re-fitted to fight against aircraft as well as other war ships.

The USS Arizona had an interesting history:

Built in the Brooklyn New York Navy Yard in 1914-15.

October 1916 - assigned to the Atlantic Fleet: WW I training in Chesapeake Bay.

November 18, 1918 - with naval force in British waters; April-July, 1919 Mediterranean Cruise.

1918-1921 - with the Atlantic Fleet; 1921-1929 with the Pacific Fleet.

1931 - carried President Herbert Hoover on cruise to the West Indies.

1936 - the filming site for the popular movie "Here Comes the Navy."

1931-1941 - with the Pacific Fleet for normal Fleet maneuvers.

Ralph Corbin reported to the Arizona and immediately started as a boatswains mate, carrying supplies and unpacking equipment aboard ship.

They worked around the clock, everyday, gaining liberty only one afternoon per month. Ralph's general quarters (in combat) was a loader in the rear turret, operating the lever that rammed the steel shells and bags of gunpowder into position for firing. It was exciting and tedious, but he accepted the Navy regimen and hard work. And, he appreciated the thirty-two dollars a month Ordinary Seamen's pay as he did not have to share it with any one. If he made Seaman First Class, he would get a whole sixty-four dollars a month.

Corbin became good friends with three young men in his division aboard the Arizona and they hung around together as buddies. Ray Crosby from Boston, Massachusetts, Don Anselmen and Robert Heinz, both from Denver, Colorado, and Corbin were usually in the same detail and in Division Four aboard the Arizona. These three friends were all Seamen First Class.

Refurbishing completed, the Arizona finally left dry dock and completed loading fuel, ammunition and supplies and left Seattle for the home port, Pearl Harbor, Oahu, Hawaii. The shakedown cruise was one long training exercise to prepare the crew for any un-expected battle. They were busy times, maintaining the ship, making adjustments in storage, and responding to general quarters. For the Missouri farm boy it could not get much more exciting.

Entering Pearl Harbor was a thrill. The assembled flotilla of naval craft was bewildering, as there were battleships, cruisers, destroyers and support ships everywhere. Once inside the harbor the USS Arizona was maneuvered into place by tugboats, and anchored in "Battleship Row" near Ford Island. It was directly behind the USS Maryland and the USS Tennessee. Paralleling the ships were the USS Oklahoma, the USS West Virginia, the Vestal (a supply ship along side the Arizona) and the USS Nevada. A floating line was immediately attached to the Arizona, to replace the fuel and oil used on their training mission.

The Hawaiian Islands were billed as paradise for the sailors, but working seven days a week for three weeks before getting a twelve-hour liberty was not exactly paradise. On Division Four's first shore leave, the four friends dressed in their white uniforms and headed for Waikiki Beach for the afternoon. They learned there was a roller skating rink in town, got directions and moved on. After three hours of skating, horseplay and checking out the young girls, they headed back to the docks to make the twelve o'clock return. No one wanted to face their Chief Petty Officer for returning late from their first leave. Most of the sailors found the Officers to be respectful and decent. Chief Petty Officers, on the other hand, were mean-spirited, ornery, demanding and unforgiving. They literally ran the Navy and made it work. With responsibilities similar to First Sergeants in the Army, sooner or later all responsibility fell on their shoulders, because they had to keep the troops in line and functioning. They were more to be feared than loved. And feared they were.

The Navy uniforms were fitted skin tight and without pockets. As a result, the sailors remained trim without unsightly distortion from bulging pockets. The added benefit was it also made it difficult to smuggle alcohol aboard ship. It was rumored that any liquor confiscated became the property of the Chief Petty Officer, but that was hard to believe.

The four men returned to the ship and continued to perform their duties, unaware that Navy leaders were very uncomfortable about developments in the Pacific Theater. They worked hard for three weeks and next Saturday afternoon would get another leave. Now was the time to start making plans for twelve hours ashore.

The USS Arizona late afternoon December 7th, 1941. By this time, Ralph Corbin was fighting fires aboard the adjoining ship, the USS Tennessee. (Photo-U S Navy)

CORBIN • CHAPTER 3

The eruptions and large plumes of smoke on Ford Island were followed by sounds of aircraft coming from several directions. An explosion rocked the Arizona. A bomb hit the control room knocking out the communications system. The band and marines scattered, while the four young sailors sat wide-eyed. A number of planes flew over with a large red dot under each wing.

"Those Japanese planes?"

"Hail, yes!"

"What the hail is going on?"

A deck officer came running to the fantail. Corbin asked "Sir, should we go to general quarters to the gun turret?"

The deck officer shouted "The turrets don't have any ammunition. Get below and run ammunition up to the five inch guns!" The men darted down the gangway to their alternate tasks, down five deck levels where the loading elevator was located. Suddenly the Arizona shook from a series of violent explosions.

Japanese planes dropped three 500 pound bombs directly over the Arizona, sending steel and debris flying in all directions. The third bomb exploded, igniting one and a half million pounds of gunpowder in the powder magazine of the Arizona, blowing away the forward third of the ship in a huge fireball, violently shaking the remaining carcass and sending water gushing through the compartments below water. All persons in the bow, forward turrets, and the bridge were killed, including Admiral Kidd and the ship's Captain Van Velkenburg.

Corbin had just reached the elevator compartment when water began to rise. The lights flickered, and the men found themselves in complete darkness. They felt their way to the passageway hatch and managed to force it open. They found the ladder and scrambled up with the water gurgling up behind them. Handrails and rungs were almost too hot to touch, but the sailors continued their climb. The acrid smoke of gunpowder filled the causeway, limiting visibility, causing them to cough violently and their eyes to burn. At each level men were screaming and moaning, crying for help. The smoke made them nauseated and dizzy as they groped upward. Reaching the main deck they were surprised to find the door hatch unlocked, and stepped out onto the debris-strewn deck. Bodies of sailors and marines were scattered about on the deck with one marine almost split up the middle, and, as the ship listed, blood and saltwater flowed in strange patterns. Corbin sat on a motor housing, hacking and coughing, clearing his lungs of the smoke, replacing it with fresh Hawaiian air. Men ambled about in a stupor, shocked by the concussion of the exploding magazine. An officer wandered by, and Corbin shouted, "Sir, what do you want me to do?" The officer looked at the chaos and with a bewildered look shouted back, "Get the hell off of the ship. It's sinking!"

Corbin worked his way through the machinery, smoke and bodies, to the rail and looked down. The sea was on fire with burning oil, dancing from oil puddle to puddle. Certainly other ships were bombed, but there was not time to look around to view the carnage inflicted by this sudden and deadly attack. Corbin saw the floating connecting supply line some distance away and decided that if he could make it safely to the line, he could work his way to shore. Spotting open seawater, free of oil, he jumped feet first through the flames and swam underwater until he could see sunlight, then broke through for air. He swam hard for a bit, then commenced to dogpaddle for several hundred yards to the floating line. He was joined by other sailors who helped each other from floating support to floating support, and they were finally able to reach Ford Island. Wading ashore, he realized for the first time he had lost a deck shoe when he hit the water.

Corbin and the sailors caught their breath and looked at the unbelievable sight of burning battleships, buildings and docks. The enormity of the damage was difficult to comprehend. If the Japanese had decided to eliminate the United States Navy, they had a damned good start. There was so much smoke it was hard to see how much damage some vessels had actually sustained.

Corbin and the men were still catching their breath when a launch came by with two sailors in it. They called out, "Get in. We need help in rescue operations!" Several men clamored aboard the launch. Corbin looked at his watch. It was only 8:30 in the morning, only one hour after the planes had first started to drop their deadly bombs.

The launch avoided the burning oil and pulled alongside sailors treading water, some severely burned. The sailors gingerly pulled them aboard. Some were fortunate enough to have found life jackets, but most were at the point of exhaustion, barely hanging on. When the boat was full, they headed to shore and helped the men up on the dock. One man headed for a maintenance hanger where there might be a vehicle to take the men to refuge. The dining hall was undamaged, and became an instant aid station. The launch pushed off for another trip around the line of battlewagons, once neatly lined up, but now in disarray.

The Vestal, a supply ship alongside the Arizona, managed to get underway, slowly heading for open water. Conditions aboard the other battleships were not so good. Flames and smoke were pouring from all of them, as their crews sprayed them with water trying to get the main fires under control. The bombing attack had lasted just thirty minutes, but the damage to facilities and ships was so great that each element had to deal with its own horrendous problems. Assistance from another source was impossible.

The launch repeated to search among the row of battleships, rescuing the living, and bypassing the young sailors showing no signs of life. Trip after trip they deposited the wounded and whole to the docks, where an ambulance had arrived to haul the men to the mess hall where they were treated. Men were burned on their hands and feet, and some had severe head burns from swimming through burning oil. Before long the launch reeked of burnt flesh, making it most uncomfortable for the rescuers as they continued their search.

By early afternoon most of the living in the immediate area had been pulled out of the water and taken to the dock. Now they began the distasteful task of pulling aboard the dead who were still floating, as well as body parts that were scattered about. The rescuers treated the men with great respect, and laid them out on the plank seating. They, too, were taken to the dock on Ford Island.

After several hours and numerous trips, another launch pulled aside with an officer on board who directed the men to report to the USS Tennessee anchored immediately behind the Arizona, to assist in suppressing the fires surrounding the ship. The launch pulled aside the battlewagon ladder and the men climbed aboard.

Most of the worst fires aboard the Tennessee had been put out, and the crew searched for trouble spots where the steel had overheated and could again start a blaze. Corbin and the men were given coffee and sandwiches and an opportunity to catch their breath. Their task aboard the Tennessee was to keep the burning oil in the harbor from reaching the sides of the ship. After a brief respite they were taken to the fantail, where they were given a fire hose under high pressure to force back the oil and the flames. The water did not put out the flames, but was forceful enough to push the oil away from the boat a safe distance. The oil was like an amoeba, crawling and creeping, following its own course as if searching for a vessel to consume. The pressure on the hose was so great that at times it almost lifted the young sailors off the deck and they struggled to maintain their footing. Several hoses worked in tandem to keep the fire not only away from the Tennessee, but from forcing the burning oil to the USS Maryland immediately behind. Opposite the Tennessee, the USS West Virginia and USS Oklahoma were battling their own fires. Throughout the night they managed to keep the burning oil from getting close to the Tennessee.

As dawn approached, they turned their hoses over to other sailors. Climbing aboard a launch, they went ashore to find a place to catch some sleep. Finding a quiet area in a shipping and receiving building, they stretched out on some packing crates too exhausted to look for something soft.

After four or five hours of sleep, they were awakened by a Chief Petty Officer who told them to carry equipment and supplies from ships stores to the dock, where it could be distributed to ships still operating in Pearl. Finding coffee and sandwiches, they started on their new assignment to haul box after box to the docks. This continued for a week, sleeping in the receiving station, and working sixteen hours a day. Fortunately, the Japanese did not make any return trips.

Every day the four buddies checked the big bulletin board, looking for another ship. A call was posted for sailors to sign onto the crew of the USS Chester, a heavy cruiser that was ready to leave port. The four friends from the Arizona decided to sign on. Checking in at the supply room, they replaced all of their lost clothing and equipment, and caught the first launch headed for the USS Chester. Finally, they would go to sea.

CORBIN • CHAPTER 4

The USS Chester, a heavy cruiser, that participated in several invasions ion the South Pacific.
(Photo-U S Navy)

The four young sailors, with duffels thrown over their shoulders, climbed the ship's ladder and with a "Permission to come aboard, Sir!" were now crewmen of the USS Chester. Not as big as a battleship, it was still imposing, and carried enough firepower to support amphibious landings throughout the Pacific. Commissioned July 3, 1929, it was built during peacetime, anticipating needs based on the Great War. A few years later, it was modified to carry six seaplanes on deck that were used for scouting and observation, with cranes necessary to place and retrieve them from the water. The ship was 576 feet long and had a beam of 66 feet. It had a range of thirteen thousand miles, traveling at fifteen knots.

The Chester carried nine 8" guns and twelve 5" guns, and later added numerous 40mm and 20mm anti-aircraft guns for protection. Once again, Corbin "general quarters" duty was to be a loader for a 5" cannon inside a turret. He settled in with the new crew and prepared for a training cruise.

The Chester left on a two-month training mission; calling to general quarters, firing their artillery, and familiarizing the crew with emergency and firefighting responsibilities. Every morning about 7:00AM, the crew stood muster where they received the orders of the day, and then went about their respective duties.

Returning to Pearl Harbor, the ship refueled and replenished the food locker, then joined a convoy headed for action in the South Pacific.

Ralph's duties as a loader inside a turret on a 5" gun required coordination and training. Each gun had a crew of four or five to service the cannon.

When a green light came on a shell would come up from below on an elevator, and roll into the loading tray. The loader would ram it forward into the chamber. Then followed one, two, or three charges of gunpowder encased in cloth bags that were also rammed into the breech by the loader. When the breech closed a red light came on, and the firing officer on the bridge would assume control over the operation. Radar aimed the cannon, and gyroscopes kept it on target when the ship was pitching and rolling. The crew would stand aside, since the cannon recoiled when fired, returning five or six feet. After firing, the breech was opened, and a jet of compressed air cleared the cannon of residual smoke and fumes. The breech operator wiped the breech clean of dirt or oil that might affect the firing process. A good crew could fire every two to three minutes. Amazingly, the crew did not wear earplugs inside the turret, even though two or three weapons might fire simultaneously.

Divisions held muster, and each Division performed their duty as assigned. Ralph took his turn in the 'crows nest' as a lookout, using powerful binoculars. Even with radar, visual sighting was very important, during both day and night. When in port Ralph was often put on Shore Patrol, the police of the Navy. Slightly built, Ralph did not fit the image usually associated with policeman.

The USS Chester supported landings on both the Marshall and Gilbert Islands, throwing heavy shells several miles inland in support of invading troops. The task force consisted of aircraft carriers, heavy cruisers, destroyers, LSTs and supply ships, everything it took to support the marines on the island. The Chester also protected supply lines, the additional ships delivering men and material. During one engagement in the Gilbert Islands, as in every battle, the task force was attacked by Japanese airplanes. This time, the Chester was singled out and attacked by several dive-bombers. As the bombs rained down, the captain of the Chester executed several tight maneuvers to avoid the dropping bombs, but finally took a direct hit on the fantail. The explosion did considerable damage to the rear structure, killing eleven men. As a result, the USS Chester withdrew from battle, returning to Pearl Harbor for a patch job to make it seaworthy.

The USS Chester underwent immediate repair. The four young sailors again checked the bulletin board and discovered the Navy was looking for volunteers with battleship experience to assist in commissioning a new battleship under construction in the U.S. Preferring to serve on 'the big ships,' the four sailors volunteered, before the Chester was scheduled to leave port. They received notice of acceptance and orders to report to the USS Massachusetts, a brand new South Dakota Class battleship

The USS Massachusetts battleship that supported landings in North Africa and the Mediterranean. (Photo-U S Navy)

nearing completion in Norfolk, Virginia. The men had a thirty-day delay-en-route travel schedule, enabling them to spend a few days at home before reporting for duty.

Ralph returned to Seattle on a liberty ship, rode the train for three days to Kansas City and finally to Lucerne, to spend a relaxing two weeks with the family. Home cooking and sleeping late were enjoyed with great relish. Also, there were no Chief Petty Officers chewing on him.

Boarding a train for Norfolk, Ralph checked into the Navy Yard upon arrival, where he was immediately put to work loading supplies and ammunition. The big battlewagon left Norfolk and traveled to Boston Harbor, where the grand commissioning ceremony was to take place. Ralph and members of the re-stocking crew moved into an old fur warehouse used as a receiving station for the goods and supplies that were to be loaded aboard the Massachusetts.

The USS Massachusetts was a magnificent new battleship. At 690 feet long, with a beam of 107'-11", it was designed to knife through the water at twenty-seven knots. The basic crew of one hundred seventeen officers and one thousand sixteen hundred seventy enlisted men increased to two thousand five hundred persons under wartime conditions. The keel was laid July 20, 1939, prior to the war, and the launch date was September 23, 1941. Displacement of thirty-five thousand tons stabilized the nine 16" cannon capable of firing armor piercing shells over forty thousand six hundred yards or twenty-three miles. In addition, it carried twenty 5" cannons, six quad 40mm cannons and twenty-two 20mm cannons. Turbines producing one hundred thirty thousand shaft horsepower turned the four big propellers, almost fifteen feet in diameter. Large turrets protected by eighteen inches of steel plate, mounted two three-gun turrets fore and one three-gun turret aft. It was the epitome of a "battlewagon."

The commissioning on May 12, 1942 was a grand event, as only Bostonians can do. There were flowers, speeches, and the christening bottle of champagne launched by Mrs. Charles Francis Adams.

The maiden cruise took them to New York, followed by a training cruise of three weeks testing all systems after which engineering adjustments were made. The ship sailed up the coast of Maine as winter approached, and the men on deck had to wear masks to protect their faces from the freezing salt spray.

After the commissioning, the USS Massachusetts joined a large convoy of troopships, supply ships, and ships of the line headed for North Africa. Supporting the Army on the first European-African invasion against the Axis, they shelled the beach and interior artillery emplacements as the landing troops advanced. On one occasion the ship was notified to stop firing their big guns, since the troops had advanced so fast they were now in range of shells fired from the Massachusetts. During the cease-fire, a German shore battery managed to bounce an artillery shell off one of the turrets. Fortunately, it did not explode, but the steel on steel made everyone's ears ring.

During the engagement, the Massachusetts dueled in an artillery battle with the French battleship Jean Bart and silenced its big guns. In another action, the Germans scuttled a German battle cruiser in the harbor alongside the docks. The cruiser's propellers were inoperable, but the ship's power was maintained in order to keep its artillery operating. The USS Massachusetts, ordered to take out the stationary ship, quieted its big guns in short order.

The big battleship then moved into the Mediterranean where it participated in several landings. During the Sicilian invasion, the battlewagon took a direct hit from an armor piercing artillery shell that penetrated the hull, exploding inside a meat storage locker. The damage was severe enough, the ship retired from battle and returned to Norfolk for repairs.

Repairs made, the ship was re-supplied, the fuel tanks holding two million eighty-five thousand gallons re-filled, and the battlewagon given a new assignment. In March, 1943, it was transferred to the Pacific Fleet and ordered to proceed to the Pacific Ocean through the Panama Canal. As the first battleship to pass through the locks, the tight squeeze was delicately handled, and the big ship made it through without incident. Now battleships played a different role, since the aircraft carrier had become the main strike force in the Pacific Theater. The ship escorted convoys, and participated in task forces, patrolling the Gilbert Islands from November 1943 to February 1944.

Ralph Corbin was promoted to Boatswains Mate Second Class, and received orders to return to the U.S. Placed aboard a troopship carrying soldiers and marines, he returned to San Diego, California. There were many wounded troops aboard, as well as soldiers being rotated for their length of service. The reassignment was disappointing to Ralph, since it broke up his group of four buddies who had served together for several years.

Arriving in San Diego, Ralph was assigned to the USS ATR-68, a sea-going tug about to be commissioned. The large tugboat, with its powerful screw propellers, sailed for the Aleutian Islands, with a homeport of Kodiak, Alaska.

The northern Pacific currents and extreme varieties of weather made delivering supplies to Aleutian outposts most difficult. Because of the volcanic origin of the islands, islands that extended over a thousand miles into the Pacific, there were no natural ports on any of them. The hidden rocks with rugged features would tear the bottoms out of ships, lessons learned from experience with great distress. The currents were unpredictable and variable, requiring a ship to remain under power at all times. Even more unpredictable was the weather. Alternating air currents from the Pacific Ocean and the Bering Sea changed weather conditions every thirty minutes; from sunshine to freezing rain, wind blasts at seventy miles per hour, dense fog, snow whiteouts or intense downpours. The unpredictability of currents and weather kept sailors busy and ship captains in a constant state of fear.

One of Ralph's duties in Kodiak Harbor was to prepare seagoing machine shops, ships with a variety of machine tools, for delivery to the Russian Navy. After installing the equipment, the ships were moved in convoy to northeastern Russia ports. After instructing the Russians how to operate the equipment, the sailors returned by plane or by boat to Kodiak. On one return trip, Ralph flew in a PBY plane that could land on water. The return flight ran into bad weather and the plane was tossed violently for several hours. Ralph became so scared he has never flown since.

Delivering supplies to Aleutian outposts was quite an exercise. The tugs would position themselves offshore, then fire a rope line to shore. The line was attached to other lines of increasing size until a rope capable of carrying the intended load was anchored. Supplies were then stacked inside a harness on a pulley and winched onto shore for unloading. Because the tug could maintain a relatively stable position in the strong currents, most deliveries were successful.

After a tour in the Aleutians, Corbin returned to the U.S. for a 30-day leave. While at home the atomic bombs were dropped on Hiroshima and Nagasaki, and the war with Japan officially over. Ralph received orders to report to the Ottumwa Naval Air Training Station in Ottumwa, Iowa, and stayed a week. He then received orders to report to Astoria, Oregon, assigned to LST-11. With a number of LSTs in port, Ralph's duties included cleaning up the ships, chipping paint, and repainting them; preparation for putting them in "moth balls" for extended storage. Since the LSTs were no longer a necessary part of the working fleet, they were placed in storage for future use.

This proved to be tedious, boring work, so Ralph put in for shore duty of some kind, or sea duty of any kind. His current assignment was not fun. His request was denied, and more LSTs were placed in moth balls.

Ralph Corbin finally received orders to report to the U.S. Navy Receiving Station, Seattle, Washington, to a separation center. He was officially discharged from the United States Navy December 2nd, 1946. He had accumulated a good deal of leave time, and was sent home, where he continued to receive military pay, clothing allowance, and other considerations until the terminal date.

Ralph's six-year enlistment was completed. He had served on two battleships, one that still rests on the bottom of Pearl Harbor. Of all of the battlewagons damaged in Pearl Harbor, only the USS Arizona, USS Oklahoma, and the USS Utah were not returned to service. Ralph Corbin had been to the Pacific Ocean, Atlantic Ocean, Mediterranean Sea, Panama Canal and the Bering Sea. He was a reluctant participant in the Day of Infamy, supported invasions in the Mediterranean and South Pacific, and participated in supply operations and escort missions. The Navy experience took Ralph Corbin a long way from rural Lucerne, Missouri.

CORBIN • CHAPTER 5

Ralph Corbin was now out of the service and searching for work, along with the other sixteen million young men and women who had left their homes to serve their country. While on leave after returning from the Aleutian Islands, Ralph had met a young lady, dating her several times before returning to duty. Violet Pauley was born in Missouri, but moved to a farm between Hampton and Alden, Iowa, at an early age. Her father worked as a hired hand on several farms in the area, but finally found steady work as the school custodian for Milford Township School, north of Nevada, Iowa. Violet attended grade school and graduated in the ninth grade in nearby Fernald School, which is also north of Nevada.

Corbin returned to the Fernald area, working as a carpenter on a variety of projects. Ralph and Violet decided to wed, and were married in Mylan, Missouri, by a Justice of the Peace, June 4th, 1949. Returning to Fernald, Ralph took a job with Walter Smay, who was manufacturing laminated members in a half-round configuration used for farm buildings and barn roof framing. Thin strips of wood were glued together with waterproof adhesive, usually one and one-half inches wide and depths ranging from two inches to twelve inches. It was an extremely efficient system designed for enclosing space used for corn storage units, machine sheds, chicken houses, and other farm structures. They were sometimes used on large corn storage units could later be converted to machine sheds, an attractive convenience for farmers.

Violet worked for Nevada Poultry for a number of years, then worked for R.H. Donnelly, a large printing firm located in Nevada. Ralph and Violet were blessed with three children. Nancy Lee, was born June 18th, 1951, Dwight Earl was born July 9th, 1953, and Dennis Dean was born September 21st, 1959. Dennis served in the military briefly, returning home after boot camp.

Ralph continued building laminated members, but after thirteen years decided he needed a raise in salary. He approached Mr. Smay, asking for a twenty-five cent per hour raise. Mr. Smay felt that ten cents per hour was adequate, and there was a marked disagreement. Ralph left his job and went to Des Moines working as a union carpenter. Ralph worked for a number of union contractors in the Des Moines environs until he retired in 1980. He continued to live in Fernald, commuting to construction sites in the area, helping to erect a number of prominent buildings.

Ralph looks back on his service experience with fond memories, and still communicates with one of his buddies from the USS Arizona and the USS Massachusetts. His living room displays memorabilia from the Arizona, including an American Flag and a list of the USS Arizona survivors. The list of the 1088 men who are still aboard the USS Arizona are on the walls of the Memorial enclosure that sits atop the remaining structure in Pearl Harbor. Also inside the rusty hulk are Ralph Corbin's personal belongings and a stack of pictures from basic training.

Ralph Corbin, who was awarded the Asiatic Pacific Medal with two stars, the American Area Medal, the European-African-Middle East Medal with two stars, the American Defense Medal with one star, the Good Conduct Medal, and the World War II Victory Medal, has never visited the USS Arizona Memorial. He states, "They keep sending Senators and Congressmen over to see the Arizona Memorial, but I have never been back."

The Arizona Memorial sits upon the remaining structure of the USS Arizona and is visited by thousands of tourists annually. A symbol of the Day of Infamy, it represents even more: of eight battleships, three were sunk and four severely damaged. Three cruisers and three destroyers were damaged. Of 394 aircraft stationed there, 188 were demolished and 159 damaged. 2403 Soldiers, sailors and marines lost their life, and 1178 were wounded. The Japanese lost twenty-nine aircraft, five midget submarines and one full sized submarine. Of the original approximately 2100 crewmembers, 1102 still remain aboard the Arizona.
(Photo-National Park Service)

BOOK 2

John C. Phillips

First Lieutenant
E Company, 2nd Battalion
424th Infantry Regiment
106th Division

*"I had many Guardian Angels
who looked after me!"*

~ John Phillips

PHILLIPS • CHAPTER 1

Fighting from house to house flushing out the German troops had taken its toll. Every corner offered a challenge, every window might conceal a sniper in the shadows, and every shot came from somewhere and went somewhere. From where to at what seemed irrelevant. To the infantryman caught in the middle, it meant a lot.

For twenty-four days the men had advanced under constant fire. Slogging through the wet snow, attempting sleep in foxholes half filled with snow and ice, and answering bullets with bullets continued day after day. The German offensive in Belgium started on the morning of December 16, 1944, with the German Army expending a full effort to drive to the city of Antwerp. There they hoped to seize the Allied fuel and supplies, as well as divide the Allied armies. They succeeded in creating a "bulge" in the Allied lines almost 60 miles deep.

Now the Germans were stopped and a counterattack initiated by cold, tired soldiers to push them back. The German Army expended its full effort in the Ardennes Forest surrounding Bastogne, and now reluctantly withdrew as it reorganized its ability to resist.

On the 24th day of the Allied counterattack, the 2nd Battalion of the 424th Regiment of the 106th Division was told to take the village of Medell, Belgium. Company E soldiers fought their way through several intense skirmishes before gaining control of the town. As night fell, the infantrymen verified the Germans were no longer in the village, and found shelter in houses, sleeping out of the weather for the first time in weeks.

Lieutenant John Phillips was totally exhausted. As executive officer of Company E, he was up early every morning assembling the men and urging them on. While searching house to house he discovered a relatively undamaged home with a bed on the second floor, and a stack of blankets. Calling to the first sergeant, he said, "I'm going to sack in. Don't let anyone bother me. Let me sleep as long as possible."

Shedding his muddy trench coat, he took off his still wet boots, loosened his shirt collar, grabbed a blanket and stretched out. His exhaustion was evident. Two deep breaths and he was sound asleep.

The sergeant was reluctant to do it, but it had to be done. He shook the lumpy form until it showed signs of life. "Lieutenant, sir, you and the Captain are ordered to report to Battalion HQ immediately."
"What time is it?"

"It's about 2:30 A.M., sir."

Phillips uttered a few choice words and rolled out, grunting as he pulled on his combat boots, tucking in his trousers and buckling the tops. He pulled on his trench coat, grabbed his metal helmet and carbine, and left the building for HQ. Finding the Command Post converted residence, he entered to find the company commanders of the regiment scattered about the dimly lit room. The Battalion Commander began. "Men, I have to know the make up of your units."

One by one the company commanders reported. The Captain of Company E responded. "We have two officers and forty-nine men."

As the company commanders finished their reports, the BC reported, "OK, Company E, your company wins the prize because it has the most men. The rest of you are excused." The commanders shuffled out. The BC continued, "Captain, Company E has to move out at dawn to secure a ridge about a mile out of town. We don't want to give the Germans a chance to counter-attack, and want to be prepared to protect the village. Have your men in position soon after dawn."

The BC continued softly, "Captain and Lieutenant, we have been attacking for over three weeks and it has not been easy, and we are all exhausted. Let me know when the ridge is secured. Rumor has it that we will remain here and will be relieved the day after tomorrow."

"I know the men will be happy about that. We'll get the men up and move out."

"Good luck, men."

Phillips found his sergeant and they started rounding up the company. As they assembled, Phillips told them their orders and the rumor that relief was on the way. The men grumbled but grimly accepted their duty, gathered their equipment, ammunition, and started hiking in the cold darkness, just as the eastern sky began to lighten.

Phillips mused aloud as they trudged along. "God, my men need rest!"

PHILLIPS • CHAPTER 2

Mac's Pharmacy was the place to hang out in West Waterloo, Iowa, if you were an athlete or hung around with athletes. After a big football game, or Sunday afternoons, and most days after school, there would be fifteen or thirty kids hanging around, doing what kids do when they hang around. In 1941, it was no different. That is until December 7th, 1941, when word was received that the Japanese had bombed Pearl Harbor. The seniors knew their lives would probably change and they just might be called into service.

John Phillips was going to graduate at midyear, in January 1941. He had hoped to go to college, but did not want to start at midyear, so he took a job at Rath Packing Company at forty cents an hour in order to accumulate enough money so he could enter college in the fall.

John was born in Henry, Illinois, where his father was president of the Henry National Bank. Clarence Phillips was a veteran of the Great War, now known as World War I. He fought in France in the battle of the Ardennes Forest with the 84th Division of the American Expeditionary Force. Clarence met Orpha Dunivan of Scranton, Iowa, when he was in training at Camp Dodge, and Orpha was attending Drake University in Des Moines. He returned after the war to marry Orpha and attend Business College so he could go into banking. Clarence and Orpha Phillips were blessed with their second son John on April 25th, 1923. One brother, William, was older by eighteen months and brother Clark was seven years younger.

Clarence A. Phillips had committed all of his funds to the Henry National Bank, and when the banks failed in 1929 all of his resources were lost. In desperation the family moved to Scranton, Iowa, to live with Orpha's parents until Clarence could find work. As a child, and later as a teenager, John loved visiting his grandparents' farm in Scranton. Grandfather Dunivan was a rural mail carrier, a valued job in those days. The Dunivan home was located on the west edge of town, right on Highway 30, known as the Lincoln Highway that ran from coast to coast.

In those days the highway always went straight through the main business district of every town. To do that in Scranton, Highway 30 made an abrupt 90-degree turn at the edge of Dunivan's backyard. Every year several large semi-trucks would misgauge the speed of the curve and roll over, dumping their contents on the grandparents' vegetable garden. It was upsetting to grandmother to see her garden ruined, but terribly exciting to the grandchildren who watched the activity of righting the truck and transferring the cargo.

Later, when John was in high school, he and brother William would spend part of the summer at their grandparents and work on a farm owned by Uncle Gordon and Aunt Mary MacDonald about five miles away. The MacDonald's had two ponies that the boys loved to ride. They would do chores and herd the six or eight milk cows while riding the ponies; for this they earned twenty-five cents an hour. The farm had many farm buildings to explore, and Aunt Mary's homemade ice cream was very special. The boys also made twenty-five cents an hour detasselling corn for the Garst and Thomas Seed Corn Company. The Garst farms in Coon Rapids, Iowa, later became famous when Russian Premier Nikita Khrushchev visited them in September of 1959.

Clarence Phillips finally found work in northeast Iowa, and moved his family to Waterloo where John attended West Waterloo High School. John loved attending high school, where he was president of the student body, and participated in football, basketball, tennis, band and orchestra. Although his two brothers were six foot two, John was five foot eight and one hundred fifty-five pounds, but that did not keep him from participating and doing his best. During John's senior year, Clarence Phillips became the manager of the Chamber of Commerce in Algona, Iowa and the family moved to the small town. John wanted to finish school in Waterloo, so he lived with friends until school was over. When he went to work at Rath Packing Company he lived at the YMCA for four dollars a week.

In September, John attended Iowa State Teachers College in Cedar Falls, taking pre-law. While attending ISTC, some friends who were attending the University of Iowa learned that the Federal Bureau of Investigation was desperate for workers and was advertising nationwide for employees. Those hired would be deferred from the draft and military service. John and five of his young friends sent in their applications, and soon FBI men questioned the young men's neighbors about the boys' loyalty, veracity, and matters of security. They were all accepted by the FBI, boarded a train for Washington, D.C. and reported to FBI headquarters. They managed to find housing in a private home in Tacoma Park, Maryland, a suburb of Washington, DC. The men received their assignments that covered most of the activities of the bureau; one worked in Files, one in Finger Prints, one in Special Files, one in an Administrative Office, and one became a Messenger. John worked an eleven-to-seven shift, so he slept during the daytime. He discovered he could take classes at George Washington University, and signed up for one class during summer session.

During their internship the young men watched an interesting event unfold. Eight German saboteurs were in custody at headquarters. Four had been put ashore by the German Submarine V-202 near Amagansett Station on Long Island, New York, and the other four landed on Ponte Vedra Beach, Florida, just south of Jacksonville, on June 13, 1942. They were captured on June 17th and placed on the sixth floor of FBI headquarters for interrogation. Tried by a military commission, six were sentenced to death, and two were spared and returned to Germany for giving testimony that aided the authorities. John, as a potential law student, was most interested in the trial that lasted from July 8th to August 4th. He was so intrigued that he managed to finagle the task of delivering food to the prisoners, just to see what saboteurs looked like.

ROTC cadet John Phillips served on the University of Iowa Rifle Team, sinning several events.

Wearing suits to work every day was not without some peer pressure, since Washington D.C. was filled with military personnel. Taunted as draft dodgers and 4-F slackers, they were continually sneered and laughed at by service men and women. Near the end of the summer, the six decided they had had enough and decided to return home and enlist. John returned to Iowa City, enrolled in the University of Iowa for the fall semester, and visited the Air Corps Recruiting Station. The thought of being a fighter pilot and wearing the cap with a fifty-mission crush was most appealing.

He was scheduled to report to Des Moines at the KRNT Theater where he would take a written examination. Of the twenty-five men who sat for the exam, John was one of five who passed. He was taken immediately to Camp Dodge where he was given a physical examination, passing with flying colors. In the last test, John was handed twelve cards covered with colored dots and told to read the numbers. John raced through the cards only to find out he only got two correct. He repeated the test and again only got two right. John discovered he was red-green color blind, and these 'flying colors' cost him his dream of being a fighter pilot.

He returned to Iowa City to finish the semester. He continued in the mandatory Reserved Officer Training Program (ROTC) and served on the rifle team where he excelled in accuracy and made the traveling competitive shooting team.

In the middle of the first semester his older brother advised him to enlist, since his draft number would soon be called. John took a number of math classes to help his enlistment chances. William was already in service, an officer in anti-aircraft artillery, and recommended John enlist in that branch of service. It appeared to be a safe assignment, away from the front, out of the foxholes, and shooting at targets overhead. After some thought, John again visited a recruiting office, and on February 3rd, 1943, enlisted in the anti-aircraft artillery. He was nineteen years old.

John Phillips was inducted into service from Algona, his parents' official residence. Twenty-five young men from Kossuth County boarded the Greyhound Bus that evening, and as they boarded each lad was presented with a small pocket New Testament from their local Pastor. John slipped it into his breast pocket. The bus arrived at Camp Dodge, Des Moines, about midnight. Assigned a barracks, the new recruits found their building and crawled into bed. About 4:00 A.M. John was awakened and told to report to the Mess Hall for Kitchen Police (KP), where tall stacks of greasy pans awaited for a thorough scrubbing. John had not yet been sworn into the army and already he was on KP. The recruits managed to finish just before breakfast, then returned to the barracks to get a brief nap before the processing began.

John's uncle, married to his father's sister, was the Adjutant General of the State of Iowa and Commander of the National Guard at Camp Dodge. General Grahl was one of John's favorite uncles and a fine gentleman. John was in the process of taking his physical, standing naked in line with twenty other naked soldier candidates, when a sergeant entered the room and said, "Is John Phillips here?" John acknowledged his presence and the soldier continued, "Get dressed and come with me." Suspecting more KP duty, John dressed and went outside to find a staff car waiting. The soldier drove him to the Officers Club, where General Grahl treated him to lunch. His first day in service found John on KP scrubbing pots and pans and dining in the Officers Club, an anomaly if there ever was one. He did not see the General again until he returned from service. Getting off an airplane from St. Louis, he was met by the General and was again a guest for lunch at the Officer's Club.

Basic training took place in Camp Haan, California, where they went on maneuvers in the Mojave Desert. The training in the desert ended with a twenty-five mile hike carrying a full field pack and only one canteen of water. After Basic Training, John was sent to Camp Davis, North Carolina, for Anti-Aircraft Artillery Officer training.

The Officer Candidate School (OCS) for Anti-Aircraft Artillery was politely described as "excessively difficult." It was all "spit and polish" and every effort made to 'wash out' potential officers. Although they were all corporals, they were addressed as "mister" and wore no rank insignia. The first day an officer aligned the men in formation, called them to attention and remarked, "Look right and left. Two of the three of you will not be here at the end of this training." This presaged to constantly challenge the limits of their endurance academically, physically, and psychologically. If the wall lockers were not perfectly aligned, the contents of the one out of alignment was thrown out the window, requiring re-washing and re-pressing all uniforms. An officer would enter the barracks at 9:20 P.M. and pour some lye on the floor, making it considerably lighter in value than the rest of the floor. He would then announce, "Soldiers, I want the entire floor to be the color of this spot by 6:00 AM inspection."

One outstanding officer candidate slipped out on a weekend pass and got rip-roaring drunk, returning to the barracks Sunday afternoon for a 4:00 P.M. class. The young man could barely navigate, so when marching to class he was placed in the middle of the formation, and the men alongside tried to hold him up. Caught by the Lieutenant affectionately called "the Birddog," he was removed from formation and marched to the barracks. When the men returned from class, his locker was cleaned out and he was gone.

During inspection an inspecting officer, usually "the Birddog," would touch a shining belt buckle and demand, "Mister, what are you doing with a thumbprint on your buckle?," or would scuff shined shoes and order, "Your shoes are not shined. You will stay in your barracks this weekend and clean the latrines!" On one occasion, Phillips was ordered to scrub the latrines "…so clean and polished you could eat off of them." Phillips proceeded to scrub the toilets, and when done, liberally doused them with aftershave lotion. When the inspecting officer came by, he gave it his usual snarled-look inspection and then started laughing, the only laughter Phillips heard from the Lieutenant in thirteen weeks. It was literally thirteen weeks of hell.

When the training was completed Phillips received his commission. Trained to fire 90 mm anti-aircraft guns with knowledge of trajectory, charge, explosive shells, and pattern firing, he was next assigned as training cadre at Camp Stuart, Georgia, and again at Camp Edwards, Massachusetts.

Then one day the training officers were assembled and the announcement was made. "Men, the Allies are now in control of the skies in Europe and the Far East. There is no more need for anti-aircraft artillery officers. You are all being transferred to the infantry!" That day four thousand highly trained artillery officers were transferred to the infantry, where the life expectancy for officers was a day and a half.

The next stop was Fort Benning, Georgia, for eight weeks of infantry officers tactical training. Ultimately, all the men would be sent overseas as replacement officers. Completing the training, Phillips went to Ft. McClelland, Alabama, where the new arrivals trained as a unit. Fresh out of civilian clothes, the young men came by the hundreds, many of them away from home for the first time. They were given thirteen weeks of training after which they were shipped overseas as replacements in depleted infantry units. New infantry officers, like Phillips, worked long hours and conscientiously in the Alabama heat, attempting to train the men as best they could, knowing that a few weeks after leaving Ft. McClelland they would be in battle.

After training two such groups, Phillips, now promoted to First Lieutenant, received orders to report to Ft. Meade, Maryland, for shipment overseas as a replacement officer.

He reported to Ft. Meade, and the night before they embarked, Lt. Robert Spillane who attended AAA OCS with Phillips approached John with a special request. Spillane's wife, who lived in Newark, New Jersey, had come to Maryland in hopes of seeing her husband before he went overseas. Bob asked John to help him crawl over the fence the night before they were to leave, for one last nightly visit. John helped him over the fence, with strict orders to be at the same spot at 3:00 A.M. when he returned. John met him at the appointed time, and helped him back across the fence. When they arrived in Europe, Lt. Spillane was assigned to the 104th Division, known as the "Timberwolves," Spillane assisted in taking Cologne, and the Remagen Bridge, and while taking the town of Altenkirken, was hit six times by a machine gun in the lower legs. His shinbone was shattered, arteries cut in two places, and his leg was amputated at the knee on March 28th, 1945.

Phillips traveled to Europe along with ten thousand soldiers needed as replacements, aboard the Queen Elizabeth, the famous English liner that had been converted to a troop ship. The trip was relatively fast and uneventful, except for changing directions frequently to avoid any torpedoes that might be sent their way.

Arriving in Europe, Phillips landed in Scotland. They boarded a train for the trip through England, and by boat to Port Le Havre, France, to find the town practically leveled, with a only a few walls left standing. The men were trucked to a holding area and replacement depot in Belgium, where John was assigned as Executive Officer of E Company, 2nd Battalion, 424th Regiment of the 106th Division. Arriving at the depot, John started coughing violently and running a temperature. He was diagnosed with double pneumonia at the depot Aid Station and placed in a hospital at Leige, Belgium, where he was treated with sulfa drugs. Although quite sick, he welcomed the nice warm bed and hot food. After a week he was recovering nicely, when an officer entered the ward and announced that all men who could walk had to vacate, as there was a big battle going on near Bastogne in Belgium. The wounded would be coming in any minute. A few moments later, while John was packing, a badly burned tank man was brought in, completely wrapped in bandages with only his eyes showing. It was the first seriously wounded man Phillips had seen. It was most unnerving. Numerous wounded soldiers in various states of pain and decimation joined the burned soldier.

On December 16th, 1944, the Germans started a massive offensive that would fill many wards in many hospitals. It was the beginning of the Battle of the Bulge.

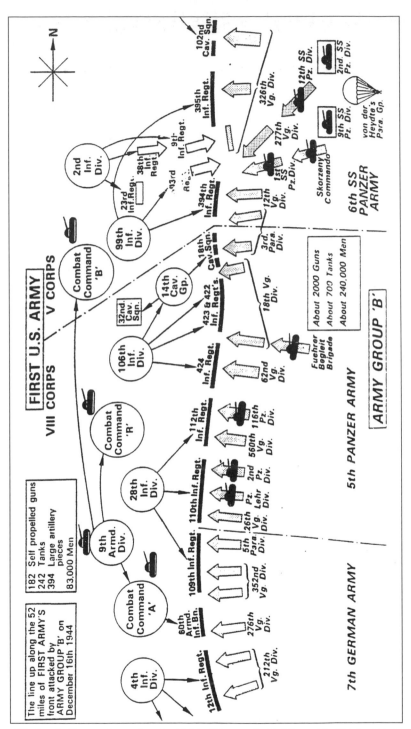

The battle line on December 16, 1944. The 106th Division with 424th, 423rd, and 422nd Infantry Regiments never stood a chance against the attacking two hundred fifty thousand German soldiers. Allied Headquarters dismissed reports of increased German activity at the front reported by members of the division.

PHILLIPS • CHAPTER 3

First Lieutenant John Phillips crawled out of his hospital bed, returned to the replacement depot, and was delivered to E Company, on January 1st, 1945. The Battle of the Bulge raged on, with front lines still indistinct, but Allied resistance started to define areas of security. Most members of Phillips' assigned division had simply disappeared; the 422nd Regiment and 423rd Regiment no longer existed.

Hitler, himself, had planned this supreme effort, a final big assault by the Germans forces against a broad front in Belgium to defeat the Allies. A new replacement division had moved into position to defend that broad front. The 106th Division's three infantry regiments, the 422nd, the 423rd, and the 424th, as well as regiments from the 28th Division, were spread out over a broad twenty mile front. For a week, forward observers and patrols reported to Battalion HQ, and on up the chain of command, that they could detect noises of trucks and tanks moving about. The HQ responded that the Germans knew there was a new division at the front and were playing recordings over loudspeakers to frighten the infantrymen.

On December 16th, 1944, 240,000 elite German troops hit the twenty mile front with everything they had. It included the 5th Panzer Division, two thousand guns and over seven hundred tanks. The two regiments of the 106th Division, the 422nd and the 423rd, never had a chance. During the first five days of fierce fighting, the 106th Division's toll was four hundred sixteen men killed, one thousand two hundred forty-six men wounded, and seven thousand men missing in action. It was the beginning of the Battle of the Bulge. It was also the beginning of the worst winter experienced in that area in over twenty-five years, with below freezing temperatures and an inordinate amount of snow.

The 424th Regiment managed to fight its way out of encirclement by joining forces with elements of the 7th Armored Division and the 112th Infantry Regiment of the 28th Division nearby. Together they amassed enough firepower to hold their area and contain the German advance. In the counterattack, the 424th Regiment was teamed with the 7th Armored Division as a task force to recover land lost in the Battle of the Bulge.

On January 1st, during this action, First Lieutenant John Phillips finally caught up with 424th Regiment, 2nd Battalion, 106th Division. Listed as Executive Officer of E Company, it was "in name only" because of officer losses, and John performed all tasks required of officers in battle. It was the day Lt. Phillips began twenty-five continuous days of combat.

Spending precious little time meeting his charges but trying to understand their area of responsibility in counterattacking, Phillips began adjusting to the physical conditions. The men were not equipped with winter boots, and frozen feet were a severe problem. More men were lost from the front lines with frozen feet than from battle injury. Digging foxholes in frozen ground, sleeping in snow with frozen water in the bottom of the excavations required a real adjustment. During the night, body heat would melt the snow or ice, and as a result, some part of the men's uniforms was always wet. Weapons were constantly checked to insure they would work when needed. Carbines worked fine for close quarters, but the officers really needed sidearms, .45 caliber pistols, for house-to-house fighting. Winter footwear and side arms were received at the front lines until several months later. Some days the company faced severe resistance, and other days they could move ahead a mile or three with little or no resistance. Coordinating artillery was difficult since communication systems were intermittent. Fortunately, the skies cleared and not only could fighter planes support the ground forces, but supplies could be dropped to isolated troops below.

On January 7th, the infantrymen were awakened by the loud rumble of airplanes. Overhead, large formations of bombers flew in a never-ending stream. Phillips lay in the snow on his back and marveled at this incredible display of air power. The flights continued until mid-afternoon. Thousands of airplanes rendezvoused from England, France, and Italy, passing overhead; Germany was going to suffer from the tons of bombs dropped that day. It was as if the Allies were getting even for the attack on December 16th and were paying the Germans back, with interest.

The 424th Regiment and E Company pushed ahead day by day, making progress. After twenty days of constant fighting, pushing and maneuvering, the Company Commander called Phillips on the radio. He said, "Phillips, you need a break. We have a soldier who is ready for rotation (enough points to go home on leave). Why don't you take a jeep and drive him back about ten miles to Regimental HQ?" Phillips grabbed a nearby jeep and drove the soldier to Battalion Headquarters. Phillips noted that all the men at headquarters were wearing winter boots, and wearing side arms. He had been begging regimental HQ for them and getting no response. After processing the soldier's papers, an officer asked, "Lieutenant, why don't you stay for dinner?" Phillips looked at his crusty uniform and mud caked boots, but agreed to join them, and the officers went to a recently captured large estate.

The dimly lit dining room was very elegant. Crystal goblets and newly liberated fine china and silverware were in place, along with cloth napkins. The waiters were German POWs in dark pants and white shirts. Phillips looked around at the grand dining facilities and the well-equipped soldiers and hesitated. "Colonel, Sir, I don't think I can do this. I have men up front sleeping in foxholes with no winter footwear or sidearms, and you guys are back here with hot meals and a nice warm bed. I appreciate your invitation, Colonel, but if you will excuse me, I will go back to my men."

The officers stared in silence as John turned and slowly made his way to the door and out into the bitter cold night. The jeep trip back without headlights was tedious and frigid, and he fumed at the thought that his men who needed winter clothing and proper equipment to fight the enemy would continue to have to do without.

Sniper fire was a constant threat. Germans would hide in the shadows or in buildings, fire a few shots then move to a new location. E Company had a Sergeant Richard J. Maslankoski who Phillips believed deserved every medal the Army presented. When the company or a platoon was pinned down by a sniper, the sergeant would always call to Phillips and say, "Lieutenant, let me get him!" There would be a long period of silence, then a rifle shot. The sergeant would return and say, "It's OK! Let's move on!"

The towns were small villages, some a few buildings along the side of the road, others fifteen or sixteen American blocks in size. The soldiers had to check every room of every house still standing. Phillips was shocked one afternoon when he entered a second floor bedroom to find an elderly couple lying in bed, each shot through the forehead. The bodies were frozen and preserved. It was an image Phillips has never forgotten.

The men were constantly on patrols, probing the strength and location of the enemy. During one patrol at night, Phillips, a sergeant and two infantrymen were moving out through the snow to evaluate the terrain in an attempt to locate the enemy. As they made a loop around a field to return not following their original tracks, they heard noises of men talking. Crawling through the snow looking over a small rise, they discovered twelve German soldiers with rifles stacked, warming themselves over a low fire. Phillips signaled the sergeant to approach and they discussed their options. The sergeant observed that since they had been out for four hours crawling through the snow, there was a good chance their weapons were frozen, and would not work. If one weapon did not work, they would be at a disadvantage once the Germans recovered and returned fire. They could have killed all twelve soldiers, but instead, withdrew and worked their way back to camp. Phillips later rationalized that sparing those lives may have helped his cause at a later time.

Once the counter-offensive was initiated, the army had to replenish the infantrymen that were killed, wounded or captured. As a result, every spare cook, typist, quartermaster, supply man, and mechanic was handed a rifle and sent to the front. The men had no training, had not fired a gun since basic training, had no proper uniform for the weather, nor any tactical training. The losses suffered by these replacements were substantial. The members of the Allied High Command wanted to keep pressure on the retreating Germans and get back to the front where it had been established on December 16th. Fighting a defensive war was to the German advantage, and the Americans paid a very high price for the real estate they recovered. Even experienced units like the 424th Regiment had an inordinate amount of casualties. When John Phillips joined E Company, there were two hundred men and officers. After twenty-six days of fighting, E Company consisted of forty-nine men and two officers. At the end of twenty-five days of continuous fighting (paradoxically January 25th was known as the end of the Battle of the Bulge) the real estate gained was near the line where the Germans had originally attacked.

On January 24th, the battalion was told to capture the town of Medell, Belgium, which was a few miles away in a beautiful valley only six miles from the German border. As they approached the town, only one hundred yards out, E Company was suddenly pinned down by machine gunfire and artillery explosions. Taking refuge behind a hedgerow, they could see the machine guns shooting from a church tower, and where an observer was very likely directing artillery fire from that same spot. They called battalion HQ and requested artillery support repeatedly, but got none.

About mid-afternoon, they managed to make radio contact with several P-51s that were in the area. One pilot on the line said, in a decidedly southern drawl, "What do you-all need?"

Phillips responded, "The company is pinned down just outside of town. Blow down the church steeple, drop a couple of bombs on the town, and strafe the Krauts as they run out the other side of town!" With a "Rajah! Wilco!," two P-51s suddenly roared over the treetops strafing and knocking down the steeple. Another pass produced violent explosions within the village. The pilot reported, "We got'em runnin' out of town like rats."

Phillips thanked them for a job well done. When the pilot inquired, "Where you-all from, soldier?"

Phillips replied, "I'm from Iowa!"

"I don't see any cornfields around here. If you dawg-faces need any more hep, you-all jus call, you heah?" With that, the pilot headed home for a shot of whiskey, a hot meal and a warm bed.

That night, First Lieutenant John Phillips found a second floor bedroom with a bed and a stack of blankets. Tonight there would be no snow in his foxhole.

PHILLIPS • CHAPTER 4

It seemed unfair, but the battalion commander had a job to do and numbers count. At least Lt. Phillips could rationalize these facts to his troops, but he was as tired and mentally fatigued as they were. Just before dawn the men started filing through the snow toward a firebreak in the forest. They reached the ridgeline about a mile from the village. The company commander waited for his men to gather around. He issued terse orders for the men to disperse along the ridge and dig foxholes. He then called Lt. Phillips to his side and instructed him to take two machine gun squads and move ahead about 100 yards to find a good field of fire locations where they could sweep the area and protect the ridge. The low ridge opened to a large pasture with clusters of trees on both sides and a small forest about one-half mile ahead. Gathering the machine gun crews, the men walked to where they could observe the snow covered field. Spotting two good locations, Phillips gave directions for setting up the machine guns, and was talking about being relieved when suddenly all hell broke loose.

The patrol had walked into an ambush. Germans were in the trees, behind shrubs, and rising out of the snow in the open field. Everywhere! A machine gun began to chatter only thirty-five yards away, hitting Phillips who immediately fell, with his six foot two, two hundred forty pound, Sergeant falling on top of him. Five bullets hit Phillips; three times in the stomach, once over the heart and once through the bicep of his left arm. He was carrying the small New Testament presented to him when he left Algona in the left breast pocket of his shirt, and although a bullet penetrated his clothing, it lodged in the small book over his heart without breaking skin.

The sergeant was hit in the legs and both kneecaps were shattered. The men lay still, bleeding in the snow, hoping the Germans would pass them by thinking they were dead. Soon, two SS troopers came by, stuck a bayonet in Phillips' back, and demanded they stand up. The Sergeant rolled over, and Phillips managed to stagger to his feet. They were prisoners of the SS, a fearsome Nazi organization noted for its brutality and disregard for human life. The previous week about ten miles away in Melmedy, Belgium, the SS had lined up a whole platoon of infantry prisoners and machine-gunned them in a ditch. The bodies were discovered three days later when the Americans retook the village.

The men were now captives and, prodded with bayonets, told to move out. The sergeant could not walk, so the SS troops told Phillips to carry him, or they would shoot him. Slightly-built and still bleeding from stomach and arm wounds, Phillips managed to lift the sergeant on his back and they staggered through the snow and rough ground for about 100 yards. It was apparent he could carry the sergeant no further, so Phillips placed the wounded man down next to a tree, propping him in an upright position. After making a slight adjustment to the tourniquet on each leg, Phillips gave the sergeant a full canteen of water, encouraging him to hang on until the Americans arrived.

Phillips was marched about a mile, taken into a farmhouse, and seated in a chair. One of the soldiers pulled out a knife and proceeded to cut off the left sleeve of all of his clothes: his trench coat, jacket, sweater, shirt, and long winter underwear. After inspecting the wound to his arm, they had him strip to the waist and drink a glass of water to see if any of it ran out of the bullet holes. Finding no apparent damage to the intestines, the soldiers proceeded to relieve him of all of his valuables: watches rings, money and insignia. When John graduated from high school, his parents gave him an expensive Elgin watch. John also had an inexpensive military issue watch, and for fear of losing the Elgin, usually wore both of them. When first captured, he managed to loosen the strap of one watch and slide it up his sleeve to conceal it. Unfortunately, it was the military watch, and the Germans relieved him of his prized Elgin. They also found a small address book with the names and addresses of all of the men in his company. It was valuable to the German intelligence, but personally extremely valuable to John, since later he could not contact any of his men or their families. The Germans were very excited about capturing an American officer. John grew weak from loss of blood and thought he would soon pass out, but fought to stay awake.

After stripping him of his valuables, the German soldiers told John to get dressed, so he reversed his underwear and sweater, so there would be some protection for his left arm. They walked about five more miles to a field hospital, and entered the waiting room where John laid down on a pile of straw distributed along the outer walls of the room. The low block building resembled an auto repair shop, with an entry space, and a large room with a row of eight or ten operating tables. He was one of several persons, the rest German soldiers, waiting to enter the operatory from which screams, moaning, yelling, and crying emanated in one constant song.

A German medic walked by, and Phillips asked what was going on inside. The medic said in broken English, "Ve haf no anesthetic."

Phillips winced and said to himself, "Dear God, I don't think I can handle this one." He was feeling pain, but was amazed he had managed to walk this far. As he waited, he thought about his wounds. He knew that an M-1 rifle shell would penetrate a six-inch pine tree at 100 yards. Shot from thirty-five yards by a .31 caliber German machinegun, the bullets that should have penetrated his body. Surely there was a Guardian Angel looking out for him. The Guardian Angel worked it's magic a second time when the Germans made him walk to the farmhouse instead of shooting him. What about the Guardian Angel who lodged the bullet in the New Testament?

A German medic stepped out of the operatory and helped Phillips to his feet. They entered a long room with eight operating tables, each with German doctors and medics in green rubber aprons covered with blood, and all wearing surgical masks. Told to undress, he took off all of his clothes and the medics helped lift him onto the table. Screams and cries were still coming from the German soldiers on adjoining operating tables. At that moment a German Colonel appeared from the other side of the room and asked in perfect English, "Are you an American officer?"

Phillips replied, "Yes, I am an American First Lieutenant."

The Colonel said to Phillips, "I was educated in the United States." He then turned to the doctor and said in German, "Doctor, give this officer an anesthetic!" Another Guardian Angel had raised its lovely head. Injected with morphine, Phillips immediately lost consciousness.

John awoke the next morning lying on straw in the entryway, completely naked, with his clothing piled neatly next to him. Inspecting his wounds, he discovered they were un-sutured, and his torso was completely wrapped in crepe paper. A guard sat nearby, so he inquired about his condition. The guard replied in broken English, "Number one, ve haf no bandage. Number two, ve are out of medicine, and number three, ve haf no thread and cannot sew you up. And number four, crepe paper is the only bandage material we have left."

A few hours earlier in Medell, Belgium, one of the few standing houses had been about to provide a dry bed for Phillips, when his company was selected for one more patrol. Now, he was wrapped in crepe paper with open wounds, stretched out on a straw pallet. A German non-com entered the room and motioned Phillips to get dressed. He laboriously put on his clothing, again reversing the sleeves so there might be some protection and warmth. At least his stockings had dried out overnight. The soldier and John walked about fifteen miles to Koblenz, where they would spend the night. Arriving late in the evening, John lay down next to a building on a side street, and fell into an exhausted sleep.

The next morning, he was placed with other American prisoners. As they were marched out of town, the townsfolk, mostly old men and women, gathered to swear and spit on them as they paraded by. The Nazi youth were guarding bridges, and they taunted the prisoners, threatening to shoot them. The prisoners continued for about ten miles to Limberg; Phillips, the only officer, was separated from the men and placed in solitary confinement in a small room in sort of a castle-like building, complete with a moat. Even though there were prisoners in the adjoining rooms, they were told not to speak. John later found out the building was a Roman Catholic Monastery, and the small rooms formerly housed the resident monks.

This was the only time as a prisoner that Phillips was "roughed up." As they interrogated him, they used every psychological trick to get him to talk. Raw meat was thrown on the floor once a day, but John was not capable of eating it. Interrogated continuously day and night for six days, he was placed in solitary confinement, awakened in the middle of the night, and usually thrown down the stairs on the way to interrogation. They would be nice to him, then mean to him, then nice, then threaten, deprive him of sleep, then push him against the walls of the room. Phillips' greatest fear was they might shoot him, and no one would have an idea where he was or what had happened. Occasionally they threatened to shoot him, and would take him to a window where he could see naked men lined up against a wall. They would then pull him away and take him back to confinement, where he would struggle with what he had seen.

It was obvious this was routine interrogation, as the walls of his cell were covered with the admonitions of other prisoners. There were calendars and notes of reassurance; "don't give up," "you are going to be all right," and "keep your chin up."

A German Colonel who was educated in the United States and spoke perfect English performed the interrogation. While in the monastery/prison, Phillips received no medical attention for his wounds. When Phillips left the castle, the Colonel gave him some parting words, "Hitler did not really want to fight America. He was really fighting communism. And remember this; I will probably be dead, but when this battle is over, your real enemies will be Russia and China. Don't you ever forget it!"

Finally released from the castle, Phillips joined other officers for a march to the railroad yards. There they were loaded on a boxcar, seventy or more per car, and the doors nailed shut. The conditions were so crowded that the men leaned against one another, standing as the train slowly lurched along. There was no room for anyone to sit down. Every so often, the train pulled off onto a siding where American P-51s strafed it with fifty caliber machine guns. Many of the men had diarrhea and were very sick. There was no way to relieve themselves by squatting, or avoid vomiting on one another. Without food or water for four days, the soldiers were seventy animals crammed into a boxcar trying to breath and survive. On the fifth day they arrived at Hammelburg, the nails were pulled from the doors, and the desperate, humiliated, men could finally breathe their first fresh air.

PHILLIPS SON PRISONER OF THE GERMANS

Parents Now Hopeful of News Reporting Liberation.

C. A. Phillips, Chamber of Commerce secretary, and Mrs Phillips, late Thursday received a government telegram which follows:

Washington, D. C., May 5— The secretary of war desires me to inform you that your son 1Lt. John C. Phillips is a prisoner of war of the Ger-

man government. Report was received through International Red Cross. Letter of information follows from Provost Marshal General.— J. A. Ulio, Adjutant General.

Lieutenant Phillips had been officially reported 'missing-in-action' as of Jan. 26, and since that time his parents here had no word from or about him till two weeks ago, when a woman at Waterloo wrote to say that her husband, an officer overseas who was captured, had written of having talked with John and said the latter had suffered a right arm wound somewhat like his own. ∎

Won Combat Citation.

After receipt of that news, Mr. and Mrs. Phillips were encouraged with renewed hope that they would hear from their son in due time. They believed that if it were at all possible he would try to communicate with them April 25, his 22nd birthday. However, no word came till receipt of the Ulio message.

The young lieutenant was en route overseas at last Thanksgiving time, and from letters he later wrote home it appeared that he went into combat almost immediately. He was in 106th division of the 424th infantry, Co. E.

In one letter the lieutenant mentioned a combat citation. It is known that he fought in the original Luxembourg offensive, because he told of having been or being in Germany. About that time he suffered an attack of pneumonia, and was hospitalized at Liege in Belgium. Later he wrote that while he was convalescent there he helped evacuate bed patients to the rear.

Served in Rundstedt Push.

That coincided with the Runstedt counter-offensive, which started Dec. 16, and it is presumed that when re recovered sufficiently he was ordered back to combat, for it was only a little ore than a month later that he is reported "missing."

The 106th division was almost annihilated in the Runstedt push. There were 8,000 casualties. In the fighting the men of that division did much, it was claimed by reporters on the scene, to lay the foundation for the later victory now at hand.

FATE OF PHILLIPS SON IS A PUZZLER

Chamber of Commerce Secretary and Mrs. C. A. Phillips received a message from the government Saturday announcing that their son, 1st Lt. John C. Phillips, had been missing in action in Belgium since January 26. However, on Wednesday, February 7, a cablegram was received from him which said, "All well and safe, please don't worry." This message was not dated, and it is not known whether it was sent before or after Jan. 26. The young man is in the infantry.

The Algona Newspapers account of Lt. Phillips' capture

PHILLIPS • CHAPTER 5

Hammelburg Prison Camp, known as Auflug XIIIB (also known as Oulflug XIIIB and Stalag VIIIA) was the destination of this trainload of prisoners. Two fences of barbed wire, twelve feet apart and twelve feet high, surrounded a collection of hastily constructed wooden barracks set upon brick stilts. Guard towers twenty feet high were located every one hundred fifty feet, and occupied at all times by guards with machine guns trained on the prisoners. The prison, originally constructed to hold three thousand prisoners, now housed three to four times that many. The soldiers were marched to the prison where they joined fifteen hundred officers and eight thousand other prisoners of war, most of whom were Yugoslavian Serbs. The conditions were terrible, and morale was extremely low. Dysentery was prevalent; there were no medical facilities nor treatment of the wounded. A Yugoslav doctor did the best he could without medicines or bandages. An old Yugoslav dentist tried to help, but had no equipment or supplies since the International Red Cross was not able to service the camp. Food was scarce since the American Air Corps had bombed all the railroads, bridges and transportation routes, but even if food were available, it could not be delivered. Food was also in short supply for the German military and civilians, so prisoners of war were the least of the German concerns.

The men lived in crowded barracks, forty to sixty persons in two-tiered buildings that contained one stove and little fuel. The cold was penetrating and bone-chilling. Everyone had lice or fleas, and the straw-filled mattresses on beds were full of a variety of bed bugs. Since some of the prisoners had to share bunks on a rotating basis, the vermin problem was not about to improve.

Phillips sent his first letter to his parents from prison.

"I suppose you have received word by now that I am missing and am now a prisoner. I am a prisoner in Germany and have been treated and fed pretty well. I have written a letter prior to this and hope they got through to you. I have been moved from where I last wrote you and will eventually end up in an officer's prison camp. From here I will be able to write you regularly once a week, I think. Anyway, I will write as often as possible. Say hello to everyone for me, and do not worry as I am well and everything is all right. Keep your chin up and keep smiling. Love and kisses to all.

The German staff told him what to write.

Always concerned about escaping prisoners, German Commandant General Gunther Von Goeckel called the prisoners out in the middle of the night for an 'apell' or head count. The commandant took delight in making the men stand at attention for several hours during the night in freezing weather. He often made them stand in formation day or night during bombing raids, hoping to reduce the prison population with a few errant bombs; fewer mouths to feed would please the commandant. The tower guards would fire at the prisoners going to the latrine at night to see how close they could come without hitting the prisoner. On some mornings the prisoners would find a dead comrade hit by the guards during the night.

Breakfast consisted of 'ersatz coffee,' warm water flavored by beans of unknown origin. Lunch consisted of a loaf of bread made with sawdust, shared by six people. For dinner, each prisoner's tin can was half-filled with a weak turnip or rutabaga soup, usually enhanced with weeds or grass. Once a week they added bread for twelve or a potato for two. Each prisoner was supposed to receive a food parcel from the International Red Cross every week, but late in the war, availability and distribution were nonexistent. The amount of food in the Red Cross parcel intended to sustain one person's diet for one week barely met one day's needed intake - if it arrived!

The prisoners were known as "kregies" from the German word "Kriegsgefangener" or "prisoner of war." German guards were called "goons," and were convinced by kregies it was a complimentary term.

For a military prison, there was surprisingly little or no military discipline in the group of fifteen hundred officers. Most were exhausted and humiliated for having been captured, and morale was very low. There were no facilities to relieve the boredom of being penned up and herded about, no reading material or sports equipment so the men could organize a game, nor space to do it in. A few men exercised or walked the fences, but most sat around and talked about food, or the lack of it. Men would make up menus and recipes hour after hour, and John even brought some of them home and had his mother try them. They were essentially inedible, but the recipes sure sounded good at the time.

Phillips still carried his New Testament with the bullet hole in it, one of the few books and the only Bible in the prison. To keep his mind active he started a 'Sunday School' discussion group, reading a chapter and inviting a group of prisoners to talk about it. It kept his mind active, and the discussions took some interesting directions and kept some of the men occupied.

46

What military discipline existed in the prison was under the command of Colonel Paul Goode, one of the chief officers of the 106th Division. His executive officer was Lt. Col. John Waters. Waters was thirty-nine years old, and was captured in North Africa during the African Campaign, and a prisoner for several years.

Meanwhile, Commander of the Third Army, General George S. Patton, summoned two of his generals to his command post with an assignment. General William Hodges, Commander of the 4th Armored Division, and General Eddy, Commander of the 12th Corps, were to assemble a task force under the command of Captain Abraham Baum to liberate officers in a prison camp. Captain Baum was to lead a task force of three hundred seven men, ten medium tanks, twenty-seven half-tracks, three self-propelled 105mm assault cannon, seven jeeps and one cargo carrier. They were to go to Hammelburg and liberate the "three hundred officers contained there." General Patton decided to send along his aide, Major Alexander Stiller, on "Operation Baum".

Generals Hodges and Eddy were very opposed to the task force and argued against it, but General Patton finally ordered them to proceed with the mission. The task force was assembled and started for Hammelburg, encountering no resistance because the Germans were caught by complete surprise. All of the Allied attack activity was in one direction and the task force proceeded in a totally different direction. When they reached Hammelburg Prison they mistook the Serb soldiers for German soldiers because of the similarity in uniforms, and began firing at them. The German commandant asked American officers to intercede to stop the firing that was killing the defenseless Serbs. The commandant asked Lt. Col. Waters, under a white flag, to leave the compound to convince the task force to stop firing. Col. Waters succeded in his mission, but ironically was seriously wounded in the hip when hit by a stray bullet. He was placed on a litter and carried back inside the compound.

The task force tanks knocked down the fence compound and were warmly welcomed by the prisoners who streamed out of the barracks cheering, ecstatic because they thought the war was over. Phillips happened to be standing next to the fence where they broke through. When Captain Baum jumped out of his tank, he asked Phillips, "Where is Lt. Col. John Waters?" Phillips directed them to what was loosely called a hospital where Waters was taken after being hit. Major Stiller appeared and ran over to the building, returning a few minutes later. He told Captain Baum, "His wound is serious. He cannot be moved."

Captain Baum crawled up on the tank, and shouted, "All of you prisoners who want to return to our lines sixty miles to the west, climb aboard the tanks and half-tracks." Phillips gave serious thought about climbing aboard, but given his physical condition, he was not certain he could sit up on the rough-riding tank that long. As an infantry officer he knew anyone riding on the tank would be a sitting duck for any sniper. He decided not to go. The Task Force swung about and returned up the road to the west.

The Germans considered Patton's task force attack a brilliant move, catching them completely off guard, since the main thrust was northeast. As the task force drove through small villages on their way to Hammelburg, they did considerable damage to the villages with artillery and machinegun fire. On the return trip, the Germans had already reacted and in a few hours had roadblocks set up along the way. Four hours later, they either killed or captured the entire "Operation Baum" task force, plus all the prisoners accompanying them. Any soldier still alive returned to the Hammelburg Prison Camp.

Military strategists are still discussing today the wisdom sending the task force to Hammelburg on the orders of General Patton. Was he attempting to rescue his son or was it a brilliant maneuver? The Germans thought the task force assault on Hammelburg was a major breakthrough and rushed many of their troops from the north front to that area. As a result, the 11th Army was able to move one hundred miles in a matter of days with limited resistance.

The camp commandant realized the war was nearly over, and thinking the American task force was a only a few miles away, decided to abandon the camp. Two days after the visit from the task force, the prisoners were marched to the rail siding where once again they were loaded aboard freight cars headed for Nurnberg. Phillips had the option to remain with the wounded for later evacuation, or go with the prisoners. He decided there was safety in numbers, and opted to go with the group. This time the guards were friendlier and more helpful. When American fighter planes strafed the train, the guards let the men out of the cars so they could find refuge. The guards gave them water and treated them much nicer, because the war was about to end.

After four days the train arrived at the Nurnberg Stadium, and the prisoners were marched to the stadium to sleep on the track. Unfortunately, that night Allied bombers hit Nurnberg hard, and the prisoners subjected to a two-hour bombing attack. The city was literally leveled while the prisoners huddled under the stadium seating, hoping it was not a target. After the bombing, they slept on the running track and center field.

The next morning, the prisoners again started on their way, walking in a long column, thinking they were going to Munich. Instead, the column headed toward Moosburg Prison Camp, over one hundred miles away. The column was two and three abreast, containing over two thousand men. As they passed the devastation at Nurnberg, dense smoke filled the air. That night fires were visible, still burning all over the city. As the men marched along they stripped the countryside of anything edible. At first they begged farmers for food; later the farms were ransacked. Chickens were killed and eggs gathered. All the cows along the way were milked for just a taste of milk, and ended up being milked 24 hours a day as the prisoners walked by. The prisoners discovered farmers fed their pigs boiled potatoes and barley. Prisoners fought pigs often during the day just to get a few boiled potatoes to eat. The tin can from a Red Cross Package was the only eating utensil the prisoners had. It was used for bathing, shaving, and washing clothes, as well as eating and drinking.

As they marched along, each morning the column was strafed by American P-51s, and the troops would scatter into the fields, ditches, and trees to avoid being hit. They had no way to communicate with the pilots to let them know they were Americans, and could not understand why the pilots did not figure it out themselves. There evidently was some contact with our forces, since Colonel Goode would send back by word of mouth that "a little bird just told me that ..." Finally one POW made a grand sacrifice and spelled out "POW" in large letters on green grass in a pasture with his secret cache of toilet paper, a precious commodity owned by only a few. Colonel Goode was informed about it, and the Colonel ordered that the next morning when P-51s flew over, the prisoners stand fast in line on the road, and waive anything white instead of diving into a ditch. The next morning when a P-51 started down the line, the pilot suddenly saw the POW sign and pulled up. Communicating with other planes in the air, the pilots dropped their wheels and flew over the men tipping their wings. The men cheered, because the strafing finally stopped. From that day on a plane flew cover twenty-four hours a day, followed their progress, and was able to direct the 'great white fleet,' trucks from the Red Cross with food parcels, to their location, providing the prisoners something to eat on the remainder of their trip to Moosburg.

Arriving at Moosburg Stammlager VIIA, they found conditions better and cleaner than at Auflug XIIIB. The prison was crowded with thirty thousand prisoners, fifteen thousand who were Americans, of which six thousand were American officers. The remainder of the prisoners was a mixture of enlisted men, airmen from several other Stalags, and French and English soldiers who had been prisoners for several years. The officers were kept in a separate area from the rest of the POWs. Colonel Goode kept sending word to the men not to try to escape because he was receiving word that the end of the war and liberation were near. The one saving circumstance was the Red Cross arrived often with parcels of food for the men.

Once again, John would produce his New Testament, read a few chapters aloud, and the conversations would begin. In all of the humiliation, it was one touch of sanity.

On April 29th, the 14th Armored Division under the command of General George Patton, arrived at the gates of Stammlager VIIA. A group of American soldiers under a white flag approached the prison to talk to the Commandant. They reported, "We are taking this camp one way or the other and would prefer that none of the prisoners get hurt!" The German staff, a collection of older soldiers and a number of wounded men who could not stand the rigors of the front lines, indicated they would not give up without a fight. The "little bird" informed the prisoners that at 6:00 A.M., two P-51s would fly over the prison, indicating the 14th Armored Force was coming and everyone was to lay down on the floor or crawl under bunks.

At exactly 6:00 A.M., two P-51s did a slow roll over the camp, just as tanks broke through the barbed wire. A GI jumped out of a tank, took down the swastika from the main flagpole and ran up an American flag. The soldiers ran out of the barracks and cheered. A "little bird" passed along word to get into an orderly formation, since General George A. Patton himself was going to arrive. As the men lined up, six motorcycles roared into the compound, driven by Military Police in glistening white helmets. Then a jeep entered the compound, and there stood General Patton, with his polished riding boots and pearl handled pistols. Word went out that all officers would fall out and stand in formation to be inspected by the General. Climbing out of the Jeep, he entered several of the barracks to see what the living conditions were like and to visit the critically injured and sick; he then emerged to address the prisoners. The men were a sorry looking bunch with no insignia or rank, in the rag-tag uniforms that they had lived in for months.

The General was driven in his jeep to the front of the formation, and as he stood up to address the prisoners, tears began rolling down his cheeks, unusual for him. The speech he had practiced could not come out. Instead, he said in his own profane manner, "Now listen, you #%$## men. I'm going to get you home as soon as $&**#$## possible. I'm going to get you some hot food. The 14th Mobile Kitchens will roll in and start to feed you."

Another staff officer then addressed the crowd and explained the prisoners were to remain in camp until the kitchens and transportation could be arranged. He told them not to eat too much at first until their stomach had time to adjust to 'real food.' The relief soldiers wanted to kill the some of the guards, but the prisoners intervened, saying the "goons" had carried out their orders and were not nearly as ruthless as they could have been.

The next day life in the prison really started to turn around. The food trucks arrived with plenty of supplies to feed the thirty thousand men in the camp. Of course, some soldiers ignored the warning, ate too much, and got extremely ill. The next day trucks arrived to take prisoners to Ingolstadt Air Field in Germany, to arrange for a flight to Reims, France.

Ingolstadt Field had been bombed many times. The field was full of craters, and there were only the shells of buildings standing. With the lack of facilities, one crater was designated a latrine, and most of the soldiers made a deposit at one time or another. Two days later, while waiting for planes to land, a German Stuka dive-bomber suddenly appeared over the trees. Suspecting they were going to be bombed, men dove for the nearest crater for protection. Phillips thought twice and headed for a crater in the open field. A number of men, without thinking, found themselves knee-deep in what they would have liked to avoid.

The Stuka pilot wanted to surrender himself and his airplane to Americans rather than the Russians, and landed, taxiing to the end of runway. As the German pilot stepped out of the Stuka, soldiers wanting a souvenir to take home immediately stripped him naked.

Airplanes of every size and description transported the men to Reims, France. The field was without a control tower and there were at least fifty airplanes circling in the air at all times,. Phillips was amazed that there were not "collisions all over the place." For an entire week hauling thirty thousand soldiers, there was not one single accident.

Reims was set up to process the prisoners. The men disposed of their clothing, took hot showers, were deloused, and given standard issue uniforms. At the far end of the base, the pile of prisoners' clothing burned day and night. The mess hall was open twenty-four hours per day, and the ex-prisoners could eat any time and as many times as they wanted. German POWs served the food. Phillips made many trips, eating mashed potatoes and gravy in small quantities. He was finally sleeping off the ground in a clean bed and eating hot food.

After several days of processing and getting used to more food, John and a few other officers decided to visit the Officers Club in downtown Reims and try their first alcohol in six months. Entering the club, he went to the bar and ordered a whiskey and seven. The bartender, seeing the standard issue GI uniform with no bars, said, "I'm afraid I'm going to have to ask you to leave!" Phillips explained he was being processed as an ex-prisoner, the supply sergeant had no officer's uniform, and he did not have an opportunity to purchase a new uniform and insignia. The bartender was insistent, as was Phillips. The club manager-officer, a Colonel, approached and asked Phillips a few questions. He then turned to the bartender and said, "Give this officer anything he wants and put it on my tab!"

It was in Reims that Phillips learned that Lieutenant Colonel John Waters was George Patton's son-in-law. In a personal meeting with General Patton after the war, Captain Baum, the task force leader, commented, "You know, Sir, it is difficult for me to believe that you would have sent us on a mission without artillery or air support just to rescue one man." General Patton replied, "That's right, Captain. I wouldn't have."

However, in General Patton's diary, The Patton Papers, he wrote his wife on March 25th, 1944, he "...hoped to send an expedition tomorrow to get John." On March 30th, he wrote his son George Jr. "The other day I sent an armored column out to recapture a prison camp. I am afraid this was a bad guess and the column has been destroyed. If so, I lost two hundred twenty-three men."

PHILLIPS • CHAPTER 6

When it was time to return to the United States, John Phillips had a big decision to make; should he fly home or travel by boat? John checked the aircraft and discovered they were not in very good repair. Rather than take a chance flying across the Atlantic in a marginal aircraft, John decided to option for the boat. John and other wounded soldiers were put aboard a rusty liberty ship and it turned out to be a trip long remembered. John had made a bad decision. As part of a convoy of twenty-five ships, traveling at the maximum speed for the slowest ship, the trip took seventeen days. The weather was very rough with huge swells that lifted the propellers out of the water, causing the boat to shudder violently when they re-entered the water. The prow was spraying water over the decks, and for several days, the passengers were not allowed on deck. Most all of the men were terribly seasick for most of the trip. Yes! John had made a very bad decision.

Making port in Boston, Phillips caught a train for Jefferson Barracks, Missouri, outside of St. Louis, for processing. After filing a myriad of forms, he returned to Algona for a needed rest with his family. John spent most of his time catching up on lice-free sleep. After a sixty day leave, he then was to report to Hot Springs, Arkansas, for corrective surgery and repair.

On a trip to the local drugstore he ran into friends who introduced him to several young ladies home from college for the summer. Louise Wadleigh had just completed her junior year at Carleton College in Northfield, Minnesota, and was home for the summer. Recuperating in Algona suddenly became fun. During John's leave there were numerous trips made to the famous Surf Ballroom in Clear Lake, Iowa, where they danced to the big bands that played several times a week. Louise was in high school when the war started, and upon graduation selected Carleton College, as it was intellectually stimulating and an academic challenge. She reminded John of this fact quite frequently.

At the completion of his leave, John reported to Hot Springs Army-Navy General Hospital where they began three months of corrective surgery on his stomach and arm wounds. Most of the hotels and motels in Hot Springs were leased by the government for use as prisoner of war rehabilitation. On his way to Hot Springs, John got off the plane in St. Louis, hailed a taxi and asked to be taken downtown. The driver said, "Are you kidding. Today is V-J (Victory in Japan) day. That place is a zoo. I wouldn't go downtown for anything."

The Presbyterian Church in Algona was the scene of Louise Wadleigh and John Phillips'
wedding on September 6th, 1947.

While at Hot Springs he met a soldier who was also in the Hammelburg Stalag, who managed to escape after the task force "raid" and made it back to Allied lines and freedom. He said he went through hell avoiding German civilians and soldiers, sleeping in barns and finding food without being caught. It was a harrowing experience, but he finally made it. He admitted the decision to escape was a bad one.

The surgery and recovery were going well when he received a call from George Neel, an uncle living in Chicago. "Can you get out of the hospital for a few days? I have tickets to the World Series in Chicago. The Cubs are playing the Detroit Tigers with Hank Greenberg." When John approached his doctor about a four-day leave, the doctor replied, "How soon can you get out of town?" John, with his arm in a sling, flew to Chicago, met his uncle, and sat directly behind the third base dugout. It was the last time the Cubs played in a world series for almost sixty-five years.

Whenever John would return home, he was always embarrassed by his grandmother who would announce in front of her lady friends, "John, show these folks the scar on your belly!" It was not much fun for a twenty-two year old to get up in front of a group of old ladies and show off his stomach. But, he had to please grandmother!

Visiting Louise at Carleton College became a regular occurrence. John would fly to Minneapolis, catching a bus to Northfield. There he stayed in an old hotel whose distinguishing characteristic was a coiled rope at the

54

window that served as the fire escape. Northfield was famous, not only for the college, but because Jesse James robbed the Northfield Bank, and there are still bullets lodged in the wall from his warning shots. Carleton College was very strict. Students were not allowed to own a car, and young girls could not ride in a car without parental approval. John and Louise would sometimes catch a bus to Minneapolis where they could attend shows and movies without being supervised. Visiting Minnesota during the winter months was trying, since John's only uniforms were summer weight, and he was more sensitive to cold from sleeping in foxholes for a winter month. If John could withstand the temperatures in a Minnesota winter wearing summer weight clothes, it had to be love! Louise graduated in the spring of 1946, with degrees in Sociology and Botany. That fall she entered Iowa State Teachers College to acquire a teaching certificate.

John continued his rehabilitation, was promoted to Captain, and was finally released from service on March 11th, 1946, at Ft. Sam Houston, near San Antonio, Texas. He arrived home in February, because of time allowed for travel (TDY), and enrolled at the University of Iowa for the second semester. With money saved from service, he purchased a new car and joined a fraternity. The fraternity house with the best view in Iowa City was Phi Kappa Psi, located high on the side of a hill overlooking the Iowa River and a city park. It was also the fraternity of Heisman Trophy winner Nile Kinnick, and later the Big Ten player of the year, Bill Reichardt.

Since the GI Bill paid enough for room, board and tuition, John attended school year-round, so he could get his degree as fast as possible. He carried a full load every semester, even summers, and graduated with a Bachelor of Science in Commerce in August 1947. In retrospect, it was a mistake. With additional GI Bill monies still available, he might have been able to obtain a Masters Degree in Business Administration or even a degree in Law, studying at a leisurely pace, and having fun.

On September 6th, 1947 Louise and John were married in the Presbyterian Church in Algona, Iowa, with friends and fraternity brothers in the wedding party. After a reception in the basement of the church, the couple drove to Duluth, Mackinaw Island, across the northern U. S., and spent their honeymoon at Niagara Falls, New York.

Now it was time to get serious about making a living. Following his father's advice, John became the Chamber of Commerce Manager in Iowa Falls, Iowa. Louise found a teaching position in the school system, and they thoroughly enjoyed living in Iowa Falls. After two years, John and a fraternity brother analyzed cities where an accounting business might thrive.

The Presbyterian Church in Algona was the scene of Louise Wadleigh and John Phillips'
wedding on September 6th, 1947.

After serious consideration of several communities, they formed a partner-
ship in the Newton Booking and Tax Service in Newton, Iowa. The young
men made the right decision, as business was active from the first day.

John remained in the Army Reserve, serving in a unit in Newton,
where he was the only person who had served in combat. His business
partner, who was a medic during the war, also remained in the Reserve.
Louise called from home one day and said, "Dear, you have a very important looking letter from the Army." John returned home to review the document, learning he was recalled to active duty because of the conflict in
Korea. He was to immediately report to the KRNT Theater in Des Moines
for a physical.

After his physical, the reviewing doctor wrote on his form, "I would
not recommend this officer for active duty." The doctor chatted with John
about his physical condition, his stomach and arm scars; noting a gym wart
on the bottom of his foot, he commented, "I would hate to walk twenty
miles on that foot." Two weeks later John received orders to report to Fort
Sam Houston, Texas.

John was stunned to say the least. With thirty days to get their affairs
in order, the partners decided to sell their thriving business, and take a

week's vacation before reporting for duty. The prospects for a long healthy life had taken a sudden turn, and he and Louise had to make the most of the few moments left they had together. They found a buyer for the business and traveled to Biloxi, Mississippi, to sit on the beach and enjoy the sunshine. After four days of relaxation John received a telegram: "Your orders have been rescinded. Reason: Wart on left foot."

John was stunned once more. No military commitment! No business! No job!

Returning to Iowa, John and Louise scoured the want ads, looking for opportunities. John noticed in a newspaper ad that Iowa Machinery and Supply in Des Moines needed a "gopher." He applied for the job and was hired. John Stoddard, the owner, was extremely successful in a number of business ventures, creating several subsidiary companies involved in machine tools, machine equipment, plumbing supplies, and similar enterprises. Phillips became instrumental in serving various capacities running the companies, both in operations and in management.

In 1958, Stoddard called Phillips and Frank Cate into his office and offered to sell them the business. They managed to arrange financing, and Frank agreed to handle sales, while John took care of everything else. The business prospered, and in 1975, John Phillips sold his interest to focus on retirement. Aware of the old aphorism, "Idle hands are ...etc" John spent a short time with the Iowa State Energy Department as the State Energy Conservation Director, the Iowa Retail Hardware Association, and the National Credit Management Association.

John and Louise were blessed with two children, both daughters. Daughter Sharon (Monferdini) is a second grade school teacher in Colorado, and Susan (Larsen) serves as principal of an elementary school in Houston, Texas. Susan's husband, Chris, played on the University of Iowa's golf team and is a PGA professional.

John Phillips has never attended any of the military reunions of his units for several reasons. Because of the nature and length of his service, moving back and forth to a number of assignments, he never really got to know his compatriots. He did not train with the 106th Division, only joining them as a replacement officer later in the war. When the Germans took his address book, a valuable resource for them, he lost the only record available for future contact with the men with whom he spent time in the foxholes in battle. He feels he owes them a lot.

For his service to our country, John Phillips received the European-African Theater of Operations Medal with three battle stars, the Combat

Infantry Badge, World War II Medal, Prisoner of War Medal, the American Campaign Medal, and the Purple Heart.

John frequently is asked to address church and service groups about his experiences in service. Invariably, he concludes with the following comments:

"Of course, the real heroes of WWII are the four hundred five thousand young men who died during the war. When talking to school administrators and teachers, I get mixed signals about teaching history and what happened during the various conflicts in which our country has been involved. The teachers say, "Oh, yes! We are definitely teaching them a lot of history." When I talk to the students, many do not know what happened at Pearl Harbor, or Normandy, or the Battle of the Bulge, or in the Philippines, on Bataan, or Corregidor. So I think it is imperative that you tell your children and grandchildren, so they know what went on during those conflicts. Insist that they read the history of all of our nations wars that have gone on, because what they enjoy now is the result of the sacrifice of the many who fought in those wars."

The New Testament which stopped a German machinegun bullet resides in a special class case in the Phillips' home.

BOOK 3

Clark Anderson

Clark W Anderson

Pharmacists Mate 2nd Class
United States Navy

I have heard people say
"There are no atheists in foxholes!"
I say, there is no God!
No God would let things happen to the young men
whom we tried to put back together!

~ Clark Anderson

ANDERSON • CHAPTER 1

David E. Anderson was a very skillful man. He could build anything. His accumulated knowledge in the construction trades, whether it was sawing, welding, assembling, cutting sheet metal, or finishing, made a profound impression upon his son. It inspired the boy to emulate his father's skills in any manner he could, and his father encouraged him to work with his hands. It was an "old world" tradition, following in father's footsteps, assimilating his father's knowledge.

The boy's family life was not dysfunctional; it just was not as stable or inspiring as the prospect of learning to work with your hands building something. Family life was confusing. Building something was safe, productive, and energizing.

When Clark Anderson walked into the recruiting office, he knew exactly what he wanted to do in the Navy. He wanted to be a Carpenters Mate. The recruiting Petty Officer explained that by enlisting he could select his activity in the Navy and be assured of his choice.

Clark was working in a Montgomery Ward Store in Denver, and he felt his draft number would soon be pulled from the container. Whether pulled out of a bucket, can or hat, it made no difference; his number would be selected and he would have to report for induction, assigned to the service of their choice. Remembering his father's skills, he now had an opportunity to pursue a dream. He decided to enlist in the United States Navy Reserve for three years or the duration of the war. He signed the enlistment papers. It was May 26th, 1942.

Great Lakes Naval Training Center near Chicago was the basic training location for the great central plains of the United States. The seventeen-week training was a rigid routine experience, suffered by all Navy recruits. However, early in the war, the Navy needed men for specific tasks fast. After three weeks of indoctrination, Clark's name appeared on a list slated for gunnery school. The Navy needed radiomen, signalmen and gunners aboard the merchant fleet now hauling enormous quantities of supplies and material to England and the South Pacific.

This did not particularly please the young carpenter to be, so he complained to his commanding officer about his commitment and desire to follow his enlistment intent. His commander recommended that Clark take a standard navy test to determine areas of capability and Clark assented. The results of the tests showed intellectual skills that would suggest other areas of service. The Navy made the decision for him, placing him in the Hospital Corps School, training him to become a Navy Corpsman. Entering the pharmacy class along with five hundred other sailors, he worked hard, applying talents mostly dormant in high school. At the conclusion of the school, Clark finished 15th in the class.

Portsmouth, New Hampshire, was the next stop for Clark, where he attended classes and lectures in the hospital. He was training to become an Operating Room Technician, an assistant to doctors in the operating room. He was also assigned to the "Lock Ward," where prisoners with mental problems were contained. One of his duties was to march twento or so prisoners to the gymnasium, where the men played basketball for exercise and recreation. On the return trip he was responsible for placing them back under confinement.

For his first operating room experience he observed the repair of a broken finger. He watched as the fracture was opened and a silver splint was screwed into place. Clark observed with great interest then fainted, falling to the floor. He was removed from the operating room to recover.

Later exposure to the most hideous operations did not bother him, and he was never sick again. This is to his credit, as he had plenty of opportunities to become violently ill.

ANDERSON • CHAPTER 2

Norfolk, Nebraska, was good for the Anderson family. David Anderson met Ruth Cordela Boone, a student nurse, while serving in the U.S. Navy during the Great War. David was one of eleven children, and it seemed only natural that he would return to his roots in Norfolk, not unlike a family of prairie dogs returning to their hill. Ruth accepted the move to be with her husband, but underneath resented the relocation from the east coast. When Clark was born September 17, 1921, three sisters were added to the family in short order, later joined by another sister. David and a first cousin exercised an opportunity to move to Tilden, Nebraska, where they operated a pool hall. Recognizing an additional business opportunity, they dug a pond, and in the wintertime harvested ice that was stored in a large barn, covering the ice with sawdust to preserve it for selling during the hot dry Nebraska summers. It was ten years before refrigerators became a fixture in most homes.

Clark Anderson's high school graduation photo

When Clark was six, his curiosity ended in a great adventure. David owned fishing tackle that was purposefully hidden from the children. On a beautiful summer day while exploring an outbuilding, Clark found the fishing pole and decided to try it out. He did not know how to swim, but stood on the bank throwing the line into the water. Clark's mother suspected what Clark was doing, and when David returned home from work, demanded he retrieve Clark from the pond and punish him for borrowing the equipment and going against strict orders. On the way to the pond, David pulled out his pocketknife and cut a willow branch, skinning it as he walked along, preparing it to dispense punishment. Arriving at the pond, he discovered Clark sitting on the bank with the pole bending into the water as he tried to retrieve a fish. The father dropped the switch, grabbed the pole and reeled in a good-sized fish. When the two did not immediately return, Ruth went to the pond and found father and son sitting side by side on the bank, fishing. This time, both got a scolding.

David sold his interest in the pool hall to his cousin, bought a new 1928 Ford Coach, loaded Ruth, four children and a dog into it, and went to Fredrich, Maryland to visit Ruth's parents. While visiting in Maryland, the stock market crashed. After using up all their money, they decided to return to Norfolk, and David worked as a farm laborer, harvesting crops on farms along the highway. Ruth was a very good cook, and spent her waking hours finding food for her family. She also nursed them through their childhood diseases and kept their clothes clean and repaired.

During the depression, David was forced to work for the Works Progress Administration (WPA), a "make work" program by the government to provide money for families. David sought additional income by building a form to make cement block. He mixed the concrete and poured blocks to sell to local builders. He would make stacks of them, setting them on pallets to cure. Coping with the depression was very difficult for the family after their move back to Norfolk.

David began drinking heavily, which bothered Ruth who was now trying to raise a family of five. Ruth experienced some mental problems and, in fits of despondency, would verbally intimidate and harass David until he would lose his temper and strike her. The children had a difficult time understanding the pressures on the family during these trying times, and suffered dramatically.

Consumed with guilt, Ruth filed for divorce. David moved out, leaving Ruth to raise the family. She worked as a waitress, did cleaning for neighbors, and took in ironing. One day she received a letter from David indicating he had found work in Lead, South Dakota, with the Homestake Mining Company, extracting gold from the South Dakota Hills. He was working as a miner at the five thousand foot level and making a fair salary. He asked them to join him in Lead, as he wanted to help raise the family. Ruth packed a trailer with their belongings and pulled it behind the 1928 Ford. Grandfather's old four-door Durrant car was also packed full, and accompanied them to help Ruth. Grandfather bought a side of beef to take along, and a crate of oranges for the children to eat on the trip. Traveling the dusty back roads through the Nebraska sand hills, they spent the first night with friends of David. Arriving in Lead, they rented a house right next to the mine. David worked down in the mine for ten years, and then transferred to the Homestake Company shops, an above ground job, where he learned welding and ironwork. To David's credit, he continued to support the family until all of the children graduated from high school.

The family life remained unsettled, full of dissension, causing Clark to move out of the household several times to live with friends. His schooling was intermittent during this period, as he worked at various jobs to pay his way. Clark ultimately finished his schooling, hopping from family to family, finally receiving a high school diploma at the age of twenty-one. His grades suffered during most of his school experience, but attending school his senior year in Lead, South Dakota, he got straight "A's."

Once the family had graduated from high school, Clark's father moved to Burlington, Iowa, where he met and married a woman who had accumulated a modest nest egg. David began buying rundown buildings, fixing them up, subdividing them, and renting out apartments. In a few years, David was a millionaire, owning many properties in the Burlington area. A few years later his second wife passed away, leaving David very well-off financially. Unfortunately, he met and married another woman in Burlington who was much younger and very demanding. Even though she separated from him after a few years, she inherited all of his money when he passed away. His children received nothing.

Clark's mother, Ruth, never did remarry. Her life was forever influenced by the strain caused by the uncertainties of the economic depression. It was distressing. It was overwhelming. It was debilitating. Life was definitely not fair. But the family survived; most of the children went on to college and two sisters became nurses.

After high school graduation, Clark started working in the Montgomery Ward Store in Denver. Fortunately, he had received a deferment from the draft during his schooling. He knew his time was limited before he would be going into service. His father was a Navy man. He had always admired his father's skills. Perhaps he should consider the Navy. It might be an opportunity to learn to be a carpenter.

ANDERSON • CHAPTER 3

After completing training as an Operating Room Technician in Portsmouth, Clark Anderson went to Camp Algiers, New Orleans, Louisiana. Located on an island off the coast, the navy facility contained a clinic, where Clark gained further experience in the medical field. After a short tour of duty, he traveled by train to Moffit Field, California, where he became a part of a CUB-9 unit, serving all aspects of the medical community. The huge airbase generated a good deal of activity, embracing all the medical practices found in a medium-sized community. Clark finally received his orders for overseas duty.

Navy corpsmen served in many capacities in both the Marines and the Navy. One duty was to be assigned to the Marines as a field medic, wading ashore and providing immediate assistance to the wounded. This was special service, demanding bravery and commitment of the highest order. Other options included serving in permanent hospitals and stations throughout the world. Another option was to serve in forward aid stations, supporting ground troops, and another was to serve aboard naval vessels at sea. Clark's assignment would not be known until he arrived at his duty station.

Late in 1943, Clark traveled to San Francisco, marched to the docks, and boarded the American Legion, a World War I troopship, headed for the South Pacific. The ship did not meet the usual Navy standards as it was very old, very dirty, and efforts to clean it up en route were not successful. Traveling alone, moving at a slow pace, meant many days at sea. Clark was initiated into the Navy's exclusive Neptune Club as they crossed the equator. Early in the war, sailors celebrated crossing the equator with a special ceremony, usually in some form of "hazing" or disgustingly distasteful activity, such as retrieving an apple from the bottom of a barrel of fresh chicken guts, and eating it. Clark was one of the many sailors who passed from "pollywog" to "shellback" on that particular day.

The American Legion landed in New Maya, New Caledonia, and Clark reported to a base hospital located in the capitol city. The hospital staff included many Navy nurses, and it was Anderson's first opportunity to see them in action. This Navy hospital was as close as the Navy nurses got to the front lines. The hospital was buzzing one day with the news a high-ranking official would visit them. Clark was working in a ward, standing next to the entrance, when the door flew open and in walked Mrs. Eleanor Roosevelt, the President's wife, who bumped into him. Clark stood six foot one, and he was surprised to be looking UP at Mrs. Roosevelt, who was quite tall. Mrs. Roosevelt stepped back, said, "So glad to see you heah!" and hurriedly moved on down the ward. Mrs. Roosevelt's reputation for extensive travel, and showing up in unexpected places, was confirmed this day.

After an appropriate tour of duty, Clark packed his gear and boarded a transport for his next assignment, Guadalcanal. The island fighting was in its last stages, but still intense. The Japanese refused to surrender and fought viciously in certain pockets, even though the island was considered secure. The jungle proved to be as big an obstacle as the Japanese defenders. The island was covered with lush, tangled, jungle plants, and contained many sinkholes filled with insect infested scum. These were contrasted with huge bougainvillea plants with large red flowers in lush full bloom. Attempts to re-supply the Japanese garrison with convoys of supplies were turned back by the Americans in a series of fiercely contested naval battles. The Japanese-built airfield was renamed Henderson Field to honor an American pilot killed in the battle of Midway Island. The airfield was the main stronghold for control of the island and was under constant siege by both parties, exchanging ownership every two or three days.

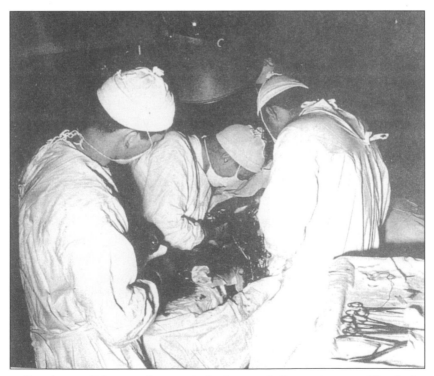

Aboard an LST-the type where surgical suites were built to put young soldiers back together, and treat other afflictions. (Photo-U S Navy)

The Guadalcanal beach was piled high with supplies, containing everything from K-rations to cement, extending for a half-mile down the beach. Success at taking the island would not be hindered by lack of supplies. Success in taking the island was credited to the courageous soldiers of the 3rd Marine Division, who overcame the environmental obstacles and a tough, relentless enemy.

Clark was living and working in an aid station clinic in a tent close to an area known as Maggot Beach. After the first few days of the invasion of the island, many of the dead Japanese were collected, a huge hole bulldozed on the beach, and the soldiers buried in a mass grave. Land crabs, big red creatures six inches across the back, would dig to the remains and not eat them but excrete an enzyme that dissolved the flesh. The beach was literally crawling with millions of land crabs that reproduced in great quantities because of their enormous food source. The constant movement of the sand crabs resembled maggots attacking a decaying carcass, thus the name.

When Clark left San Francisco, he was issued a bolt action 30.06 Springfield rifle that he carried from station to station. At Maggot Beach, he not only worked in the clinic, but occasionally stood guard duty protecting the supplies. After a standard four-hour shift, he would awaken his replacement. One of the men in his unit was an young lad from New York City of Italian descent, who exhibited the New York bravado personality of being a really "tough guy." As the scheduled relief, Clark approached his cot and announced, "Arsenio, get up. The Japanese are coming." The young man leapt out of bed, destroying his mosquito netting, and totally naked, ran screaming down the beach. Clark called the Master at Arms, who sent a detail out to find him and bring him back, while Clark tried to locate another sailor to stand watch.

While on Guadalcanal, Clark contracted a strain of jungle rot on his feet, which proved to be very difficult to cure. It started with a small pimple which when mature would pop open releasing small parasites that would start to eat the flesh. He first treated it with gentian violet (KMNO4), but the parasites seemed to feast on the medicine. He tried iodine and many combinations of ingredients he could think of to get rid it. With constant treating of iodine and alcohol at different strengths, he finally conquered the parasite - four years after returning to the United States.

The sailors grew very excited one afternoon when a Japanese Zero fighter plane suddenly zoomed over the treetops and landed on the airstrip. The severely-wounded pilot was removed from the plane and the plane was stored for study by members of the Air Corps. Clark and a friend visited the plane, and had the thrill of climbing into the cockpit and sitting in the enemy plane. Constructed of very thin sheets of aluminum, the plane did not have the same feel of the solid American planes. However, it was an effective and capable fighting weapon.

Work in the clinic was intermittent and varied. A majority of time was spent on common problems; diarrhea, lacerations, different types of rash, jungle rot, foot fungus and Dengue fever. However, there were still perforations, shrapnel, shattered bones and torn muscles from engaging the enemy in mop-up operations. The remaining Japanese never wavered in their intent to do as much harm as possible.

Guadalcanal housed a plantation of coconut palms, owned by a well-known soap company, especially planted to produce copra, the white meat of the coconuts, for processing into a number of products. There were strict orders not to bomb, strafe, or damage the trees on the plantation in order to preserve them for production after the war. This proved to be costly for the Marines, since the ingenious Japanese snipers would position themselves in the treetops and inflict a good deal of damage, with individual snipers sneaking back into the plantation after the main force was driven from the area. Protecting the investment of the plantation's owners was not commensurate with the taking of young men's lives. The action of the snipers continued until the island was totally secure.

Clark's medical unit was placed aboard an LST and moved to Bougainville Island, where they had to perform many more difficult surgical operations. Saving lives and sewing young men back together became an hourly task. With fighting still in progress, it was necessary to take special precautions for protection. The Seabees excavated a large hole, covered it with coconut palm logs, and then covered the logs with several feet of dirt. The entrance was constructed in an "S" curve of fifty-five-gallon steel drums filled with sand, so a rifle shell could not enter the operating room in a direct path. A small power plant provided electricity, and wood walls and floor made it relatively clean. In this underground chamber the team performed a large number of amputations and other serious surgeries caused by the continued fighting.

A number of Nisei (citizens of Japanese-American origin) marines performed invaluable services. They could speak the Japanese language and could interrogate the few Japanese who surrendered. Because of the presence of the Nisei marines, a Japanese soldier would occasionally sneak into the American food lines for a meal. The desperate thieves had been educated in the United States and could speak perfect English. A few of the

Japanese soldiers were captured while in the mess line, but not all.

At night the Japanese brought a cannon out of concealment and randomly shelled the secured hospital area. The Seabees decided to help solve the problem by bulldozing a small airstrip right through the center of the jungle. A Piper Cub observation plane delivered to the island scouted for the artillery's location. The Japanese cleverly concealed the cannon inside a cave on the active volcano on the island. Steel tracks permitted the artillery piece to be rolled out at night, fire a few rounds and then be pulled back inside the cave. Once the cannon was located and silenced, the Seabees built several Quonset half-round buildings, permitting the medical team to utilize their skills above ground.

The volcano was still active, and every morning a small coating of ash covered all exterior surfaces. Clark was happy the top did not blow off the volcano while he was stationed there. The airstrip continued to function, and on one occasion, an observation plane's wingtip caught a mahogany tree, and the plane pirouetted into a treetop. The plane was still hanging there when the team left the island. The medical team stayed on Bougainville for six or eight weeks before moving on.

Orders were received specifying a group of ten people was needed for a special assignment. Clark, along with seven other corpsmen, a surgeon, Lieutenant Commander Dr. Trimbur, and a medical doctor, Lieutenant Dr. Jackson, were selected. They boarded a C-47 bound for Port Moresby, New Guinea, and transferred from there to Hollandia, New Guinea. The team was placed aboard LST-1027 to be used as a hospital ship. The second level of the LST had rooms for the crew on the starboard side of the ship and ward rooms and operating rooms on the port side. The LSTs had two interior decks; a lower for carrying tanks and loaded trucks for delivery on the beach and the second level usually allowed for rolling equipment of lower clearance. Landing craft and troops were normally transported on deck, with the six invasion craft lowered by cranes.

The LST had to be sanitized and prepared to receive the injured, no small undertaking for the incoming medical team. Clark and the assistants built the operating room amidships with three wardrooms on each side, each housing six men in stacked bunks.

There were no operating tables available, so Clark decided to build one. Rounding up pipe, sheet metal and boards, he designed a table that would adjust to various heights. Borrowing welding equipment and tools, he proceeded to cut and weld the pipes together. His inexperience showed when he was welding galvanized pipes, when any seasoned welder knows galvanized pipes cannot be successfully welded together. However, Clark proceeded, completed the welding, and the height-adjustable tables worked just fine throughout their stay on board.

He also built stands for the lap packs to hold the sterile goods that were available. However, there was no way to sterilize used medical equipment. An autoclave was not available, so the medics used soap and water, heat, and ten percent denatured alcohol to prepare surgical tools for their next use. They acquired "lap packs" from the U.S. Army Depots for use aboard the LST. Lap packs contained everything necessary for one operation.

Putting out to sea, the LST proceeded to the invasion beach on the east coast of Leyte, Philippine Islands, where they landed with the second wave of the island invasion. As the big ship nosed into the beach, a number of wounded were already waiting for their arrival, some ambulatory and some on stretchers. The men were immediately taken aboard, and when the number of wounded that could be accommodated was reached, the LST backed off the beach and headed for Hollandia. The 100 or so wounded were evaluated for seriousness of the wounds, and once categorized the operations started continuing without interruption. As they had learned in their Great Lakes training, the least wounded were attended to first, since their survival rate was higher. The doctors and assistants would catch a bite to eat or a quick nap whenever they could, since attending to the wounded was continuous. The LST-1027 made four and one-half trips to Hollandia and back. Traveling in convoy, the trip would take about a week, with several stops on the way. On the return trips, the bottom hold and upper deck were filled with jeeps, trucks and materials needed to resupply the units.

The team used large quantities of "lap packs" consisting of sheets that would permit abdominal surgery. The men suffered a good deal of stomach wounds caused by shrapnel. Working on the intestines, the shrapnel would be located, removed and the damage assessed. The intestines would be separated from viscera, pulled out, inspected, sutured and stuffed back in; more intestines were then pulled out and the process repeated. Repair of shrapnel tears was made using the "Bull Durham" technique. Bull Durham was a small sack of inexpensive tobacco used for rolling one's own cigarettes, a measure of economy during the depression. The top contained a string through a lapped edge that puckered together as it was drawn close. The technique worked on the intestine since it was fast, and Mother Nature helped in healing. As they worked their way down the intestine sewing and stuffing, they were assured of finding all of the perforations, locating most of the shrapnel.

While taking on wounded on Leyte, they were visited every night by a Japanese bomber that would brave the anti-aircraft to drop a few bombs on the beach. The plane's engines made a funny noise, and the daily happening became known as "another visit from Washing Machine Charley!" Also, there were daily broadcasts on the radio by "Tokyo Rose," whose dulcet tones and homespun chatter were aimed at breaking the U.S. Soldier's morale. She played American dance records, and announced American military troop and ship movements with great accuracy. Instead of damaging morale, she actually bolstered it by giving the GI's something to focus on. And, the soldiers were kept abreast of the most recent recordings by big bands back home. How Tokyo Rose acquired the platters is unknown.

The convoy trip through the Surigao Strait and Mindanao Gulf was hazardous, since the Japanese took advantage of the very narrow passageway. The Japanese kamikaze suicide planes, loaded with explosives, were making an enormous impact on Allied shipping during this period of the war. Climbing to 5000 feet, the planes would dive out of the sun making them difficult to see, sight and shoot. A victory ship immediately behind LST-1027 was hit by a kamikaze and literally just disappeared, leaving very little debris. It blew up and immediately sank. Several of Clark's friends were on board the lost vessel.

A stop on the west shore of Leyte in Lyngayen Gulf was equally as harrowing. Anchored several hundred yards from the beach, there was a good amount of floating debris in the harbor. The Japanese would hide under crates filled with explosives and detonators, and float toward a ship to destroy it. As a result, day and night, debris of any size was suspect and fired at with a machine gun to blow up the explosives. There were many bodies from landing craft and sunken ships floating on the surface, both American and Japanese, that were retrieved daily by service crews.

Nearing the end of the Philippine campaign Clark Anderson was transferred to Admiral Halsey's flagship, the USS Missouri. General Douglas MacArthur was about to return to take over the Philippines, and the Navy was withdrawing from commanding the area. From the Missouri, Clark was put aboard a refrigerator ship in a convoy headed for San Francisco.

Clark's father, now in his sixties, had joined the Army Construction Engineers, and had been building a variety of things in the Solomon Islands. He returned to Hawaii, where he wanted to see his World War I ship, the USS Oklahoma, that was resting on its side in Pearl Harbor as a result of the December 7th attack. By pure coincidence, the son's ship en route home passed Hawaii where his father was stationed.

Returning to San Francisco, it took a week for processing, and finally Clark was sent to Camp Shoemaker, California, where he was assigned to work in a dispensary in a Navy Hospital. While in the operating room, it was the second opportunity to see the famous Navy nurses in action. Most were Lieutenants with authority over a Second Class Pharmacists Mate. Clark was particularly impressed by nurse Pondgratz, who was tough, demanding and unrelenting. And, in charge!

Clark Anderson's enlistment in the Navy was for three years or the duration of the war, whichever was longer. He had served in the Navy three years six months and was scheduled to be released. A recruiting officer approached Clark to re-enlist with the promise of promotion to Chief Petty Officer. It was tempting since Chief Petty Officers ran the Navy. However, Clark was very unhappy with the "class system" in the Navy. Some officers deserved respect, while others were purposefully snobbish and difficult to deal with. This really bothered Clark, so he decided to leave the Navy. One of the first to be separated from Camp Shoemaker, he boarded a train to Lambert Field, Missouri, for final discharge.

After three and one-half years of service life, and two years of assisting in the repairing of young men in the South Pacific who had faced a living hell, he returned to civilian life.

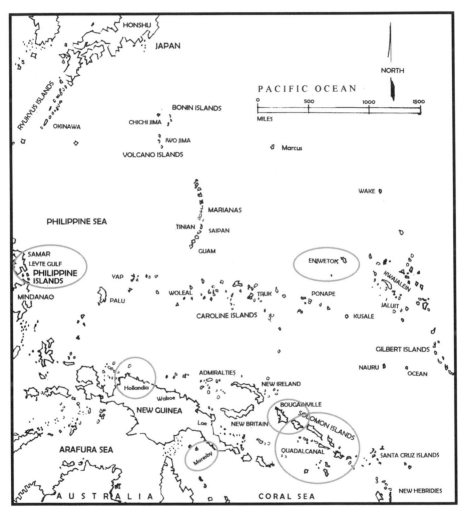

The South Pacific area where Clark Anderson's LST traveled to Guadalcanal, Einiwetok, Bougainville, New Guinea and other locations

ANDERSON • CHAPTER 4

After leaving Camp Shoemaker, Clark Anderson had leave-time to use before being finally discharged. Clark decided to get as far away from the Navy regimen as possible, and found work on a ranch in Wyoming. Located about twenty miles west of Belle Fourche, South Dakota, the ranch was remote and the scenery beautiful. Mickey Blackburn owned and operated the sheep and cattle ranch, and was an interesting person. His face was unusually scarred from burns suffered when he lit a match to look down in a fifty-five-gallon gas barrel to see if it was empty. During the summer Mickey employed a man who had lost both legs, but amazingly, could ride a horse. The fellow worked as a sheepherder back in the mountains, and when the weather started to turn cold, he would return from the mountains, go into town, write a bad check, and spend the winter in prison. The routine suited him just fine, and the State gratuitously accepted the winter tenant.

Clark worked in the hayfield, cutting, raking, hauling and storing hay. It was hot, dusty work, and the physical nature of it energized him. He spent time repairing the out-buildings, the barns and sheds, giving him an opportunity to do carpentry work he thoroughly enjoyed. Clark worked on the ranch for almost a year, finally making a decision to leave to attend college.

He enrolled in the University of Dakota Wesleyan in Mitchell, South Dakota. He enjoyed the academic work and received a double degree in Sociology and Education in 1952. Even though he had the G.I. Bill, he worked construction, framing buildings and troweling concrete for local contractors.

While attending Dakota Wesleyan, he met, courted, and married Patricia May Shipton from Mitchell, South Dakota, on July 29th, 1948. Clark always felt it would be a "cold day in hell" when he got married, and when the two spent their honeymoon in the Bighorn Mountains in Wyoming, it was "colder than hell!"

Patricia's father passed away the year before Clark and she were married, but he had an unusual distinction. Captain George Shipton served in Colonel Teddy Roosevelt's Rough Riders in Mexico, and spent several months chasing Pancho Villa through the mountains.

Two children were added to their family, Lynn Dee on June 27th 1950 and Troy Michael on March 2nd, 1952, both born with cystic fibrosis. It was a source of great anguish for Patricia and Clark.

After graduating from college, Clark took a high school teaching position at an independent consolidated school in Argonne, South Dakota, for a year. He taught English, sociology, Biology, and vocal music. Clark also coached the girls' softball team by default. The commercial teacher who normally coached the team entered a mental institution, and Clark as the newest member of the faculty got the dubious honor of replacing her. He also coached the girl's basketball team, and admittedly knew absolutely nothing about the women's game. At the first practice he asked the captain to choose up sides and play a game, watched the girls play, asked some questions, and learned the rules. The players were farm girls: mature, tough, well-fed, and good athletes. Both the women's softball team and basketball team went undefeated that year.

At the end of the school year in the spring of 1953, Clark heard that a dry climate might be better for his two young children suffering from cystic fibrosis. He drove to Albuquerque and started looking for a job. He first worked as an attendant at a gas station. His employer was very understanding, and raised Clark's salary to a level where Clark could apply for a GI Veteran's loan in order to get a new house. He purchased a three-bedroom home with the GI loan and moved his family down in 1954. Clark also worked as an assistant manager in a lumberyard, and part-time at another filling station in order to feed his family. Deciding to get back into teaching, he moved to Tularosa, New Mexico with an opportunity to teach English. In Tularosa he moved into an older adobe house, made of clay bricks reinforced with horse manure and straw. The few times it did rain in Tularosa, the house reeked of manure odors. The kitchen was about fifty feet long, with outside doors leading to the bedrooms. The heating system used coal and mesquite roots, which gave the house a special flavor.

When Clark first started registering students in his new school, he learned several lessons. The school board and the superintendent permitted the physical disciplining of the students and supported the teacher forced to use those measures. The registration room was very crowded with unregistered students, and Clark asked for silence so he could began the registration process. The students totally ignored his several pleadings, obviously showing disrespect for the teacher. Clark looked around the room and located the tallest student, worked his way over to him and told him to sit down at a library table. When the student gave him an obvious sneer, Clark slapped him on the side of the face, knocking him out. Clark then picked him up and sat him at the table with his head on his arms. The silence in the room was deafening. Students immediately lined up, sat down to fill out their forms, and registration proceeded in an orderly manner.

By default, Clark became the head disciplinarian at the high school. It seems the young man was a star athlete, greatly admired by his fellow students. Clark was also admired, but considered an ogre at the same time. He taught sociology and economics to junior and senior students, as well as eighth grade English. At the end of the school year the superintendent asked him to return to teach, but Clark decided to leave. He took a job as a cement finisher in Mitchell , South Dakota.

The tragedy of cystic fibrosis took its toll when both children passed away when they were ten years old. It was a devastating loss for the family, from which Pat and Clark suffered great personal pain. On October 29, 1961, a third child was born, a daughter Cassie, who was fortunately spared from the terrible disease.

Clark received word his father in Burlington, Iowa, was in the hospital. His wife had abandoned him, and his money was tied up in real estate. Clark traveled to Burlington and rescued his father from the hospital, with Clark's savings of 500 dollars. Without a job and without money, Clark, Pat, and Cassie returned to Mitchell, South Dakota, where Pat's father let them live in one of his farmhouses so they would not have to pay rent. Clark found work in a window fabricating company, and worked as a maintenance man on weekends. He also worked on the farm. His father-in-law did not pay him a salary but did give him a few dollars every so often. With Clark being gone all the time every day, Patricia became very isolated and alienated.

Clark put Pat and Cassie in the car and drove to Ames, Iowa, to visit a sister, the wife of a local dentist. His sister suggested Clark look for work in the Ames area, since there was a good deal of construction going on. He managed to find work with a local construction company for several years, and finally went to work for the City of Ames in Building Maintenance and Repair. For twenty years, he worked steadily, finally getting to do the carpentry work he initially sought and so thoroughly enjoyed. Retiring in 1990, he continues to work with his tools, and enjoying his grandchild who lives in Grinnell, Iowa. In 1979, Patricia and Clark divorced, ending their thirty-one year marriage.

When Clark Anderson looks back on his military experience, he has no recollection of the hundreds of faces of the young men who lay on the operating tables of his various assignments. He sees only the flesh the surgical team repaired, the plasma administered, the I V's inserted, and the constant cleanup after every surgery.

The bravery and honor of the young men who rushed into battle, facing the jungle, pestilence, disease, and violent injury were never seen by the young Navy corpsman. However, the bravery and honor of the young men, the residue of fighting in the jungle, pestilence, disease and violent injury to these young men have been a part of his memory ever since.

BOOK 4

R. Burdette Jack

R. Burdette Jack

Corporal
B Company, 1st Battalion
86th Regiment
10th Mountain Division

"Any man who can walk,
get out of bed and return to your unit.
There is a big battle going on
and we need your bed!"

~Medical Officer
Florence - 24th General Hospital

JACK • CHAPTER 1

KABLOOM!

The loud explosion caught the soldiers standing in the mess hall line by complete surprise. The long line of hungry men snaked from the mess hall past several barracks, and on this bright sunny day they joshed each other as the line moved along at a fair pace. One very uncommitted soldier in basic training lit a cherry bomb and threw it into an open barracks window hoping to startle the soldiers in the mess line. The resulting explosion achieved its purpose, causing the men to jump in surprise. The soldier's laughter was soon interrupted by a Captain charging out of the barracks with a very committed look in his eyes.

Scowling at the men in the line, the Captain stated firmly, "I know we won't find the soldier who threw a firecracker through the window, damaging a commode in the latrine. However, you, you, you and you, Attention! You four are hereby ordered to locate a new commode and have it installed in this barracks in one hour or your names will be placed on report! Do you understand? One hour! Dismiss!"

Private Burdette Jack looked at the other three soldiers, one from his company and the other two complete strangers. The men were in the later stages of the seventeen-week basic infantry training at Camp Joseph T. Robinson, Arkansas, and were shocked and surprised by this sudden turn of events. It seems this was the Army way. Someone goofed off or screwed up, and someone else had to pick up the pieces.

The men walked inside the barracks to view the damage and check out the commode. The cherry bomb had not landed near the commode, but in the commode, causing it to break into three big pieces, and scatter smaller pieces around the latrine. The Captain had stepped around the damage to turn the control to stop the water flow, and managed to spray his trousers in the process. The soldiers in line knew better than to snicker at his dilemma. The four soldiers investigated what tools it would take to replace the commode. One soldier suggested, "I worked at the motor pool last week. Let's go over there and see if we can borrow some tools." As they approached the motor pool, the young soldier approached a sergeant, and related their problem. The sergeant expressed understanding and loaned them a jeep. The four men gathered some tools, climbed aboard the jeep, and made their plans.

Since most everyone on the post was in the mess hall, they drove to one of the more remote barracks and entered, shouting, to see if it was occupied. With no one at home, one soldier was stationed at the door as a lookout, while the other three entered the latrine and shut off the water to one of the commodes. Methodically they removed the caps, screws, and flushing gasket. Loading it aboard the jeep, they took a back route to the barracks and slipped in the back door. Without caulking or a seating gasket, they replaced the commode and hooked up the flushing mechanism. Turning on the water, it worked perfectly without leaking. They gathered up the broken pieces, while one soldier mopped up the excess water. The broken commode was deposited in a garbage container outside another barracks on the way back to the motor pool. Returning to the original barracks, Private Jack knocked on the Captain's door, and reported. "Sir. We have completed replacement of the damaged commode. It is ready for inspection."

The Captain entered the latrine and gave it a thorough going over. "It took you fifty-five minutes. Good work, men! Go have your meal and I hope you have learned a good lesson!"

With a crisp "Thank you, sir!" the men turned and left for the mess hall.

As the men sauntered along, one soldier remarked, "I don't know, Burdette. Exactly what lesson was it that we learned?"

JACK • CHAPTER 2

Burdette Jack registered for the draft when he turned 18, just as every young man in America was required to do. He was working as a hired hand for George and Ruby Norden where room, board, and 35 dollars a month was a fair wage. This was a good situation and Burdette felt he was very well off. He liked the farmland around Guernsey, Iowa, and it was a good community to grow up in. The folks were friendly and helped one another throughout the depression. The year 1941 was a big one for Burdette. He graduated from Guernsey High School, got his drivers license, and started working for the Nordens. 1940 had been a good year also. He played well on the high school baseball team and developed to be a pretty good hitter. He also had his first real date. Burdette took a young lady named Irene LaKose all the way to Newton to the skating rink. There they could hold hands while skating in the dim light with a multi-faceted mirrored center globe exploding in small rays of light on the walls and ceiling. It was very impressive, and romantic, to the young Guernsey lad.

A year later he earned big money picking corn. After the Norden's crop was in, he hired out to the Schlesselman's, receiving ten cents a bushel. For eleven days straight, he averaged one hundred ten bushels a day following a team-drawn bang-board wagon, picking, shucking, and chucking. When he received his pay, Burdette felt he was really rich.

Burdette was born at his grandparents' home south of Guernsey on February 13th, 1924. George and Naomi (Grier) Jack were farming two miles west of Deep River, but Naomi chose to deliver at her parents' home, Ross and Clara Grier, closer to Guernsey. Burdette was later joined by three brothers; Melvin, born in October 1925, Lowell, born in November 1927 and Stan born in January 1932. The family moved several times in the early 30's. Burdette remembers spending his sixth birthday in the Iowa City Children's Hospital for a mastoid operation.

Burdette started school in August 1929, and that fall the stock market bottomed out. Everyone thought the world would come to an end, and for some it did. Living in the country, they were carried to the Guernsey school in a horse-drawn 'hack' that during winter was drafty and beastly cold. His mother solved that problem by heating bricks in the oven, wrapping them in a burlap sack so he could place his feet on them during the ride to school. Burdette was fortunate enough to have a beautiful brown and white pony while growing up. During the severe drought of 1934,

Burdette grazed cattle with his pony along the railroad track that went through their farm. He was very fond of the pony named 'Nellie,' and a number of years later while Burdette was home on leave from service, Nellie was kicked by another horse, breaking her ribs. Nellie died from internal bleeding, and since she was so near and dear, Burdette had the pony skinned and the hide taken to Cownie Fur Company in Des Moines, where it was tanned and made into a lap robe. Burdette owns it to this day, and considers it a family heirloom.

The winter of 1935-36 was a particularly memorable one because of the severe weather throughout the year. A hot, dry summer was followed by a winter that set records in both snow quantities and low temperatures. Several successive storms deposited six to eight foot snowdrifts across the mid-west and the temperature registered 30 below for a week, never rising above zero for 30 days. It is vividly remembered since it was the middle year of three years when Burdette delivered flyers for the Jack Spratt Food Stores to every home in Guernsey every week. School was closed for two weeks because it could not be heated to a comfortable level. The summer of 1936 was even hotter and dryer than 1935. The fifty acre pasture across from the Jack farm was virgin pasture, and ox trail ruts from pulling prairie schooners across Iowa were still visible. One side of the road adjoining the pasture and the edge of the pasture were filled with Canadian thistles, and unbeknownst to the Jacks, the county decided to spray them. The county workers lowered the fence and applied a generous dose of spray to the this-tles. Subsequently, eight of the ten milk cows in the pasture ate some of the thistles, were poisoned, and died. The county reimbursed the Jacks 40 dol-lars per cow, but it was a difficult loss for the family. Burdette still remem-bers his mother sitting at the kitchen table, sobbing into her hands when she first heard of the tragedy.

The Guernsey Alumni-Guernsey High School basketball game was always a popular event, generally held in December, usually won by the high school because they had more students and players. On this Sunday afternoon, the boys were in the dressing room, taunting each other and preparing to show off before the home crowd. Coach King entered the room and called for attention. He then informed the boys that Japanese airplanes were bombing Pearl Harbor, and that aggression would involve the U.S. in a war with not only Japan, but probably also with Germany. Coach King informed them that he was a member of the Seabees, and could be called into service at any time. The game went on, but most fans were at home listening to their radios.

Burdette continued working after graduation until February 1944, when, at the age of twenty, his draft number was drawn and he was told to report in June. Early morning on June 6th a group of young men from Iowa County gathered at Mel's Standard Gas Station in Victor, Iowa, to board a Greyhound bus that would take them to Camp Dodge in Des Moines. At Camp Dodge, they were sworn into the United States Army, given physicals, shots, and placed in a long line to get their uniforms. After a fitful night's sleep on a strange cot with an itchy wool army blanket, the men were awakened early, hurried through a food line, and marched to the train depot, where they climbed aboard a troop train. Twenty-four hours later, sitting upright and eating two meals of cheese sandwiches and apples, they arrived at Camp Robinson, Arkansas, northeast of Little Rock.

For seventeen weeks they learned Army procedures, marched, fired rifles, marched, attended lectures, marched, ran obstacle courses, spent some time in the woods on bivouac, and marched some more. There were no leaves or passes granted during basic training; it was up early, hard work, army food, and more training, seven days a week.

Returning to the barracks after one overnight bivouac, the men were unpacking, cleaning their equipment, and storing their gear, when two Military Policemen entered the building. One policeman asked, "Where is Burdette Jack?" The men called Jack from the other end of the barracks, and when Burdette approached, the policeman asked, "Are you Burdette Jack?"

"Yes, sir! I am Burdette Jack."

"Jack, you are under arrest for wrecking a jeep! You will have to come with us."

"Sir, I don't know what you are talking about. I did not wreck a jeep. I haven't even driven one."

"Jack, we have evidence! You will have to come with us to the stock-ade."

Burdette kept insisting he knew nothing about it. Finally, Burdette called his first sergeant into the room. The sergeant asked a few questions about where and how this all came about. The MP indicated the jeep had crashed the night before, and a package of laundry was found in the jeep with Burdette Jack's name in several pairs of shorts. The first sergeant verified that Jack had been on an overnight bivouac and could not possibly have commandeered the jeep. The MP's left and later acknowledged that there had been a laundry mix-up. Burdette was greatly relieved at being exonerated from what could have been an embarrassing and career costly accidental confinement.

At the completion of seventeen weeks, the majority of the young men would be sent overseas as replacement soldiers for units already in combat. In 1944 the war had been fought for two years, and for a novice army learning how to do battle, casualties were high. The army's standard procedure for post-basic leave was to allow soldiers ten days to reach their next destination (delay en route), so the young men headed for home as fast as possible.

Burdette returned home where he spent a good deal of time caring for Nellie after her accident. Visiting family and attending church in uniform gave the young soldier pride and pleasure. Too soon, however, the young soldiers in the area congregated at the Cedar Rapids Railroad depot to board a Baltimore and Ohio RR train headed for Fort Meade, Maryland. On November 11th, 1944, they moved on to Fort Patrick Henry, Virginia, an embarkation point, where they were put aboard the USS Monticello, formerly an Italian luxury ship converted to transport troops. The huge ship, over one thousand feet long, would carry troops, officers, USO performers and a navy crew; for a total of over fourteen thousand persons on this voyage. Leaving port, the Monticello was placed in the center of a huge convoy of over one hundred ships, including aircraft carriers, troopships, supply ships, destroyers, and cruisers.

Jack volunteered to serve on Kitchen Police (KP), and spent his time carrying foodstuffs from storage to the kitchen. Occasionally a few cans of tomato juice, or a case of cream-filled cookies found their way into the bowels of the troopship, and were greatly enjoyed by Burdette's unit. Burdette never was accused by the cooks for being involved in this sort of chicanery, but in a confined city of fourteen thousand people, it's easy to misplace a few foodstuffs, and difficult to locate them once they are gone.

After thirteen days at sea, the ships neared the southern coast of Spain and half of the convoy veered north to northern Europe, while the remainder prepared to pass through the Strait of Gibraltar. Suddenly the convoy slowed and destroyers began circling about. It seems a submarine had been detected. Destroyers began dropping depth charges, continuing into the early evening. The next morning the sea was cluttered with floating debris and oil, indicating something underwater had been eliminated.

Continuing through the narrows into the Mediterranean Sea, the convoy proceeded to the Port of Naples, where the troops disembarked on November 26th, 1944, and were trucked to a Replacement Depot tent city. The soldiers would soon receive their new unit assignments and be thrust into a vicious war, not of their own choosing.

Crowded conditions on the troop ship made the Atlantic crossing most uncomfortable. There were not this many smiling faces on most troop ships the entire voyage, as most soldiers were very seasick. (Photo-U S Army)

JACK • CHAPTER 3

Private Burdette Jack checked the bulletin board for several minutes until he found his new assignment. He was assigned to the 10th Mountain Division, B Company, 1st Battalion, 86th Regiment as a BAR man. The main group of the 10th Mountain Division would not arrive for another month or so. It would mean moving into a tent encampment near the front lines and becoming familiar with the new surroundings and new officers.

The reputation of the 10th Mountain Division preceded it to Italy. Trained as expert skiers at Camp Carson, Colorado, the soldiers were skilled infantrymen prepared for the winter and mountainous terrain of northern Italy. Of the twelve to fifteen thousand men assigned to the 10th Division, only twenty-five hundred men were trained to climb mountains and ski down as another tactic for engaging the enemy. The twenty-five hundred men were reputed to be the cream of the crop, trained as Special Forces, and in the peak of physical and fighting condition. The remainder of the division included three regiments of infantrymen (85th, 86th and 87th Regiments), a transportation group, mortar and machine gun companies, and a medical battalion. A quartermaster group furnished equipment, uniforms, laundry, ammunition and all items necessary to keep the division operating.

After the war, several ski troopers returned to Colorado and the northeastern states to develop ski areas, thereby laying the groundwork for our nation's very successful ski industry.

Fighting in the mountains was difficult at best, since supplying the forward troops was almost impossible. The war in the mountains turned into constant artillery battles, with the infantry advancing under heavy fire. Digging foxholes in solid rock was not possible, and there were few places to hide. Once the infantry advanced out of the valleys and forests, there was little concealment.

The men moved forward toward the front, into a camp of tents that protected them from most of the foul weather. Winter in the mountains was unpredictable, mostly cloudy and mostly wet. The men went on a few patrols to get the feel of combat and fighting under these conditions.

Jack had the additional burden of being a BAR man, carrying the twenty-two pound automatic rifle in addition to his full field pack. Each soldier had to know his weapon's description and repeat it during inspection. Jack could say it in his sleep: "U S Browning Automatic Rifle, caliber .30,

The Germans were only one obstacle to overcome in Italy. The cold, rainy weather made progress pursuing the enemy difficult.

model 1914 A-4, air cooled, gas operated, magazine fed, rapid fire shoulder weapon, weighing 22point2 pounds, 24 pounds with tripod." Experience showed that the life of a BAR man was short lived, as the Germans did not want any rapid-fire weapon pointed at them. Only a machine gunner was reputed to have a shorter life. On patrol, the BAR man had one soldier who carried additional magazines of ammunition, since any contact with the enemy meant using several clips. Burdette's carrier was a young man from Swannanoa, North Carolina, named Eugene Brank. He was a good man and they became close friends.

The men continued early morning training and patrols until the middle of February 1945, when the weather improved and the spring offensive began. The regiment was taken by truck to the docks, loaded on an LCI (Landing Craft Infantry), and transported via water to Leghorn, Italy. They performed a successful beach landing, working inland to form a pincher movement around the Germans. While moving inland they met a good amount of intense enemy opposition, but finally linked up with the inland American division, encircling the Germans. On the second night, American forces managed to capture Mt. Sasomalore, which was the second ridge before descending into the Po River Valley. During the night, Germans fired more than one hundred fifty rounds of artillery on the mountaintop, forcing the Americans to withdraw. However, the next day a concentrated push put the mountain under American control for good.

Burdette had an opportunity to write home and attempted to inform his parents of his location by writing, "How are my leghorn hens doing?" This sophomoric effort received a large black mark by the censor through "leghorn" when his parents finally received the letter.

The division was under constant artillery and mortar barrages, as well as air attacks. One afternoon Jack and members of his squad watched an American P-47 and a German Focke-Wulf 190 in aerial combat for nearly a half an hour. The battle ended when the FW 190 took a nosedive into the side of a mountain, just a short distance from Company B's emplacement.

Soldiers were always collecting souvenirs that could be kept, sold or traded. At one time Burdette had acquired five German Luger pistols, a very hot commodity in trading circles. He later managed to sell them to Air Force personnel for one hundred twenty-five dollars apiece. In true depression fashion, he was able to spirit the money away, and it came in very handy later.

Basic training at Camp Robinson prepared the young soldiers for certain aspects of combat, but not the reality of it. Sleeping in tents in sleeping bags did not prepare them for sleeping in rock strewn craters resulting from artillery, wrapped in a woolen blanket and shelter half. At least Italy was better than Camp Robinson, Arkansas, in one respect; large hairy spiders that looked like tarantulas did not try to sneak into your sleeping bag at night. Sleeping in foxholes and wearing combat boots meant you were subject to wet feet. Sox were changed at every opportunity, since foot problems for the infantry were a major concern. Wet sox were placed inside one's jacket next to the body where body heat might dry them out during the day. Fresh laundry was delivered every three or four days, and clean underwear and fresh dry sox were always welcome. The army did its best to get hot food to men at the front, but C-rations in cans and K-rations in cardboard cartons were the usual fare. C-rations were carried in their backpack, and k-rations and chocolate bars were handed out at different intervals. Occasionally hot coffee was available, but rarely.

Hearing and understanding the sounds during conflict was learned early in combat. The chatter of machine pistols was different from machine guns. The bolt action Mauser rifle had a recognizable pop. The whiz of German 88 mm. artillery as it flew toward you was very distinctive, much different from cannon of a smaller size. Mortar fire flew high and came straight down without a sound until it exploded, and was frightening since one did not know the direction or distance from which it was fired.

Once at the front, the soldiers were on patrol almost every day, probing the German lines in an attempt to determine strength and location of the enemy. One evening after returning from a long and arduous patrol, the men dug in, ready for a well deserved good night's sleep. Unbeknown to them a British artillery group of "Long Toms," huge cannon with extra long barrels for shooting extra long distances, moved in just five hundred feet behind their encampment during the day. In the middle of the night they began firing at German targets, and the loudness and muzzle compression of the big guns scared the living daylights out of the men. The concussion from firing hurt their ears, and the men could not sleep the rest of the night, huddling in their foxholes with their fingers plugging their ears.

A company runner, a soldier who delivers messages during combat when the radio is not working, was from Marshalltown, Iowa, and a good friend of Burdette. During one advance, the men were taking a break, concealed behind a tall concrete wall embankment along a roadway. They were suddenly the target for German artillery who lobbed in several 88 mm shells into the countryside. A section of the concrete wall toppled over, trapping the company runner underneath. Eight or ten soldiers hurriedly tried to lift the wall off, but were unable to budge it. They tried to find a lever of some sort just to give the soldier some relief. Unfortunately, the soldier was crushed to death because the wall was too heavy to move and the men could not respond fast enough. It was a sad experience for Burdette, losing a close friend in such a bizarre manner.

The first week of March, the troops were constantly probing German lines, with occasional exchanges of gunfire without a major offensive show. The morning of March 9th, Jack's battalion was dug in on a ridge along Mt. Sasomolare. At 5:00 AM, the Germans started a barrage of artillery and mortars on their position, with constant bombardment. A shell hit a large tree, exploding about thirty feet from Burdette Jack's foxhole, and the concussion was deafening. Burdette felt shrapnel tear into his body as he passed out from the concussion and shock. A medic immediately jumped into the foxhole and tended his wounds, injecting him with a shot of morphine.

Burdette regained consciousness as two medics carried his litter down the mountain, toward a field hospital in a large tent. He was told he had been unconscious for ten hours, and had been wounded in the back, shoulder, arm, and leg with shrapnel. At the forward medical tent, doctors proceeded to remove all the larger pieces of steel, and marked and treated the smaller wounds. The next day he was loaded into an ambulance with other soldiers and taken to Florence to a large city hospital taken over by the Allies. There he was operated on for the remaining shrapnel, and wounds were properly tended and dressed. Burdette Jack would recover in the 24th General Hospital in Florence for six weeks.

Narrow roads in the mountains meant snipers could keep squads pinned down for several hours. (Photo-US Army)

JACK • CHAPTER 4

The 24th General Hospital in Florence, Italy, was a very busy place. Casualties in the Italian theater were very high, and there was a constant flow of new wounded soldiers to be treated. Burdette Jack does not remember very much of his first few weeks in Florence, since he received medication to reduce the pain from multiple injuries. As his condition continued to improve, he learned to like the clean sheets and three square meals served daily, luxuries compared to living in the field. Recovery was slow, however, since his wounds were not only numerous, but deep.

Some of the more serious wounded were sent back to the United States for further surgery or repair. Soldiers with certain injuries were slated to return to their units to continue the fight against the Germans. The Italian Army had capitulated early in the campaign, but the Germans fought with determination and energy as the Americans neared their homeland. Fighting a defensive war in the mountains was decidedly in the favor of the defenders. Each advancing yard was expensive in terms of men and equipment. America was paying a very high price for Italian real estate.

After six weeks Burdette was feeling much better, and pleased by the scuttlebutt that a high-ranking general would soon visit the hospital. Burdette was surprised one day by the flurry of activity in the ward, when he recognized the approaching general. The Commanding General of the Italian Campaign, Major General Mark Clark, was walking through the ward handing out the Purple Heart Award for soldiers wounded in action. The tall, taciturn, humble soldier stopped at Jack's bed and removed a Purple Heart medal from the carrying case. He deftly pinned it on Burdette's hospital gown and thanked him for his service to his country. It was a task the general would repeat many times that day in the 24th General Hospital.

Burdette replaced the medal in the case, proud to have received it from General Clark. The next morning, an officer strode into the ward and glanced around. "Let me have your attention! All patients that can walk, pack up and return to your unit! We are starting a big offensive down the Po River Valley. We not only need you at the front, we are going to need your bed in a few days. MOVE OUT! This is an order!"

Burdette still had several open wounds that were slow to heal. But he could walk. He retrieved his uniform and his duffel bag that had been delivered during his stay in the hospital, and reported to several six by six trucks that were waiting outside. When the trucks were fully loaded they began following the winding road through the mountains, and soon one could hear the faint sound of artillery in the distance. Too soon, they were back near the front lines.

The drivers pulled up at a wide spot on the road, and the men promptly jumped out. When the soldiers asked the drivers where certain divisions or regiments were, the driver replied, "Beats the hell out of me! You guys are on your own." The driver then jumped back into the truck to return to Florence to pick up another load of the 'walking wounded.'

Burdette ran into a number of infantrymen who directed him to a different sector. He ran into a sergeant and enquired if he knew where Company B of the 1st Battalion of the 86th Regiment was located. The sergeant, an American Indian named John R. Winchester, sized him up and said, "Private Jack, this is Company A. I need a good BAR man. You stick with me. I'll take care of the transfer." So, Private Burdette Jack became a member of Company A, First Battalion, 86th Regiment, and finished his service in that unit. During the rest of the campaign, he never did run into anyone from B Company.

As A Company moved out of the mountains into the Po River Valley, they left a barren rock-strewn terrain, devoid of trees and cover. At nine thousand feet, the Apennine Mountains were still snow covered and cold temperatures made fighting conditions miserable. The Germans retreated up the valley but still gave ground grudgingly. They proceeded to blow up all bridges across the Po River, stalling the drive. Army engineers installed several makeshift bridges under intense fire, and the soldiers continued to be exposed to heavy fire as they crossed the open pontoon constructions. Once across they continued to pursue the retreating Germans as rapidly as possible.

Burdette's wounds still required attention, and every morning a medic would change the dressings. It was time consuming, but the wounds managed to heal without infection, a tribute to the medic looking after them. Originally he was treated with a new drug called 'penicillin.' Given in small doses, it did not seem to give much protection, so the medic continued with sulfa drug treatment. As a result of the incorrect application of penicillin, Burdette remains allergic to it today.

As the American troops proceeded through the rolling countryside, they passed through villages and farming areas. As they were marching along near one village, Burdette as usual had his BAR slung over his shoulder. A sniper's shot rang out, and a bullet whizzed past Burdette's head hitting the BAR gun barrel and ricocheting off into the distance. The BAR barrel was bent to a 45 degree angle. Deciding it was better the barrel be damaged rather than his head, he contacted the quartermaster, who issued him another BAR. Soon after, he was back with his company advancing up the valley, using his weapon frequently and accurately.

In one small town the men stopped for a break, and as they rested leaning against a bombed-out building, they observed five young Italian children playing. They were climbing a very climbable tree in a small grassy area, in front of some houses. As they teased and cajoled one another, one young lad jumping from a tree landed on a land mine, causing a monstrous explosion that literally blew the children and the tree apart. It was a very sad experience, with the children so joyous over being liberated from the Nazis, and most of their brief life having known only war and starvation. The scourge of war is the innocents and non-combatants who suffer deprivation and death caused by the actions of others.

In another small town, the soldiers found a farm on the outskirts where a farmer was raising rabbits in cages. The cages were neat and orderly, and obviously the farmer took great care and pride in his rabbits. The soldiers of Company A had lived on reduced rations for nearly a week, since they were advancing too fast for supplies to keep up with them. The temptation was too great. Several soldiers selected a number of rabbits, killed and cleaned them, while other soldiers built a small spit for roasting them. Mounted on sticks the rabbits were slowly turned, and when done, divided among the soldiers, who enjoyed the hot fresh meat immensely. The poor farmer watched the entire process close by and openly cried as the rabbits were devoured. Burdette has never forgotten the incident.

Food for the local inhabitants was always in short supply. Since the farmers relied on the growing season, when there was no growing season, there was no food. Commerce was essentially non-existent, since combat in the area scattered the local populace and chewed up the landscape. Also, the retreating Germans had looted the countryside of all available food and wine. There was nothing left for the poor Italian people. It was not surprising then how they scrambled to find food. Germans used horses to pull their artillery in the mountains, and also for other purposes since they were low on gasoline. As soon as one of the horses was wounded or killed, Italians would suddenly appear and began skinning the large animals, cutting up the horsemeat to make into baloney. It was then easier to transport, preserve, and share with others.

As the troops continued to advance, opposition was intermittent, but always when least expected. Replacements arrived daily and were incorporated into the units. Hiking along a roadway near midday, the company was fired on by a machine pistol from nearby woods. Burdette jumped into the first available artillery excavation, and was soon joined by a young replacement officer who had arrived that day. As they scoured the countryside to find the source of the firing, something caught Burdette's eye. The replacement was wearing his gold Second Lieutenant's bars. Burdette reached over and tore them off, throwing them out of the foxhole. The recently arrived Lieutenant proceeded to give Jack a stern, animated lecture about respect and treatment of officers, as well as several other violations of the army code. Corporal Burdette quietly listened, then replied, "I don't want anything on you that shines during the day or reflects light at night. You are a walking target and I don't want to be in any foxhole with you!"

The Lieutenant then acknowledged that it was probably pretty good advice. The two men became fairly good friends for the remainder of the war. It was common during combat that leadership by the officers took place in their actions, rather than rigid discipline. Respect was shown, but there was limited saluting or insignia for recognition. The good rapport between officers and soldiers continued until the men returned to a permanent camp, where strict protocol was resumed.

Once across the PO River, the German Army retreated from the advancing American Army, traveling at breakneck speed, not wanting the Germans to have time to set up defenses. Frequently it was difficult to establish a skirmish line. At dark as the moon was rising, the Americans loaded A Company on twenty six-by-six trucks in an attempt to move them forward to keep the pressure on the retreating Germans. As the convoy sped down the road, the trucks came under heavy fire. Tires blew and truck engines exploded; Germans hiding in the west ditch along the road ambushed them. Jack was riding in the last truck, and the ten men jumped down and took refuge in the east ditch. Suddenly a lone jeep came roaring down the road, and the men flagged it down and explained what was happening. Wheeling the jeep around, the ten men crawled aboard, wherever they could find a handhold, and drove away from the battle. As they came to a 'Y' in the road, they turned, only to be looking into the mouth of a cannon mounted on a tank. The men shouted and waved their arms. Finally, a sergeant crawled out of the tank, visibly shaken. He trembled as he told them, "I was about to pull the lanyard on the cannon when I caught the reflection in the moonlight of the star painted on the hood of the jeep." That instantaneous reflection saved the lives of eleven men.

As the army advanced across the Po Valley up to Lake Garda in northern Italy, the Germans, in desperation, lowered their anti-aircraft guns for use against the infantry soldiers. It caused a good number of casualties in the American ranks, until artillery and the air corps could silence the powerful cannons. The 10th Division continued to advance, and finally, on May 4th, 1944, the Americans met up with the Russians at Brenner Pass.

The next day, May 5th, 1945, the German Army surrendered unconditionally. The war on the European Continent was over.

There may have been some celebration. For the most part, the 10th Mountain Division stopped to catch its collective breath. They had been on the front line in constant pursuit of the Germans for three months without relief. Casualties were high, but they had succeeded in their main objective. Catching their breath was short-lived.

Yugoslavia was in turmoil at the Italy-Yugoslavia border. Marshall Tito of Yugoslavia was flexing his muscles, creating difficulty in settling the area. The country was about to enter a civil war as factions assembled for a confrontation. As a result, the 10th Mountain Division was dispatched to Yugoslavia in an attempt to keep law and order in the area. They would patrol the area and make their presence know for three months, until negotiations were completed.

On August 24th, the 10th Mountain Division was ordered to return to the United States. The soldiers would be given 30 days leave, then report to Camp Carson, Colorado, where they would be brought to full division and sent to the Philippine Islands to prepare for the invasion of Japan.

Corporal Burdette Jack returned to Guernsey, Iowa, for a few days of home cooking, and parental adulation. There was time for a few dates and some hugging and kissing. Finally, he loaded his 1936 Ford and started driving to Camp Carson. In the middle of Nebraska, he noticed a bump on one of his tires and pulled into an all night gas station in McCook, about 2:00 AM. The station attendant informed him that he could get a new tire only if he met with the County Rationing Board. Burdette curled up in his car and slept until morning, and was first in line when the board convened. He stood before the board in his crumpled uniform, complete with ribbons, and explained his dilemma. In less than five minutes, he was sent back to the station where two new Kelly-Springfield tires would be waiting. He thanked them profusely, returned to the station and had the two new tires installed. When he attempted to pay for the tires, the attendant told him the board chair had called and wanted to personally pay for the young soldiers tires and installation. Burdette cheerfully went on his way and reported in at Camp Carson, to prepare for a trip to Japan.

Fortunately, the atomic bomb was dropped on Hiroshima and a few days after that, another dropped on Nagasaki. Japan finally agreed to an unconditional surrender.

Once the 10th Division arrived at Camp Carson, many of the original soldiers were discharged. Since discharge from service was regulated by a point system that evaluated length of service, time overseas and other factors, not all men were discharged. Burdette happened to be one point short of the 40 points meeting the criteria. Consequently, he was shipped to Camp Swift, Texas, near Austin.

Corporal Burdette Jack, formerly a BAR man with the 10th Mountain Division in Italy, was given a new task. He was assigned to the motor pool, and five days a week, he drove officers' wives to large nearby towns in Texas so they could do their shopping. Burdette's military bearing, pleasant personality and rural deportment fit in perfectly for his newly-assigned responsibilities.

Periodically he performed as soldiers perform, and one day was told to report for inspection and review. General Douglas MacArthur and his staff were in the camp and it was traditional military fare to review the troops. The soldiers were aligned on the parade ground when the General and his entourage arrived. As they passed through the ranks, General MacArthur stopped directly in front of Corporal Burdette Jack and asked, "Soldier, what state are you from?"

"Iowa, Sir!"

The General thought for a minute and replied, "Good state! Good state!" and walked on.

Burdette Jack was one of the few non-commissioned officers in the US Army who had the good fortune to meet both General Douglas MacArthur and General Mark Clark face to face.

JACK • CHAPTER 5

Camp Swift suited Corporal Burdette Jack just fine. He was no longer sleeping in foxholes. The prospect of invading Japan and possibly dying there was long gone. Driving officers' wives was very pleasant duty. A young lady in Guernsey caught his eye, and after a brief courtship they became engaged. To top it off, while home on leave over Christmas, he purchased a 1936 Ford four-door car that gave him mobility for the first time.

The first week in April 1946, Burdette had acquired enough points to be released from the army. He proceeded to Fort Sam Houston, Texas, where he received his discharge. He found three soldiers from Joplin, Missouri, who were as anxious to get home as Burdette, and they offered to buy the gas if he would drop them off on the way home. The four piled into the car after receiving their discharge on Saturday, April 14th, and drove straight through to Joplin. Burdette continued on home, and mid-morning Monday he was driving his father's Farmall tractor on a forty-acre rented tract.

Burdette was anxious to return to farming, and made arrangements to rent farmland from Mr. Coleman, whose land was close to the Jack farm. Mr. Coleman was afraid that Burdette would not be discharged in time to get the crops in, but Burdette stayed at it and completed the planting in time.

Burdette continued to help his father farm, and during haying season, it became clear that they could not borrow a hay rake from the neighbors and it might be necessary to buy one. Burdette visited the local implement dealer to shop for rakes and finally found the one he wanted. The implement dealer sized up this young returned serviceman wanting to get into the farming business and said, "That hay rake is five hundred dollars. That's a lot of money for a young farmer starting out."

Burdette, without hesitation, said, "I'll take it!" He pulled out his wallet and peeled off five-one hundred dollar bills he had saved from selling his Luger pistols in Italy. The implement dealer was surprised, and impressed. Burdette towed the hay rake home and presented it to his father as a gift.

When Burdette returned from overseas, he began dating a few girls when home on leave, and finally got up the nerve to become engaged to a young acquaintance. Returning home after his discharge, he discovered the young woman had changed her mind while he was in service in Texas, placed his ring in a drawer, and commenced dating other fellows. After a traumatic breakup, Burdette joined his several male friends in attending dances in the area.

Burdette continued helping his father farm, and one day was using the Farmall tractor with a mounted two-row corn picker in a field close to home. Four young women, who had the afternoon off from a local beauty parlor, parked their car beside the road, walked to the fence and gave a very flirtatious wave to the tractor driver. One of the girls, Clara Martens, caught Burdette's eye. She had graduated from the Paris Beauty Academy in Cedar Rapids and recently taken a job in a local parlor in Victor. That next Saturday night Burdette attended a dance in Belle Plaine, danced with Clara and soon they were dating regularly. Their dating began in November, they became engaged in February 1947, and were married in June. Burdette knew she was the right girl for him, because on an one of

Clara and Burdette were married at St John's Lutheran Church south of Victor, Iowa, on June 6, 1948.

their first dates, he was arrested for speeding in Cedar Rapids on the way to Danceland, and Clara loaned him enough money to pay the fine and still go dancing.

On June 6th, 1948, the two exchanged vows in St John's Lutheran Church, nine miles south of Victor. The wedding was followed by a grand reception in the church parlors, after which they left in Dad's 1941 gray Chevrolet for the fancy Roosevelt Hotel in Cedar Rapids. After a four-day honeymoon trip to the Wisconsin Dells, they returned to the one hundred and twenty acre farmstead rented to start their new life together. Clara's parents presented them with a Guernsey cow and two sows. Burdette's parents presented them with fifty bushels of seed oats. All gifts were greatly appreciated. There was only one negative. Clara really hated milking the cow.

In 1950, the young couple took a huge plunge and purchased a farm. The prospect of borrowing sixteen thousand dollars at three percent interest was almost too much to conceive. However, it proved to be one of the best investments Burdette and Clara made.

As the Jack's started farming additional land, they also started their family. Son Mervin was born May 16th, 1949. The young couple was blessed with a new daughter, Marilyn, on February 10th, 1952. Myron Kim was born on September 11th, 1957 and another daughter, Mary, joined the family November 4th, 1958. The farmhouse was filled with all of the joy and activities a family of six generates.

Burdette purchased his farm insurance from a neighbor who had a small agency in Victor. When the agent suddenly passed away, there was concern with whom they might insure. Burdette took his pickup truck to town to get a load of coal, and was met by Mr. Pribbenow from Rockford, Iowa, who wanted to know if Burdette would like to become an agent for the company. Deciding to accept the offer, Burdette worked diligently to learn the insurance business, and started with seven customers. When he retired in later years, he was servicing over seven hundred policies. Farming by day, he made calls at night when he knew the farmers would have time to discuss their insurance options.

On one occasion the Jack family had an opportunity to visit Camp Carson, Colorado, the original home of the 10th Mountain Division. The division had an illustrious history fighting in Italy. Of the twelve thousand men in the division, nine hundred ninety-two were killed and over three thousand wounded; over thirty-five percent casualties. Up a mountain trail, at Tennessee Pass, stands a monument dedicated to the men of the

10th Division who gave their lives in defeating the enemy. As Burdette read the names, he found the young man from Marshalltown who was crushed by the wall, as well as several other comrades who did not return.

Burdette Jack was fortunate to return from service for a full and active life.. The medals he was awarded include: the European-Mediterranean-African Theater of Operations with two battle stars representing the North Apennines and Po Valley Battles, the Good Conduct Medal, the Bronze Star, the Combat Infantryman's Badge, and the Purple Heart.

Burdette Jack's Honorable Discharge still lists him as a member of B Company, 1st Battalion, 86th Regiment, 10th Mountain Division, although he spent more time with A Company.

There is no known medal offered for driving officers' wives on shopping trips. If there was, he would have one and wear it proudly.

Members of B Company, 1st Battalion, 10th Mountain Division, met in Colorado for the dedication of a monument erected at Tennessee Pass, Camp Carson.

BOOK 5

Melvin Harms

First Lieutenant
Bombardier
7th Air Force
30th Bomb Group
38th Squadron

*"When they returned my watch
with the shrapnel indentation,
I suddenly realized
how close I came to being hit!"*

~Melvin Harms

HARMS • CHAPTER 1

The B-24 Liberator bomber lumbered along over the water of the central Pacific Ocean toward a tiny dot several hundred miles away. It was a long flight, over seven hundred miles to find this tiny island, but they had been there before. Bombing Iwo Jima had become routine. Three airfields were located on the naked rock-strewn island, and to protect the B-52s bombing Japan, it was necessary to keep the airfields inoperative. Keeping Japanese Zero fighter planes on the ground meant greater safety for American planes on their way to Japan.

During these long trips there was not much for bombardier Lt. Mel Harms to do, except keep a watchful eye for enemy aircraft. Mel had supervised loading the twelve five hundred pound bombs into the bomb racks and inserted the wires that kept the nose propellers from rotating. Once the target or Initial Point (IP) was reached, the lead bombardier took over guiding the squadron over the target. The high altitude bombers that dropped their loads from twenty-eight thousand feet over Germany released bombs at several different lower altitudes over Iwo Jima, in order to more accurately hit the tiny target. Without accompanying fighters, they were "easy pickin's" for the Zeros on the island.

Pilot Lt. Bill Core was on his third trip to Iwo. Bill was from Clinton, Iowa, and his bombardier, Harms, was from the small town of Sumner, Iowa. They first met in San Jose, California, when the crew was being assembled, and they became good friends right away. In fact, as they were nearing completion of training at March Field, California, Bill Core came down with pneumonia. Orders came down to break up the crew, and add a new pilot. Lt. Harms decided to go to the Commanding General of March Field, and indicated he did not want to separate from Bill Core, since they were both from Iowa. The Commanding General asked "Is there was anyone else who could take his place?" and Harms replied there was an instructor who was available. The General said, "Tell the instructor to pack tomorrow. By the way, I'm from Iowa too!"

Now the two were flying in the Chambermaid over the Pacific waters. The plane had already served one crew for its quota of missions, and now Lt. Core's crew was flying their sixth mission, the third to Iwo Jima. Weather in this part of the Pacific was always unpredictable. However, the 38th Squadron of the 30th Bomb Group kept a tight formation. Fifteen minutes before reaching the island, and finding "Mt. Sunovabitchi," as Mt.

MELVIN K. HARMS OF SUMNER, PICTURED HERE
AFTER SUCCESSFULLY COMPLETING TRAINING
AS AN AERIAL GUNNER,WENT ON TO RECEIVE
HIS WINGS AND RATING AS A BOMBADIER
AND A COMMISSIONED OFFICER AND
SERVED IN THAT CAPACITY IN
COMBAT IN WORLD WAR II.

Melvin Harms successfully completed training as an aerial gunner and went on to receive his bombardier wings and commission.

Suribachi was affectionately called, a group of eight Zeros was spotted well below the formation. Usually the Zeros would not attack until the bombs were dropped, and the bombers surged upward after releasing their six thousand pound load. That way they were not in the way of the flak rising to meet the bombers as they made their bomb run.

Today an Intelligence Officer, Lieutenant Doscher, was along to observe hits on the island. Lt. Glen Beatty, the co-pilot, leaned toward the window looking at the red flashes of anti-aircraft firing up at the squadron. The navigator, Lt. Clarence Wasser, moved up to the flight deck, and along with Lt. Doscher watched the bombs fall from the bomb bay toward the island.

Bombardier Harms released his bombs upon visual recognition of the lead plane release. The crew felt the big bomber adjust its flight, when a minute later the overhead turret gunner shouted, "What the hell is going on? I can't see a thing!" It was immediately obvious to Lt. Bill Core. The plane had been hit!

*Flight crew of the Chambermaid, with Lieutenant Bill Core as pilot and
Mel Harms as bombardier.*

HARMS • CHAPTER 2

Mel Harms moved uneasily in the cramped nose of the B-24. Having to slide around the Norden bombsight and avoid hitting the .50 caliber machine gun that projected inside the nose area took some careful maneuvering. Of course the view was spectacular, although knowing only one-quarter inch of Plexiglas kept you from falling into the Pacific was a bit disconcerting. The plastic nose was also not the best protection from .50 caliber shells and whirling steel from exploding anti-aircraft shells. But that's how these flying machines were built.

The B-24 was designed in response to the need for a boxcar to carry a large payload long distances. The big bomber flew faster than the Boeing B-17 and carried more armament and a bigger payload. Originally designed by Consolidated Aircraft, later known as Convair, the ultimate construction happened in a number of production facilities. The B-24s were built by Consolidated, Ford, North American, and Douglas Aircraft, and a total of 18,481 planes were built, more than any other aircraft during the World War II. The design of a new wing configuration permitted more lift and carrying capacity: six thousand pounds of bombs as well as six thousand pounds of ammunition used for defense of the aircraft. The plane could reach two hundred eighty miles per hour, twenty five MPH faster than the B-17. The plane was not as stable in flight or as solidly built as the B-17, but was reliable enough for use in all theaters of operation during WWII.

Mel Harms, as in the case of most navigators and bombardiers, did not plan to become a bombardier but wanted to be a pilot. When the Japanese bombed Pearl Harbor on December 7th, 1941, Mel was 17, driving back to Sumner, Iowa, from Clear Lake, Iowa, when he heard the news flash. His twin brother Calvin and he decided that when they turned 18 they would enlist in the Air Corps. The Army initially required a four-year college degree for consideration for pilot training, reduced that to two years of college, and finally modified the requirement to passing a rigid examination. Mid year in 1942, Calvin and Melvin enlisted with Cal passing the pilots exam, and Mel selected for bombardier's school.

Basic training for Mel in the Air Corps was at Mission, Texas, close to San Antonio. Since one duty of the bombardier was to fire a .50 caliber machine gun defending the aircraft from frontal assault, Mel spent two weeks of training in Harlingen, close to Houston, Texas, where he earned his gunnery wings. From Harlingen he traveled to Midland, Texas, where he earned his bombardier wings. The men practiced with the Norden bombsight, flying over the target at a variety of altitudes attempting to land a certain number of dummy bombs inside a one thousand foot circle. When the cadets passed their training they received their bombardier wings. There was no graduation hoopla; the cadets were called to formation where the Assistant Commanding Officer distributed Bombardier Wings. Returning to Sumner for a few days' leave, Mel then reported to San Jose, California, where his bomber crew met for the first time.

Growing up in Sumner, a rural community in north central Iowa, had many pluses. The educational system was better than average, the community better than average, and the opportunity to grow up with a minimum of trouble better than average. The farming community provided lots of assistance in keeping the young twins in line, well fed, and physically active. And there were enough pretty, young city and farm girls to go around.

Lt. Bill Core of Clinton, Iowa, and Harms were close friends in service and remained so after the war.

Marian Sorg was two years behind Mel Harms in Sumner High School and they began dating during Mel's junior year. She was still attending high school when Harms left for service, and they did not exchange letters during his training or while Mel was in service. The banker's daughter was very popular and enjoyed her high school experience. She later attended Iowa State College. She was unaware Mel was a bombardier, and certainly not aware how many lonely hours he would spend flying over the vast Pacific Ocean.

Once Bill Core's crew was assembled and sent to March Field in California, they began intensive training, learning to work as a team. Each man had responsibilities, and it was the pilot's job to know them all. This group of young men from various parts of the United States, would now share an aluminum assemblage designed to haul explosives, and in turn protect it so it could return to make another trip to haul explosives. They were nineteen to twenty-two years old, entrusted with a quarter of a million dollar vehicle, and facing a fearless enemy.

One crew at March Field was composed of men of the Jewish faith, apparently assembled through their own choice. Once the crews were scheduled to join units overseas, last minute plans were made for leaving the base. One of the crew who lived in Mel's tent was so distraught at going overseas, he committed suicide by slashing his wrists. It was a startling revelation for the young Iowa bombardier, who had never experienced this sort of an event. The dead soldier was replaced and the new crew trained for another month, then heading to England as a replacement crew.

Overseas assignments finally came through. Pilot Core and his crew flew to Hawaii, on to Kwajalein and Eniwetok Atoll. From there they flew to Saipan, part of the Marianas Islands that were clustered with Tinian and Guam. At Saipan, the crew was assigned to an airplane, the Chambermaid, and training began. They were to be a part of the new 7th Air Force, which was composed of elements of the 5th and 13th Air Forces.

Their first training mission was to Johnston Island. Leaving at midnight, they flew the entire mission over water arriving at 8:00 AM. The navigator was very inexperienced but found the small island without difficulty.

On Saipan the men lived in two-person tents. Bill Core and Harms shared a tent and spent a good deal of time together, becoming close friends. Each would occasionally fly with another crew, but flew together as often as possible. It rained every day on Saipan, and the island was a sea of mud. Harms was bitten by a mosquito and came down with Dengue Fever, and suffered for a few days. The island was sprayed with DDT every week to kill the swarming insects, but it only lasted for a few days. Sooner or later every airman came down with "dingy" fever.

When they first arrived on Saipan, Harms flew one mission with another crew for bombardier training under actual conditions. The mission was to Truk, where a squadron of planes bombed an airfield and Harms dropped his bombs upon visual sighting of the lead plane's release.

Now Harms was on his seventh mission, while the rest of the crew was on their sixth. It was their third trip to the island of Iwo Jima. Harms and the Chambermaid's assigned target was the storage facilities next to one of the three airfields. The eight Zero fighters followed them in, flying well below, occasionally darting toward the squadron's formation in a threatening move. One Zero got too close and was hit by .50 caliber machine gun fire from another plane, exploding immediately. Maybe this was not going to be such an easy trip after all.

*Tent accommodations on Saipan
kept out some of the rain,
but insects and crawling critters
had easy access.*

*Living conditions on the islands
were quite primitive,
but a hot shower was always welcome*

Distances between targets in the South Pacific made flights tenuous or boring,
depending upon the welcome they received over target.

HARMS • CHAPTER 3

After "bombs away," the huge B-24s usually initiate some sort of evasive action. It takes twenty seconds for a shell fired from the ground to reach the bombers, so when the anti-aircraft flash is first seen, some change in direction or elevation is called for. Releasing the bombs causes the planes to rise, and since the bombardier is controlling the airplane from the IP to the target, it is his responsibility to initiate evasive action. Each squadron is briefed prior to the flight on evasive action. After only three missions Lt. Harms was assigned to develop evasive action plans for the squadron to present at the briefing, even though there were officers with more seniority. It was an assignment Harms took seriously.

Lt. Doscher, the Intelligence officer flying as an observer on the Chambermaid's seventh mission, stood looking down through the bomb bay doors as the bombs made a direct hit on the storage facilities, scoring one hundred percent hits on the target.

A few seconds after Harms released the cargo, the turret gunner shouted, "What the hell is going on? I can't see a thing." At the same time, Sergeant Mil Howard called on the intercom, "Why won't my turret turn?" It was apparent they had been hit, and the hydraulic lines severed with hydraulic oil squirting all over the place. The floor became so slippery the airmen could not stand up without holding onto something. Harms left his post to investigate, and discovered flak had passed through the nose cone, cutting the hydraulic line.

While co-pilot Beatty flew the plane, Pilot Core called out locations of attacking fighter planes. Now both turrets were out of commission. Other Zeros were circling ready, to attack the crippled airplane, relishing the thought of another kill. One Zero did a half-roll and dropped a phosphorous bomb that hit the wing and fuselage at the same time his guns were firing at the B-24. Navigator Lt. Clarence Wasser stood behind the pilot and co-pilot with his hands on their seatbacks. A dull explosion behind the co-pilot opened a hole in the roof above the co-pilot's head. Small pieces of glass and aluminum showered the cabin and the flight deck below. The explosion blew Lt. Wasser through a narrow opening, back to the flight deck. Seeing no visible damage, Bill Core assumed they were all okay, not yet realizing Richards was also standing behind him. As fighters kept coming in, Core continued calling locations on the intercom to those guns still capable of returning fire. Co-pilot Beatty, dazed by the explosion, touched his back and was surprised to find his hand covered with blood. He twisted in his seat so Core could check him out, who found Beatty's shirt was torn to shreds, and lots of blood. Core could not see that a piece of aluminum had been driven into Beatty's back, and it was not discovered until later. Core took over controls of the plane from Beatty, who was flying the plane while Core was watching the Zeros anticipating their action. Core soon realized things were worse than he originally thought.

The throttle control for the left outboard engine, number one, was loose and waggled back and forth. Engine number two's throttle was jammed; both engines were running full blast. Engine number four was throwing oil, and Core was positive that it would be only a matter of minutes before the engine would be of no further use. Core gave up on the prospect of getting back home and began contemplating a sea landing with only one engine.

Core checked the instruments and noted his airspeed. He recognized the damage to the plane was more than he first realized. Core contacted the squadron leader for assistance in protecting his aircraft from the attacking Zeros. Captain Robert Valentine, the flight leader, deployed four aircraft around the Chambermaid, one on each side, one above and one below, and all reduced their airspeed to match the crippled airplane. This added a good deal of firepower to fight off the Zeros who tasted a kill, but maintained a safe distance from the assembled armada.

Lt. Harms crawled back from his nose position to check the damage to the rest of the airplane. He found Sgt. Ted Richards, the radio operator and top turret gunner, and the observer, Wasser, lying on the flight deck in a pool of their own blood mixed with hydraulic oil. A second explosion in the top turret shocked the men, tearing out the plastic dome and throwing it into the slipstream, where it hit the right vertical stabilizer, tearing out a large chunk of its leading edge.

Harms found the wounded men to be in serious condition. During the first explosion, forty three pieces of shrapnel had penetrated Wasser's shoulder and back, and he had three bullet holes through his right hand, and two through his shoulders. The shell that exploded in the top turret was only three feet from Richards' head. He was bleeding profusely from facial wounds, and his windpipe was severed. In addition, his right knee, left knee, shoulders, and neck were punctured with bits of glass and shrapnel.

Harms decided to take the men to the waist area where they could be laid down and treated. Harms managed to get Wasser to his feet, and half-carried him across the slippery narrow steel beam over the bomb bay doors. Since the beam was coated with oil, any misstep would send them both through the lightweight bomb bay doors, to the Pacific below. It was agonizingly slow, as hydraulic fluid was still flowing down the beam, but with considerable cautious effort they reached the waist area where Harms helped him to lay down. Removing a sleeve from Wasser's flying jacket, Harms made a tourniquet for his bleeding arm. He then treated the other wounds with sulfa. Staff Sergeant Michael Versack, the waist gunner and engineer, made his way forward and found Richards lying on the flight deck. Versack gave him a shot of morphine and began dressing his wounds.

While Harms was bandaging Wasser, Verscak slid down the steel beam to grab a machine gun to ward off the Zeros. Harms began to question whether they would make it or not, since a lone gun could not stop all of the Zeros. However, they fortunately had flown beyond the range of the fighter planes who no longer were a threat. Verscak kept firing out of frustration and sheer rage over the Chambermaid being violated.

Core called for Sgt. Robert Martin, the left waist gunner, to come forward. Martin, as most of the crewmembers, was a frustrated pilot who, after one hundred and five hours of flight training, washed out of pilot training for "lack of flying ability." Core needed him forward to help fly the airplane. On previous training missions, Core had permitted Martin to sit in the pilot's seat for brief periods, just in case he might need those skills at some future time. Now was the time.

Co-Pilot Beatty moved back to the waist area to have his wounds treated. Lt. Doscher made his way over the catwalk's slippery beam, found some iodine, took down his own trousers and treated a deep gash in his right thigh caused by the shell that exploded in the flight deck. Most of the crew was now in the waist area either being attended to, or doing the attending.

Core redirected his efforts to keeping the airplane aloft. He had full control over the number three engine. Although the cowling was full of shrapnel holes, the engine functioned perfectly. There was no throttle control over engines number one and number two. Number two would periodically go wild, speeding to full capacity, causing the plane to vibrate wildly. It would then slow to operating speed. Engine number 4 was trailing smoke and throwing oil. Every forty minutes it would burst into flames, feeding on the surface oil, then burn out. Bill Core knew that engine number 4 would soon burn out, or stop. Fortunately it continued to run without oil, hour after hour.

Core knew he would have to cut down on the propeller speeds or he would run out of gas well short of Saipan. The experienced pilot started to experiment. He first worked with Number 1 engine and fed it air from the turbocharger used to feed oxygen to engines at high altitudes, and discovered he could slow down the propeller. He found he could control engine number two using a feathering button, usually used to hold the propeller motionless on a bad engine by changing the pitch. If the propeller was not adjusted, it would rotate wildly and tear itself from the engine mounting. By adjusting the propeller pitch and the turbocharger, he could maintain speeds comparable to engines three and four. Every so often Core would turn in his seat and look at Richards, lying on the floor, and give him a wink. Richards would smile and wink back, unable to speak because of the severed windpipe.

Sgt. Martin continued to steer the lumbering B-24 while Core manipulated the engines. They managed to maintain an air speed of one hundred forty miles per hour, only fifteen miles over stalling speed. The Chambermaid engines continued to consume gas at an alarming rate, and the plane was dropping toward the water about 40 feet per minute. In the waist area the unwounded crew began to lighten the plane by throwing things out the windows. Machine guns, ammunition, flak suits and extra radio coils were tossed. Attempts to detach the machine gun mounts failed when the only available wrench, doused with hydraulic oil, slipped out of an airman's hands and fell overboard.

They decided to shift weight in the plane, so the men moved forward to the flight deck, while Harms and Shahein remained with Wasser, tending to his wounds. The plane continued on its path, running into a weather front, and since they were unable to take alternate routes, the plane shook violently from the turbulent weather. The men on the flight deck held on to each other and gritted their teeth. Fear of the plane breaking up from the turbulence was a new hazard.

Lt. Core continued to keep the plane on course, manipulating the engines, contemplating all of the options, he suddenly realized he had new worries. Should they make it to Saipan, how would they land? Without hydraulic pressure they had no brakes, and the plane would probably overrun the landing strip. The other option was to bail out over water, but with four severely wounded men aboard, this was not an option. Ditching at sea would put all of the men in jeopardy. The best opportunity for everyone would be to try a landing.

Verescak crawled into the bashed-in nose of the plane and attempted to repair the hydraulic lines. He wrapped the damaged area in adhesive tape, then poured oil from the emergency tanks into the system. The tape gave way and most of the oil was lost. Core called the flight leader and explained the predicament. Capt. Valentino remembered an instance used by the Texas Belle on Tarawa, when parachutes were tied to the gun mounts and thrown out of the windows to help reduce air speed. Valentine told Core to rig three parachutes the same way.

The able men busied themselves making preparations for landing as directed, found parachutes, tied them securely to the gun mounts, and then sat down to consider their dilemma. Lt Core and Sgt. Martin were struggling to adjust the engines to keep the plane airborne. Each man frantically reviewed his experience and training to improve his chances for survival. As they looked down into the endless Pacific waters, they refused to consider anything other than Lt. Core bringing them home safely. It was their only hope.

Five hours passed between the time the Chambermaid was hit over Iwo Jima and the time Saipan appeared on the horizon. Dusk was approaching, and visibility was slowly fading away. Core could not reach the Saipan control tower, so all communications had to go through Capt. Valentine in the escort plane. Three of the accompanying planes left the formation to land at alternate landing strips, while the flight leader remained with the Chambermaid.

Sgt. Martin continued to fly the airplane while Core went to the rear to oversee preparations for landing. Chutes were securely attached to the side gun mounts. Corporal Robert Harriff, the tail gunner, volunteered to sit in the tail position and pop the parachute at the critical time, hoping the tail section would remain attached. It was essentially a suicide mission.

Since the hydraulic system was defunct, the landing gear could only be lowered by an emergency hand crank. Verescak tested the landing cables with his full weight to be sure they would hold when lowered. As the first wheel was cranked, it lowered into place. As they cranked the second wheel, the cable snapped, locking it in its wheel well. The airmen who had nursed their plane for almost seven hundred miles over water for five long, tedious hours, and were now only five minutes from safety, were stricken. They realized what was about to happen.

Landing without brakes and shot out instruments was difficult enough. Sliding a thirty-ton bomber in on its belly might still save the occupants. However, landing with one wheel down and one wheel up predicted a total disaster. The best they could hope for was a very bad crash.

They tried once again to fix the hydraulic line with Versecak holding the line, but oil squirted through his fingers. Verescak and Shahein managed to kick the nose wheel down into position. It would not help much, but might keep a wing from hitting the ground and causing a ground loop that would kill everyone on board. Core returned to the pilot's seat, called Valentine and reported his predicament. Valentine called the tower and told them to clear the runway on the right side for a crash landing.

Core ordered everyone back into the waist, except for Martin in the co-pilot's seat. Once again, the men helped each other across the slippery beam, with Richards hopping along on one leg, with two men holding him. All of the men lay down in the waist area, with the able men adjoining the wounded to cushion the shock. Two men stood adjoining the gun mounts with parachutes in their hands, while the tail gunner prepared to respond on command.

It took a long time, or so it seemed, to clear the runway. The double row of field lights now seemed brighter and sharper as the dusk settled. Core could make out dim outlines of planes being moved from near the runway. Ambulances and crash trucks emerged from under the control tower and moved down the runway, stopping at critical points with their motors running.

Now Martin and Core strapped themselves into their seats, and Core called Valentine and reported quietly, "Coming in!"

The Chambermaid approached high and straight at the runway. Martin hand-pumped the flaps down. Core turned on the landing light, the one that had not been hit by machine gun bullets. Martin cut the No. 1 engine, as Core braced all of his weight against the left rudder.

The Chambermaid touched the ground at one hundred and five miles per hour and swerved sharply to the right. Martin cut the power with the master switch as the men threw the parachutes into the air. The chutes popped open and slowed the plane's motion a bit, but could not stop the wild surge over the field lights and off the runway. The big plane held its balance for a short time with one wheel, then caught the right wing in the ground, shearing off the propeller of No. 1 engine, which skidded down the runway in a shower of sparks. The plane plowed ahead to hit a jeep trailer outfitted with a rack of floodlights, sending bits and pieces of lighting equipment flying through the air.

Lt. Core noticed the instrument panel collapsing on top of him and turned halfway out of his seat, only to be restrained by the belts. The plane continued sliding with an earsplitting, crunching roar of metal on metal, plowing through dirt, throwing dust and debris until it blasted sideways into a dirt mound…and suddenly, violently, stopped.

All was quiet.

The men were jarred by the abrupt jolt, then shook their heads as they regained reality. They slowly responded, not certain if they were alive, hurt badly, or hurt at all. With the sudden silence, they had to convince themselves they were on the ground and alive. Core and Martin sat motionless for a while, and then slowly became aware of fire crackling. Number one engine showed a few flames, but Core decided it was not serious and would go out. Core and Martin un-strapped themselves, broke out a side window, and carefully wormed their way out of the plane. As they walked to the back of the airplane they found some of the men already out, helping others out through great gaps in the fuselage.

Harms began to count the crew, but could not find Harriff, the tail gunner. He ran toward the plane's rear, noting something hanging from the gun mount. It was the empty parachute that had been deployed as they landed. Looking around for a few minutes, he suddenly recognized the tail gunner wandering around in a daze, mingling with spectators who arrived to view the crash.

Each of the crewmembers had experienced a variety of cuts and bruises. The wounded, it appeared, were no worse off than before they landed, but were still in serious condition. Ambulances arrived, the wounded attended to, and the severely wounded prepared for transfer to the infirmary.

The crew chief of the Chambermaid arrived to survey the damage. He was proud of his airplane and kept it in first class flying condition. After every flight, he would question the crew to see what needed to be serviced, and made a variety of improvements permitting the crews to perform better. As he surveyed the fuselage, broken in half behind the bomb bay, the drooping wings all but torn off, with parts and debris scattered through the furrow alongside the runway, he knew there would be no further repairs to this airplane.

The crew chief stood next to co-pilot Beatty, lying on a stretcher near the ambulance. As the medics lifted Beatty towards the ambulance, he sadly looked up at the crew chief and said, "Chief, I'm sorry we wrecked your plane!"

Inspecting the remains of the flying Chambermaid, it was hard to believe that all eleven men survived the crash.

HARMS • CHAPTER 4

It was amazing! All eleven men survived a crash landing that predicted no survivors. The seriously wounded were treated immediately, then flown to hospitals in the United States for further treatment and rehabilitation. The walking wounded were bruised, strained, lacerated, sore and exhausted. In addition to miscellaneous cuts and bruises, Harms had bitten through his lower lip and severely strained his shoulder. After initially being treated for their ailments, the men were debriefed about the mission, and then received their usual shot of whisky to jumpstart the unwinding process. They then reported to the hospital for additional care, tests, and to have their lacerations sutured.

After a few days in the hospital, the remaining crew was put on a plane bound for Hawaii for ten days leave, to regain their equilibrium and prepare them to return to once again bomb the enemy. In Hawaii, the 7th Air Force had a recreation building and housing for the men. However, Bill Core and Mel Harms found a small house across from the beach where they could get away from the military demeanor for a few days. They would drift over to the recreation building occasionally to see how their friends were relaxing. Also, they were required to check in every day to confirm a return flight.

There was a rigid curfew imposed on the islands, with all lights out and no one allowed on the streets after 10 PM. Core and Harms were together all of the time, and spent a good deal of time on the beach. One evening they were at the recreation building, and headed back to their bungalow near the curfew deadline. Stumbling along in the dark, they were very close to their living quarters when they were stopped by the Hawaiian police for being on the streets four minutes past curfew. The police were very understanding; they both were given a ticket. The next morning they made their appearance at the police station where they each paid a five-dollar fine. In Hawaii, being a "surviving hero" did not result in waived fines.

The men finally verified their flight back to Saipan. The day arrived when they collected their gear and climbed aboard a C-47 for the trip back. The plane, usually used for carrying cargo, was fitted with bucket seats, making the return flight much more comfortable.

Returning to Saipan, a new crew was put together, and they were assigned a new airplane. Harms and Core remained together, although they were occasionally scheduled to fly with other crews. The new crew included a new navigator, radioman and engineer, and soon they were back in to mission rotation. Once more they listened to "Tokyo Rose" and her nightly program. She would accurately predict the next day's missions with, "Hello 38th Squadron. We know where you are going. Tomorrow it is . . . !" Playing the latest big band recordings in an attempt to ruin soldier morale actually improved it. She had the latest recordings before Armed Forces Radio did.

Targets changed daily, but it was always a long trip over open water to attempt to blow up one small isolated dot on a very big map. Usually the target was an airfield, in an attempt to keep Japanese planes grounded. However, the strategy was the same for the Japanese. Every night Japanese bombers would visit Saipan in an attempt to damage the runways. Spotters noted the Mitsubishis would always approach from the same direction, at the same altitude and time. Contacting the Navy, a destroyer patrolled the waters five miles offshore in the path of the approaching bombers. As the Mitsubishis turned for their bombing run, they received a very rude welcome, and became a permanent part of the Pacific bottom debris.

Iwo Jima was one of the islands most frequently visited by the B-24 squadrons. Bombardier Harms made twenty-three visits to Iwo Jima, Haha Jima or Chichi Jima. Countless other squadrons visited the islands

THE CREW WALKED AWAY FROM THIS

It's a tried and proven axiom in flying experience that no wreck is a bad one if the occupants of the plane are able to walk away from it. Among the 11 members of the crew of this wrecked Liberator bomber who escaped cut and bruised but alive and walking were two Iowans, Lieut. William V. Core, pilot of Knoxville, Ia., and Second Lieut. Melvin K. Harms, bombardier of Sumner, Ia. The ship was struck by flak and Zero interceptors after making a bomb run over Iwo Jima, 650 miles from the Jap homeland. Lieutenant Core crash landed her on one wheel on their Marianas island base with the crew's parachutes attached to gun mounts to serve as a brake.

daily without successfully eliminating the military garrison who lived in extensive caves and tunnels throughout the rock mass. They did not bomb Mt. Suribachi on Iwo Jima, but concentrated on the three airfields. The island was shaped like a pork chop, with the old volcanic mountain on the narrow end. The island was basically a large rock dome with very little vegetation, unusual for a Pacific island. Chichi Jima, the island just beyond Iwo Jima, housed the Japanese warning and communication systems in the Pacific theater; it was also a major target. Haha Jima and Marcus Islands were other military targets most frequently visited.

When bombing airstrips, the bombers usually carried one hundred pound bombs, in order to spread the damage across the target. Occasionally they carried anti-personnel bombs and incendiary bombs, but mostly bombs that could damage runways. Anti-personnel bombs are usually set with delayed timers, exploding after they are on the ground for a set period. Bombs are triggered by contact or by a small rotating propeller located on the nose. A wire inserted through a small hole keeps the propeller from rotating during flight that would cause them to detonate before they are dropped. It is the bombardier's job to pull the wires before arriving at the IP (Initial Point) when he takes over control of the plane's flight. Occasionally a bomb might hang up in the bomb rack, requiring the bombardier to walk out on a narrow beam between racks, without a parachute, to somehow release the bombs.

One of the toughest targets for Harms was Marcus Island, a small island also shaped like a pork chop, and very well protected. The Navy established a system of rescue called "dumbo" and "jumbo," for planes that had to ditch at sea. One was a submarine that coursed the flight path, and the other was a two-engine PBY aircraft that could land on water. Harms never found out which was dumbo or jumbo, but both were successful in retrieving downed airmen. One submarine managed to pick up nine men from a ten- man crew forced to bail out over water. In another recorded instance, a PBY flown by a Lt. Gordon picked up so many men from the water, his plane was too heavy to become airborne. He managed to taxi for sixty-five miles to a nearby small island, where another plane could fly in to assist in the rescue. That effort won Lt. Gordon a Congressional Medal of Honor.

One pilot assigned as a co-pilot on another plane was shot down on a bombing run. Core's plane was sent to search for survivors, and found the area covered with debris floating on the surface. None of the ten man crew were sighted or rescued.

The distances to targets were far enough that fighter planes could not accompany the bombers to engage attacking fighter planes. The Japanese would send an interceptor that would fly just outside gun range, radioing the number, altitude, and speed of the approaching bombers to the communications base, so island targets could be prepared for the attack. One day as a tactical surprise, they stripped down three P-38s and added gas tanks so they could accompany the bombers to the target. Flying above and behind the bombers, the P-38s waited until the interceptor appeared, then pounced on him. One pass eliminated the Japanese observer, and the P-38s headed home, low on gas.

The big, new B-29's began arriving on Saipan, and since they could reach Japan from that island, the B-24 Bomb Groups were moved to the island of Guam. Flying from Guam, the flights lasted about an hour longer each way; with briefing and debriefing it meant twelve to fourteen hour days. Concern for returning with a damaged plane over water added that much more stress.

During the return flight on Harm's thirtieth mission, the stress began to show. The night sky produced images that caught the gunners off guard. The gunners were so "antsy" they began shooting at every cloud and star, expending a good deal of ammunition. When the incident was reported at the debriefing, the commander grounded the crew for a few days to calm the men.

Harms continued to fly with Bill Core's crew, and after his thirty-third mission received orders to transfer to Okinawa. Since Harms had only seven more missions left to complete his tour of duty, he went to the camp commander and raised a little hell. He again expressed his desire to serve with Lt. Core. The commander relented and Harms finished his tour on Guam.

On Guam the airmen lived in tents next to the airbase. However, it was five miles through a sugarcane field to get to the supply tent. Since it rained everyday for a few minutes, the area was always a sea of mud. Core and Harms visited a small town some distance away, tearing down a house in order to get enough wood to build a platform to raise the tent floor out of the mud.

During the invasion of Iwo Jima Harms flew with another crew. The plane's location in the squadron was flying in the D position, the last plane on the outside edge of the formation, the most dangerous position. The bombing run went in at four thousand feet, flying over the waves of marines in Higgins boats, aligned and positioned to hit the beach after the bombs were dropped. Because of the altitude, it was the first time that Harms wore a parachute while performing his duties. As he looked down at the marines crouched in their small craft, he felt reassured that if shot down, someone would be available to rescue him. As they dropped their bombs, huge naval cruisers and battleships continued to pound the island. After making their bombing run at the island, they returned to their base, fortunately still in one piece.

The standard tour of duty for flying airmen in the Pacific Theater was forty missions. Few crews ever flew their fortieth mission since they were reluctant to take any more risks after completing thirty-nine missions. Most crews on their fortieth mission would attend the briefing, file a flight plan, fill out a flight log, and return to their bunk for some sack time. However, the pilot of Harm's assigned plane called his crew together and indicated there was a Japanese convoy that needed a visit, and "we had better go get them." The squadron took off, found the convoy, and decided to bomb them at four thousand feet. The convoy escorts were sending up a lot of flak as the men released their bombs. The machine gunners had all guns firing at ships' decks in what was complete mayhem. Harms looked down through the plastic nose of the B-24 and thought, "What the hell are we doing here?" Harms suddenly realized how precipitous this mission was. However, Harms did fly his fortieth mission.

Completing his missions, Harms received orders to return to the U.S. However, Lt Core still had three missions remaining. Once again, Harms appealed to the base commander to stay on Guam until Core had completed his missions so they could return to the U.S. together. Once Core flew his fortieth mission, orders were cut for the two men to fly to Hawaii, then to the west coast, and finally to Jefferson Barracks, Missouri. Mel Harms gave serious consideration to, and finally decided to, sign up to return to Okinawa for another tour of duty. However, after further consideration, he changed his mind, withdrew his application and received his discharge from service on V-E Day, May 1945.

On one mission, the plane was over target when they were forced to abort the mission and return to their base. He later learned the crew did not receive credit for that mission. Since airmen received an Oak Leaf Cluster on their Air Medal for every five missions, Harms was one mission short of an even seven clusters. Consequently, he received only six oak leaf clusters on his Air Medal.

In addition to the Air Medal, Harms also received the Asiatic Pacific Medal with three Bronze Stars, and a Purple Heart.

He also received the Order of the Fallen Sparrow, for having survived the crash landing. It is not a coveted award, but is highly cherished by those who receive it.

The crash received wide attention when it happened, with a five-page article describing the event appearing in the sophisticated "New Yorker Magazine" in 1945. Accounts of the crash were later included in several books, as well as a number of 7th Air Force histories.

The attention is well deserved. Due to the extraordinary effort of Lt. Bill Core, the other nine crewmembers and the accompanying observer survived, even though each received a Purple Heart.

A unique document of which Mel Harms is very proud.

HARMS • CHAPTER 5

Melvin Harms received his discharge in June 1945 and he returned to Sumner to determine the next phase of his life. Gone were the long anxious trips over open water, the time-compressed intensity of combat over small parcels of volcanic rock projecting out of the Pacific water, and even longer tedious return trips. The twelve hour days spent briefing, listening to the mind-numbing drone of four powerful piston engines, the slow unwinding and mental preparation for the next long flight, were no longer of pressured concern. The memorable song "Coming In On A Wing And A Prayer" was no longer just another tune but a fact. Sleeping on sagging canvas, loosely wrapped like a cocoon in mosquito netting, with the constant odor of oiled canvas was, hopefully, a thing of the past. At least for a while, being able to sleeping late, driving past endless green fields of corn and soybeans, and relishing home-cooked food, were luxuries now to be appreciated.

Brother Cal was also home from service, after flying all types of airplanes for three years. Most of his service was spent flying planes that trained bombardiers to learn their craft. Deciding to take advantage of their hard earned G. I. Bill, Cal and Mel enrolled in Upper Iowa College, a small, respected four-year institution established in 1857 in Fayette, Iowa.

While in high school, Mel occasionally dated Miriam Sorg, who started her senior year when he left for service. After graduating from Sumner High School in 1943, Miriam attended Iowa State College and received a degree in Institutional Management in 1947. Never pursuing her major, Miriam returned to Sumner to work for Dr. Whitmeier, who practiced general

Miriam and Mel were married in Sumner on August 8th, 1948.

medicine in the community. Once again, Miriam caught Mel's eye, and they began dating once more.

Mel entered Upper Iowa in the fall of 1946, and after much encouragement from brother Cal, decided to try out with the football team. It was a challenge Mel took very seriously. His sophomore season he received recognition as a third team Little All-America Team at the end position. His success on the football fueled his competitive juices, and as an all around athlete, he eventually lettered at Upper Iowa in football, basketball, and baseball. Summers were spent playing baseball for a town team that gained national success, winning regional tournaments and competing in national tournaments. One year Mel played with the Elkader, Iowa, baseball team, beating teams from Seattle, Washington, Oregon, and Dallas, Texas, and won the Western Regional Championship in Watertown South Dakota. Returning home, they were welcomed by several thousand people who celebrated their success. After washing their uniforms, the next morning they drove to Battle Creek, Michigan, where they advanced and were beaten in the tournament finals by a team from New York, who had several ex-major-leaguers on their roster. Baseball was a game Mel loved to play and he played with the town team for over twenty years. The team put Sumner on the map as the baseball capitol of central Iowa.

Mel was very intent on getting his degree, and completed his studies in three years, receiving his degree in 1948. On August 8, 1948, Miriam and Mel were married in Sumner. Upon graduation, he accepted a teaching position at Rolfe, Iowa, where he was paid three thousand three hundred dollars a year. He and Miriam bought a new car and put money in the bank. Life was good. For three years, he taught in the school system and coached, and they decided to start their family. Miriam and Mel raised two daughters, Patricia, born in 1951 and Becky, born in 1953.

In 1951, at the end of the school year, Mel and Cal were offered an opportunity to go into private business. An elderly businessman who sold insurance in Sumner approached them about buying his established insurance business. It was an opportunity that could not to be ignored, so Cal and Mel invested in their home community, servicing their many clients until Mel retired in1986.

Mel had an active community life. He served as president of the Sumner Community Club, the Commercial Club, and the Rotary Club. He was chairman of St. Johns Lutheran Church, and the building committee of Hillcrest Retirement Home. He was president of Hillcrest for the first seven years. Mel served on the board of the First National Bank of

Sumner for fifteen years, and was a volunteer fireman for ten years. He is a lifetime member of the American Legion and the Veterans of Foreign Wars. Mel Harms was elected to the Upper Iowa Hall of Fame in 1983, serves on the Upper Iowa Hall of Fame Selection Committee, and has received a number of alumni awards from that institution. Still active on several committees, Mel has certainly paid his "civic rent."

Mel and his pilot, Bill Core, remained close friends after their return from service. Most certainly, Bill Core's courage and leadership under extremely perilous conditions saved the lives of ten men as well as his own. Reflecting on that courage and leadership, Mel Harms was a lucky participant and survivor of one of the more spectacular and celebrated plane crashes during World War II.

The reunion of the crew that survived one of the more spectacular and celebrated crash landings during the war in the Pacific.

BOOK 6

Lewis Rich

Luis H. Rich

Corporal
5th Marine Division
28th Regiment
2nd Battalion
D Company

"I granted this interview,
although it is very private and personal,
in dedication to those men
who gave far more than I.
They gave their lives."

~Lewis Rich
Corporal, 5th Marine Division

"If I had aimed better
I might have saved more lives."

~Lewis Rich

RICH • CHAPTER 1

The crusty ice-over-snow crackled as the mourners left their cars and carefully stepped toward the funeral tent. The early-April storm caught everyone off guard, as earlier warm weather suggested a mild spring. The mourners entered the two-sided green tent enclosure to escape the frigid cold north wind, sitting on folding chairs overlooking the flag-draped wooden coffin. Other bundled attendees gathered around, selecting spots to avoid facing the wind for the brief graveside service.

Today they were lying to rest a decorated World War II veteran who had spent two weeks in weather similar to this, or worse, during the Battle of the Bulge. Suffering with frozen feet, this sergeant gathered twenty or more soldiers from other units, fighting side by side until support arrived to stop the German advance. Surrounded by Germans, the men fought door to door in a small Luxembourg village for eight days until they managed to meet up with other American forces. After returning to England to re-supply the decimated division, the sergeant returned to France to fight under General George Patton, where his unit took control of the Ludendorf Bridge at Remagen, and raced into Germany. Returning home, he faithfully served as a rural mail carrier until his retirement thirty years later. Besides his American medals, the sergeant received a decoration from the Grande Duchy of Luxembourg, the Croix de Guerre in "…commemoration of the defense and preservation of the Grand Duchy of Luxembourg." He also received the Purple Heart for frozen feet, but returned it since "he knew too many deserving men who had lost their feet." Today, he was being interred in the middle of a severe snow and ice storm, when in reality it might well have happened in December of 1944 on foreign soil.

Lewis Rich spent that April morning in bed with a high temperature and severe flu symptoms. He was the leader of the American Legion Drill Team that fired the honoring volley of shots and presented the flag at military funerals. He refused to remain in bed, over the protestations of his wife who was concerned over his condition. But Lewis had a job to do, honoring a decorated veteran and friend, and would do what it took to carry out his responsibilities. Dressed in two layers of long winter underwear, he wore his dark blue trousers, white shirt, dark blue tie, and Legion cap. Laced with a variety of pills to ward off stomach cramps, he reported for duty, crunching through the snow to ice and align his squad adjoining the tent enclosure.

At the appropriate time "Taps" was played. Then the distant echo resounding from a remote corner of the cemetery sent chills down the spines of the attendees, commensurate with the frigid weather. Lewis and his assistant approached the draped coffin, and carefully, deliberately, folded the flag in its traditional triangular shape. The handsome legionnaire, with his square jaw, blond hair and clear blue eyes, approached the dead soldier's wife, and half-whispered because of his raw throat. "In behalf of the United States Government and the people of the United States through Merle Hay Post Number 386 and our comrades, we wish to present you with this flag in honor of your husband's service to our country."

After the ceremony Lewis Rich returned to his home and his bed. He knew he had a responsibility. His marine training prepared him to do whatever it took to perform his duty. He had executed his responsibility without personal consideration, and with the grace and dignity needed to elevate this sorrowful occasion.

Semper Fidelis.

RICH • CHAPTER 2

Obstreperous is perhaps a bit strong. Mischievous might be closer. Certainly independent is descriptive of Lewis Rich as a young man. Some folks thought he lacked personal discipline, but when he focused on something, he was not to be deterred. If it was taking apart an alarm clock, he found interesting ways to take it apart, but putting it back together was not of paramount importance. His natural curiosity as a young man took many directions, and with a charming grin on his handsome face with clear blue eyes, he would proceed with great enthusiasm. Books and school never quite fit into that natural curiosity and he developed a stiff resistance to those who tried to involve him in topics not of his interest..

Lewis' father tilled rich farmland in Carroll County, Iowa, south of Glidden. Clyde Rich was a respected member of the community; he and his wife Lucy Rich participated in many church and community activities. Their son Bill, older than Lewis by two years, performed well in school, not only in the classroom but also in drama and musical activities. Bill was everyone's friend in school, and most folks were surprised when, as a senior in high school, he fell hopelessly in love with the high school English teacher, eight years older than he. Bill graduated from Glidden High School, became a B-17 bomber pilot, flew thirty-five missions over Europe, and returned to marry his English teacher.

As a young man, Clyde Rich worked in the local post office as Postmaster. When the Great War approached, Clyde quit his job and enlisted in the newly-formed Army Air Corps. As an airplane mechanic, he flew with the pilot, sitting in the rear seat of the open-air fabric aircraft. In case of an emergency landing, and there were many, the mechanic was available to make the necessary repairs to make the plane once again flyable. During his training in the state of New York, Clyde billeted with the Lewis family, who was most generous and kind to the young Iowan. While preparing to leave for France, Clyde had an attack of appendicitis. Although removed in time, the complications developed, causing his hospitalization in Minnesota for several weeks. Because of this delay, Clyde Rich never served overseas, and completed his enlistment in the United States. Clyde and Lucy fondly remembered their association with this generous family in New York State, and as a result named their second son Lewis.

Growing up on a farm meant many chores, but it was also full of interesting opportunities. Playing in the haymow, the two Rich boys found a long sheet of corrugated steel, and decided it would serve as a great slide from the second floor barn level to a rack full of hay below. They arranged the equipment, and Bill, the older, slid down first. When Lewis slid down the steel slide he caught a rough edge, tearing a deep four-inch gash in his arm. They rushed the eight-year-old lad to town to the doctor who cleansed the wound and indicated stitches would be necessary. Lewis wanted to go to the hospital, since he experienced such a good time there when they removed his tonsils. The doctor indicated that was not an option and he would give a local anesthetic to make the repairs. Lewis was adamant: no anesthetic. So, the doctor installed the sutures while the young man held a steady forced grin, smiled with his clear blue eyes, and never once let out a whimper.

The one distinguishing characteristic of this young farm boy's apparel was an ever-present tear in his overalls over the right knee. His first day in school in bright new overalls usually predicted his return with a tear at the right knee. It was not planned; it just happened for some inexplicable reason. Almost every pair of Lewis's trousers showed evidence where Lucy Rich attempted to stitch and conceal the damage. Nevertheless, it was as much a part of Lewis as his big grin and clear blue eyes.

Clyde Rich returned from a cattle-buying trip in Wyoming and told his sons a story of dealing with a skunk found in the hen house. It seems one of the men grabbed the skunk by the tail, threw it into the air and shot it mid-air before it could plant its feet to spray the thrower. The story impressed the young farm boys. A year or so later, Lewis and a classmate, David Lathrop, found a skunk wandering around the farmyard and decided the bold action was worth a try. Besides, they could sell the skunk fur for real money. As Lewis ran to the animal and grabbed it's tail, he received a full spray from the skunk. The two managed to subdue the animal, and Louis skinned the poor critter. When the task was completed, he approached the farmhouse, where Lucy met him at the door with a pail of hot water, soap, and a stiff brush. Lewis sat in the garage and scrubbed for several hours, only managing to moderately reduce the odiferous impact. He carried the distinctive stench for several days; in fact, wore it as a badge of honor. In addition, he sold the pelt for real money.

Emma Johnson was the Junior High Principal at Glidden Consolidated School, and had great affection for her students. Slightly overweight and of medium height, she bustled about teaching mathematics, as well as seeing to her administrative duties. Her black hair was collected in a neat bun on the back of her head. Her dark eyes, under darker eyebrows, could perceive and solve the most difficult discipline problems within her jurisdiction, and she usually charmed the erring student with her warmth and personal interest. It was generally accepted by all students that junior high was a lot more fun if you did not cross Mrs. Johnson.

Young Lewis was another matter. When Emma Johnson reprimanded him for teasing several girls in his class, she established rigid guidelines for Lewis to follow. This was not a reprimand to Lewis; it was the very sort of challenge that delighted him. Just how much could he tease before Mrs. Johnson got really upset? It finally reached a climax when Mrs. Johnson called Lewis out of class, confronted him in the hallway, and demanded an apology for the girls as well as for herself. Lewis looked at her with his clear blue eyes and smiled. Mrs. Johnson thought if she could bring tears to those clear blue eyes, he just might be remorseful. She banged his head against the wooden lockers several times, hard. Lewis stared into her dark eyes, gave her a fixed grin and his expression did not change. After numerous attempts to penetrate that grin, the exhausted Mrs. Johnson went to the Superintendents Office, called Clyde and Lucy, and put him in their hands.

While working on the farm, Lewis was riding on the back of a grain wagon, with his feet under a vertically sliding endgate for stability. As they turned a corner, he lost hold and fell off, catching his foot and distorting his toe. It was probably broken, but he never mentioned it. When taking a physical for entering the Marines, a doctor noted and inquired about it. Lewis reported a steer had stepped on it. The Marines accepted him and his condition, and, before he completed his service commitment, managed to correct the distortion.

While attending school, Lewis never could master spelling. He could communicate clearly and had no problem with mathmatics; "just don't ask him to spell anything." It probably contributed to his frustration with schoolwork, prompting him to run away from school twice. The prospect of schoolwork and mastering spelling never piqued Lewis' curiosity level, where he could focus on them. According to his Cousin Alice, "Lewis had plenty of discipline; it was just a sort of random thing. If he wanted something, give it to him, because he would get it one way or another."

Lewis was approaching seventeen years in the middle of his junior year in 1943 when he read the newspaper's glamorous accounts of the Marines landing on Guadalcanal. It inspired him to try to join the Marines, and after considerable discussion, his parents signed a release. He went to the recruiting station, lied about his sixteen years of age, and enlisted. The Marines, desperate for replacements, sent him to San Diego to boot camp within a week's time. After arriving, a bout with scarlet fever put him in the hospital for three weeks, but he finished boot camp with his enlistment class.

Boot camp in the Marines is fourteen weeks of pure hell. It is an attempt to take a young man, totally strip him of individuality and personal identity, and then rebuild those qualities that best suit the Marine Corps. Boot camp both followed and established "Marine Tradition."

As one Marine stated, "We shared everything, from our standard no-hair haircuts, to the equipment we received. We were all treated identically. We wore the same uniforms, ate the same food, marched to the same cadence, saw the same training films, suffered the same punishments. We slept in the same bunks, cleaned the same rifles, sat on the same footlockers and shined the same shoes. We did everything together, and those of us who could, helped those who couldn't, because if anyone goofed up, we all suffered the consequences. If someone was caught smoking at a forbidden time or place, we each had to put a bucket over our heads and smoke a cigarette with out touching it with our hands. Or we did "up and on shoulders" with our M-1 rifles until we couldn't lift our arms any longer. It is amazing how effective a jury of one's peers can be in dealing with the guilty party or parties in such an environment. The irony of it all is that it worked. In fact, it worked like a charm." Thus the Marine motto, "Semper Fidelis." Always faithful.

The first three weeks were filled with physical conditioning, close order drill, and the manual of arms and military bearing. They saw films on a variety of things from trench foot to venereal disease. Issued M-1 rifles, they learned to take apart and re-assemble the weapons, quickly and while blindfolded. They were called #@$##*%%# and $#%&&@$, usually nose-to-nose. The next three weeks were spent at the firing range, where they fired M-1s, .45 caliber pistols, Browning Automatic Rifles, .30 caliber rifles and grenade launchers. The men slept in tents and were up at 4:00am to work on kitchen police, clean their tents, and march to the rifle range. Back late at night, the men ate their evening meal, and had lectures for an hour and a half on military subjects before turning in. The next day was more of the same. After three weeks working with weapons, they returned to their base for additional training, inspections, and physical conditioning. At completion of boot camp, a man had been transformed to an individual who believed in himself, was a part of something outside of himself, and was bigger than a sum of the parts.

Rich next went to Camp Pendleton, California, at a camp called Little Tokyo, where marines learned infantry tactics at the squad, company, and battalion level. Lewis was assigned to the 5th Marine Division, 28th Regiment, 2nd Battalion, Company D. He was pleased to discover that two of his high school classmates were also stationed near Camp Pendleton. Bob Johnson was at a nearby Navy base. Keith Dickson was in the 3rd Marine Division. The trio frequently went on leave together. Dickson had lost three fingers on his left hand when a dummy grenade fuse went off while he was holding it. Dickson refused a discharge and insisted on remaining in the Marines.

At Little Tokyo they practiced assault landings and beach landing tactics. At the completion of their training, they were allowed a few days leave home, then boarded a troopship headed for the big island of Hawaii. Because of the prevailing winds, the big island has a desert side and a rain-forest side. Camp Tarawa was on the arid desert side, and was perfect for practicing beach landings. They would load into Higgins Boats or All-Terrain Vehicles (called alligators) and practice running up the beach to establish fire perimeters.

Lewis became part of a machine gun squad. Their water-cooled machine gun, with a metal jacket surrounding the barrel, kept the barrel from overheating and losing its effectiveness. Lewis' assigned job was an ammunition carrier, toting several metal cans with belts of .30 caliber shells. His duty was seeing that his machine gun crew always had ammunition available. His responsibility to the team was just as important as the fellow who pulled the trigger on the machine gun. Lewis also took his turn pulling the trigger during training.

After a few weeks on the Big Island, the men were loaded aboard the troopship Missoula, bound for the islands of Tinian and Saipan. A new troopship, it also carried tanks and trucks as well. The troopship zig-zagged across the Pacific for fifty-four days in an attempt to avoid submarine detection. The marines took turns sitting on the decks, and played card games to keep occupied. Once on the islands, the Marines again practiced beach landings and tactics. They knew they would soon put their training to use. It inspired many of them to write a number of letters to loved ones back home.

The day finally came when a number of LSTs (Landing Ship Tank/Personnel) appeared to take the men off the island. The 2nd Battalion of the 28th Regiment marched aboard one of the oldest, most beat-up LSTs in the Navy. Not only did the front swinging doors leak, but every time the doors were opened and the exit ramp dropped, water would pour into the boat. Twelve or fourteen gasoline-powered pumps were necessary to keep the boat afloat.

The flat-bottomed LST, even though weighted down with tanks, alligators and trucks loaded with ammunition and supplies, bobbed and tossed about like a cork on the water. The marines were very seasick, hanging over the rail most of the time. Lewis survived extreme seasickness because of a young Mexican marine in the bunk next to him. The poor soldier was so sick he never got out of bed, so Lewis helped by taking his mess kit to the mess hall for him and delivering his food. The arriving mess kit was usually missing one or two food items, like apples, oranges, or cookies. Louis felt that it did not make much difference, since the young marine never kept his food down for more than a few minutes, anyway.

The 5th Marine Division heading towards the beaches of Iwo Jima. The young men knew landing would be difficult, but did not realize what the next thirty-six days would entail. (Marine Photo-The Spearhead No. 2, Marine Public Relations G-2, published 1946. All photos)

As the convoy approached Christmas Island, the sound system played the broadcasts of "Tokyo Rose" who informed the men where they were going and what was going to happen to them. She knew the divisions, regiments, how many were on which ships, and even some of the officer's names. The Americans were proud they had secretly broken the difficult Japanese code, and knew of most of their actions. However, the Japanese information pipeline was phenomenal; the American Intelligence never did discover how Tokyo Rose got her information.

When their ship crossed the equator, several marines were put through the usually gross ritual for becoming "pollywogs." Fortunately, Lewis avoided being selected to participate.

The convoy was now nearing a small lava rock outcropping in the southwest Pacific Ocean named Iwo Jima, the translation of which is Sulfur Island. On February 19th, 1945, two divisions of marines approached the small Pacific Island, obscured in clouds and dust. Young men who rode their bikes down gravel roads, jumped out of haymows, swam in forbidden streams, and struggled with algebra, were hunkered down in small boats headed for the black sand beaches of Iwo Jima. None realized the degree of carnage they were about to experience

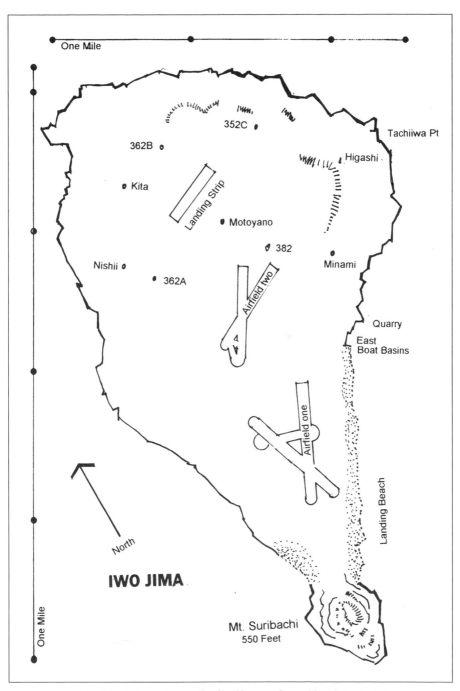

One Mile

Tachiiwa Pt

352C

362B

Higashi

Kita

Landing Strip

Motoyano

382

Minami

Nishii

362A

Airfield Two

Quarry

East
Boat Basins

North

Airfield one

Landing Beach

IWO JIMA

One Mile

Mt. Suribachi
550 Feet

Map of Iwo Jima, the small pile of lava rock considered strategic to American advances in the Pacific War.

RICH • CHAPTER 3

For several years the American forces had been island-hopping, bypassing occupied islands to only invade those where airfields could contribute to maintaining air power in support of the next acquisition. Between the Army Air Corps and the Navy, other islands inhabited by Japanese were denied supplies that were necessary to sustain the occupiers. The succession of island invasions included: Guadalcanal in the Solomon Islands-August 8, 1942; Munda in the Solomon Islands-July 1943; Bouginville, November 1, 1943; Makin and Tarawa in the Gilbert Islands-November 21, 1943; Kwajalein in the Marshall Islands-January 31, 1944; Hollandia, Aitape and Dutch New Guinea-April 22, 1944; Saipan and Tinian in the Marianas Islands-June 14, 1944; Philippine Islands-February 5, 1945; Iwo Jima in the Volcano Islands-February 19, 1945.

Once Saipan had been taken and converted to an airfield base, long-range B-29 bombers were able to reach the Islands of Japan and begin damaging their productive capacity. In order to reach Japan in a direct flight, the big bombers had to fly over or near the small volcanic island of Iwo Jima, which had two airfields housing Japanese aircraft and a third field nearly completed. A nearby island, Chichi Jima, was the "eyes and ears" of the Pacific, reporting incoming flights of American planes. Consequently, American forces bombed the two islands constantly to reduce their ability to function. Iwo was a long seven hundred miles from Saipan, and five hundred miles from the main islands of Japan.

American strategists realized after the first few raids when Japanese planes could not fly high enough to reach the B-29s and subsequently adapted their planes, the wounded B-29s would have a difficult time returning to Saipan. An intermediate landing site might save many lives. Iwo Jima became the prime target for the next leap to defeat Japan.

Iwo Jima is a small island, shaped like a pork chop, only four and one-half miles long and two and one-half miles wide. The highest point, Mount Suribachi, is located at the tip of the tail, rising five hundred fifty feet above sea level. To either side of the mountain are the island's only landing beaches, both lashed by high surf, terraced and covered with a mixture of brown volcanic sand and black cinders finer than sand. The remainder of the island is a combination of sand and lava rock with deep ravines and a very coarse terrain of rocky, inaccessible bluffs. A large area was leveled where three airfields were constructed, along with supporting hangars and gasoline storage tanks.

144

The desert island has very little rainfall, and plant life is limited to scrub bushes with large root systems. There are occasional fissures where sulfur fumes and brackish water bubble out of the ground. Numerous indentations in the surface are very hot, apparently from semi-volcanic activity still present underground.

As difficult as the terrain is, it might have been easier to take in September '44. The additional delay while the Joint Chiefs of staff of the Allied Forces were debating where to hit next gave the Japanese time to complete their intricate defenses of the island.

The Island had been under Japanese control for twenty-five years, and when finally recognized by the Japanese as a necessary link in the defense of Japan, troops were sent there. Under the command of General Tadamichi Kuribayashi, 21,000 troops, including the battle hardened 145th Regiment, were moved to the island. Kuribayshi was very impressed by defense tactics worked out in depth on the island of Peleiu in the Carolines. He set about the task of transforming the rock mass into an invulnerable fortress. He convinced the garrison of troops that each and every soldier was to fight to the death. Before dying, each man was to kill ten Americans. Even if the island was lost, the Americans would pay the kind of "bloody butcher's bill" they would not want to incur again. Perhaps the U.S. timetable for attacking Japan would be not only deterred, but America might well seek a negotiated peace.

The Japanese commander, General Kuribayashi, had two years for his men to dig three tunnels the length of the island, most of them high enough to walk through. The tunnels contained a few larger rooms and all areas had electric lights and were fan ventilated. At Mt. Suribachi they built a labyrinth of positions for artillery, mortars, and automatic weapons. Tanks were semi-concealed, firing from fixed positions, and protected by rock embankments. Numerous caves and airshafts permitted soldiers to shoot at any point on the island from two directions. From Suribachi, observers could see most of the island, and signal instructions to positions on the north of the island. Concrete bunkers with small firing slits were cleverly concealed among the rocks and sand dunes. Other islands were defended by massive "banzai" charges: three or four hundred men hurtling toward a point in the lines with frantic hand-to-hand fighting, attempting to panic the enemy and overrun his position. General Kuribayashi intended to use sniper fire and concealment to turn back the Americans.

Airplanes bombed Iwo Jima regularly; in February 1945, the island was visited daily for a week, with American planes dropping six thousand

eight hundred tons of bombs. Subsequently, Navy big guns fired twenty-two thousand rounds at the island for two straight days. On the island, Japanese soldiers hid in their caves and tunnels and were not seriously hurt by the tons of steel thrown at them.

General Kuribayashi was very philosophical about his mission. "This island is the front line that defends our mainland and I am going to die here." To his family, he wrote, "The life of your father is just like a lamp in the wind."

Because of the limited water supply on the island, American planners estimated there were between seven thousand and seventeen thousand Japanese troops on the island.. They expected to invade and control the island in four days, then withdraw the marines to invade Okinawa.

Early on the morning of February 19th, 1945, two divisions under the command of Major General Harry Schmidt went churning toward a landing beach obscured by clouds of dust and smoke. Under the cloud was an enemy unscathed by the terrible pounding of air and navy forces, hiding in the tunnels and caves.

As the assault troop's motorized equipment bogged down in the soft sand, the marines leapt out of their boats and waded ashore in the soft material. As the equipment piled up on the beach, and men tried to move ahead, confusion spread, and that is when the guns of Iwo Jima broke their silence, turning the beaches into bloody chaos.

Kuribayashi had deliberately allowed the marines to come ashore only lightly opposed. He gave them enough time to get bogged down, then opened fire with everything he had, turning the black sand blood red. The returning fire from naval ships became more accurate, permitting the marines to advance slowly to build a beachhead. By nightfall it was clear the marines had come to stay.

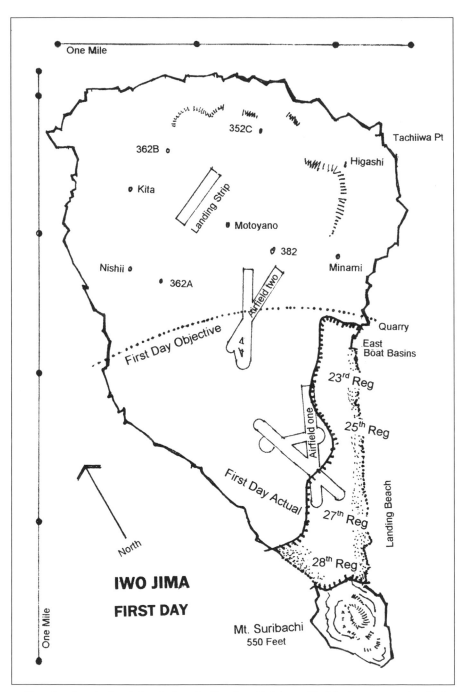

Map showing the beach-head after the first days fighting. The Marines expected to find seven thousand Japanese soldiers and fight a four-day battle. They found twenty-one thousand Japanese soldiers, and thirty-six days of hell.

RICH • CHAPTER 4

DAY ONE: The marines were awakened early aboard the LST, had a hot breakfast and donned their gear. The men who would ride Higgins boats climbed down the cargo net, difficult to do with a weapon and full field pack. Those who would ride trucks and alligators loaded their gear in the poorly-lighted hold, where the rolling equipment was ready to drive out of the LST. The invasion intent was for the 5th and 4th Divisions to lead the assault on the beach, with the 3rd Division held in reserve. A division varied from 12,000 to 14,000 men depending upon the organizational make-up for a specific task. Because of the number of men involved, marines arrived at the beach in several consecutive waves.

A machine gun platoon consists of four or five squads, each of which was assigned to a different infantry company or platoon at any one time, and might change daily. On this day, Lewis Rich's machine gun squad was attached to the third platoon, D Company. They were to ride ashore in an alligator, turn left at the base of Mt. Suribachi, drive a certain distance, and then set up their water cooled machine gun to protect the beach. As the LST approached and burrowed into the beach, the big front doors swing open and immediately began taking in water. The alligators roared out, since they could float, and headed up the beach. The pumps on the LST could not handle the water intake, and the landing ship ultimately was abandoned on the beach, settling into the soft black sand.

The black volcanic beach at Iwo Jima was very fine and had no fine clays or grit to hold it together. When the alligator reached the sand surface, it immediately dropped to its bottom unable to move forward or backward. Realizing their predicament, the marines leapt out of the vehicle, wading ashore across a low-sloped beach three hundred yards wide to a fifteen-foot high beach sand embankment. Climbing up the steep, soft surface was difficult; take one step forward, slide backward two steps. With full field packs weighing over sixty pounds, the men crawled like crabs to reach the top of the sand wall, then disbursed in the general direction of their initial orders. Because of the difficulty in climbing the sand bank, and with all vehicles ineffective, platoons and companies were in disarray. The marines formed into new groups with new leadership taking charge.

One young marine named Louis Pettigrew from Roanoke, Virginia, was the same size as Lewis, had the same blond hair, and could have passed as Lewis's brother. He was lying in the sand just ahead of Lewis, with his boot touching Lewis' shoulder. In the first ten minutes on the beach, he took bullets in the shoulder and head from a very good Japanese machine gunner. His was not a Hollywood death, with gallant motions and twitching. The young marine just did not move.

Resistance was relatively light with sporadic rifle and machinegun fire. From experience on other landings, the men were ready to receive the expected "banzai" attack by the Japanese. There was no need for banzai charges on Iwo Jima, as the Japanese defenses were dug in so effectively. The Japanese offered token resistance, and when the marines were comfortably ashore, cut loose with everything they had. The beach suddenly exploded, throwing bodies and body parts in all directions. Small arms fire came from every direction, so it was difficult to determine the source. Crawling into a mortar depression gave some protection, but crawling out of the hole made you a perfect target. The initial fulisade from the Japanese was devastating. It began an intense battle that would last thirty-six days. Five days later Lewis would be a squad leader, one of only two remaining marines in his machine gun squad. Five lieutenants in the battalion were lost the first day. Major Allen and the Battalion Commander were lost the third day.

The men crawled through the rocks and dug foxholes in the soft sand, returning fire at every opportunity. The Japanese fired from caves and emplacements on Mt. Suribachi, retreating after a few rounds, and then relocating to fire again. When the marines felt they were secure, they would suddenly receive fire from another direction, requiring them to dig deeper or relocate. The remainder of the day was spent returning fire, trying not to get pinned down, and reacting as best they could. Dust and smoke filled the air, so it was difficult to determine the direction of incoming small arms' fire. Mortar shells rained down constantly, but fortunately, the smoke kept the Japanese from accurately finding their pre-positioned targets. The snipers, however, were effective, killing fifteen members of D Company and wounding forty-five more. As evening approached, the Japanese became bolder, sneaking out of their caves to throw grenades into foxholes.

The Navy responded by firing "star shells," creating a light brighter than the sun to light up the area. Star shells fired every two minutes cast an eerie quality over the surroundings, but effectively protected the embattled marines from night assaults.

Lewis spent his first night in a shell hole with three marines from another company. They did not get much sleep. The death of Pettigrew, seeing men blown up, many dead soldiers or barely-alive ones with open wounds keeping the corpsmen busy, a day filled with mayhem, shouting, dodging snipers, and crawling about in the soft sand were all a big blur. In the early morning, just before dawn, a Japanese soldier was seen crawling toward their shell hole. One of the marines reached out, grabbed the Japanese soldier's helmet with both hands, pulled him toward the hole, and proceeded to beat his skull to a pulp with the soldier's own helmet. There was little sleep the rest of the night.

DAY TWO: Wolfing down a quick C-ration as the sky began to lighten, the men relocated in a spot where two machine guns could effectively sweep an area. The men were trying to fire into a cave where the Japanese were rolling out a cannon to shoot down on the beach below. Every fourth shell from a machine gun was a tracer shell, showing where the bullets were going. Unfortunately, it also showed the source of those bullets to the

The soft black volcanic sand made advance and use of the beaches difficult (Marine Photo. i.e.)

Corporal Rich firing his water-cooled machine gun. That day they fired over twenty-five thousand rounds of ammunition. Cpl Rich is identified because of the tear in his pants at the knee. (Marine photo i.e.)

Japanese, so it was necessary to relocate frequently. Temporarily set up on the top of a bunker taken out by a navy artillery shell, they were suddenly pinned down by a Japanese machine gun firing from an embankment. When they called for tank support, a nearby tank rolled into position, spotted the concrete "pillbox," and made a direct hit. For additional protection, the tank was modified by adding two big beams of bridge planking along the sides that held bags of sand. During the action that day it took two direct hits from a Japanese 32mm anti-tank gun that exploded the bridge planking, leaving two shiny scars on the exterior of the tank body. Powered by an air-cooled radial aircraft engine, the additional air movement was required to keep it from overheating. The tank also sported an eight-foot vertical air vent, so it could travel through water.

A water-cooled machine gun had the gun barrel located in a jacket filled with slow moving liquid, keeping the barrel from overheating and distorting. It permitted more continuous firing, and for a longer time. Company D's machine gun squad continued to relocate periodically, with their heavy weapon firing into caves and pillboxes. Rich was on a team that included PFC Evans and PFC Chapman; both were older, were drafted, and chose the Marines when Selective Service permitted them to choose their branch of service. Evans was a rubber worker in Dayton Ohio, and had a draft deferment because he worked in an "essential industry." When the plant ran out of rubber, he was immediately called up. Evans was thirty-five years old and had three children. Chapman was a cigarette salesman from Dallas when his draft number came up. Evans was the machine gun squad leader, Degraf was second, and Rich was third. That afternoon, firing into caves and bunkers, the squad fired over twenty-five thousand rounds of .30 caliber ammunition. Late in the afternoon Rich's machinegun took a slug through the water jacket; the gun overheated and had to be abandoned. Rich picked up an M-1 and served as a rifleman the remainder of the day.

Rich and a marine named Dinsmore, a kid from Davenport, Iowa, were circling the base of Mt. Suribachi when they spotted a four-inch cannon projecting from a pillbox. They approached the pillbox, discovered it was empty, and decided to disable the cannon; rolling a phosphorous grenade down the barrel would put it out of commission. Unknown to the men, the rear breech mechanism had been removed and the grenade rolled through the barrel, exploding on the ground. After dark a destroyer moved into position to shell pillboxes, using a strong searchlight to locate it's targets. The four-inch cannon Rich thought was disabled shot out the destroyer's searchlight when Japanese snuck back into the pillbox to return fire. When another searchlight was installed, it was also knocked out by the cannon. Navy artillery finally demolished the pillbox.

Rich spent the night in a foxhole, brightly lit by star shells. A destroyer firing its 40mm guns into nearby caves awakened him periodically, throughout the night.

DAY THREE: Rich and those who remained of his squad found the quartermaster and picked up an air-cooled machine gun. Returning to their assigned D Company, they spent the day moving about the base of Suribachi, firing into caves and covering advancing marines.

DAY FOUR: The next morning Dinsmore, Rich, and members of D Company, crawled up Suribachi from the backside to observe the terrain. After reaching the top, they crawled back down trying to locate the remainder of their Company. Meanwhile, members of E Company climbed Suribachi with a flag from the LST, tied it to a short pipe and installed it on a rock outcropping for all of the marines to see. E Company included a group of ex-marine raiders and paratroopers, all veterans of previous invasions. Rich knew most of the men in E Company from training exercises, and knew Ira Hayes and one or two of the flag raisers quite well. The next day, the flag-raisers were given a larger flag from the USS Missoula, found a twenty foot section of steel water pipe left by the Japanese, and used rope for attachment. The men once again climbed Suribachi, and with several cameramen in attendance, erected the flag in what is now considered one of the more famous moments recorded in American history.

D Company was working northward over the rough terrain, shooting into caves and pillboxes. Evans was crawling around looking for a new position for their gun. He stood up and called, "Rich, bring that gun up here. We have a better field of fire!" At that moment, a bullet shattered his face just below the helmet. There was no need to call a medic. Lewis used the black sand to rub the blood from his clothing. They continued relocating and firing into caves the remainder of the day.

DAY FIVE: What was left of the battalion spent the day fighting their way up the slopes of Suribachi, in an attempt to control the high ground. It was finally taken, but only after a tremendous loss of life. The Japanese were well entrenched, and caves and pillboxes could cover every inch of the mountain's surface. Flamethrowers and machine guns finally made it possible to scale the apex. Returning to the beach supply area to pick up ammunition, Rich and Dinsmore found a Naimbu machine gun on a dead Japanese, and took it with them. When they approached the beach supply area where Navy personnel were unloading supplies, a Navy Lt. Commander saw the weapon, and wanting a souvenir, traded a medi-pack for it. The medical pack included, among other items, a tin of bacon, cigarettes and twenty small bottles of 100-proof brandy. What remained of the squad went to an unoccupied area to inspect the newly acquired windfall. The men managed to reach a state completely oblivious to noise, star shells, chaos, and cannon fire. Totally relaxed, their exhausted stupor is probably what every man on that horrendous island needed. They have no idea what happened to the bacon.

DAY SIX: After munching down K-rations, the machinegun squad spent the day backing up marines trying to locate cave entrances, and sealing them up. It was a much less stressful day.

DAY SEVEN: The battalion relieved the 27th Regiment on the north end of the island. The 27th had experienced numerous casualties in taking two of the three airfields on the island. As men of the 27th walked by, Lewis was depressed by the condition of the men; green, ashen faces, gaunt and disheveled. They had all of the combat they needed. Lewis was not happy about going into battle after seeing the condition and faces of the men. Replacement squads had a day of rest, a good night's sleep, and were relatively fresh. They were to assault the big caves on the north face of Suribachi. One of the biggest caves was blown up with ten tons of explosives. The day was spent protecting marines in their attempts to dynamite other caves.

DAY EIGHT: D Company was now on the north face of Mt. Suribachi, and was told to assault Hill 362 that contained a Japanese command post. As they worked their way around the base, they found a tank trap, a ditch ten foot wide and eight foot deep. Rich and his squad had used the trap for protection several times, but now called for a tank with a grading blade to fill it in so support could move up, if needed.

Combat had reduced the squad from twelve to four people, and replacements began arriving. Rich's squad received four new men, three privates and an officer. Lieutenant Gage, a native of Maine, was a brand new Second Lieutenant suddenly thrust into his first battle. Since Rich and the squad he belonged to were some of the younger more foolhardy marines, they were often given questionable jobs requiring greater exposure to the enemy. This day the squad, along with the new men, were on the backside of Suribachi working their way to Hill 362 with their newly acquired water-cooled machine gun. The squad, under constant sniper fire, moved around the island looking for the best location for a field of fire. Lt. Gage and Rich crawled ahead in the soft sand looking for a safe location. As they surveyed

Hill 362 where Company D replaced exhausted marines from another battalion.
(Marine Photo)

the terrain, Lt. Gage took a shot through the top of his helmet, killing him instantly. At the sound, Rich raised his head to look at the Lieutenant, and a bullet kicked in the dirt directly below his face, throwing sand into his face. Rich immediately backed down, shouted to the rest of the squad, and they returned to the tank trap.

From the tank trap, the squad proceeded to climb Hill 362, since it appeared to be the best placement for a machine gun. Once there, the gun was positioned to fire down the slope. On the hill a sergeant wounded in the right hand continued to direct the troops attacking the slope. He wanted to drop grenades over the hill to a Japanese bunker located just below. The sergeant leaned way over the edge of the premonitory, while other marines held him by his cartridge belt, and he lobbed grenades down the hill left-handed. The sergeant could have returned to an aid station to have his wound attended to, but he continued to direct fire from Hill 362. An hour later he was killed by a Japanese sniper.

DAY NINE: D Companies' head cook was a soldier named Dooley. Cooks' duties were not only to prepare and deliver food, but also to bring up supplies and carry the wounded back to safe lines. This day Dooley not only brought up supplies, but also had a flame-thrower strapped on his back. The platoon sergeant said, "Here, I'll take that flame thrower." Dooley replied, "I want to use it!" Dooley proceeded to march up the hill toward a cave and pulled the trigger on the flame-thrower. Nothing happened. Marines lying in foxholes nearby shouted instructions on how to adjust the valves and turn on the pressure and ignition. Dooley stood upright in front of the cave, fumbled with the knobs and finally got it properly adjusted and ignited. He moved into the face of the cave and proceeded to fill the cave with flames until the tank was empty. Lewis thought he was one brave SOB who deserved a medal for his action.

Gunnery Sergeant Young received a field promotion to Second Lieutenant, and after visiting the command post, returned to the front lines wearing khakis instead of the green field uniforms. His lighter color stood out dramatically, placing the company in jeopardy. That night he stayed with Rich in a foxhole. About 3:00 AM, they heard and identified three Japanese sneaking up behind them. Rich did not want to rig up the machinegun, so he called to Hubbard in the next foxhole, who properly dispatched them. Lieutenant Young told Rich he did not want to sleep with him again because he was afraid of getting shot. Rich replied that he did not want Lt. Young to sleep in his foxhole because he was too bright a target.

156

Lt. Young survived the war and later fought in Korea. He received recognition when he suffered a stomach wound that opened his stomach cavity. He gathered up his intestines in his arms and walked some distance to an aid station where he was treated, sent back to the general hospital, and fully recovered.

DAY TEN: The Japanese had few mortars, doing most of their damage with very accurate sniper rifle fire. The Japanese had a lightweight mortar that rested on a bipod and steel base plate, but often Japanese would rest it on the base and wrap their knee around it to stabilize it. During early jungle fighting this technique was observed by American soldiers, who thought they rested the mortar on the side of their knee. Several soldiers tried this method, only to severely damage their leg in the process.

The morning after Hill 362, the squad moved to a new location beyond the hill and continued to establish a new field of fire. As they were firing, the barrel became over heated and warped, spraying bullets in all directions. While they were locating a new barrel and planning their new strategy, Rich looked down to see a Japanese sniper in a foxhole, firing away from them. Rich immediately pointed the warped barrel in the sniper's general direction and let go about a hundred rounds. Rich doesn't not know if he hit the sniper, but if he didn't, he certainly scared the hell out of him.

DAY ELEVEN: The next day they continued to move forward toward the north end of the island. The terrain was a combination of rock, sand, ravines, and scrub trees. Trees were stunted, since Iwo Jima was an arid island without much rainfall, and the root system spread on the surface in all directions. The island had been under Japanese control for over twenty-five years, but was inhabited by twenty-two thousand Japanese soldiers for only two years. The water from dug wells was brackish and tasted of sulfur. Consequently, the Japanese developed a complex system for capturing any rainwater falling on the island. Any rock of size had a small concrete trough built around it that flowed into a small concrete collecting-basin. Any fog or early morning dew would also deposit a few drops of the valuable liquid into the basin and the thirsty Japanese carefully collected it.

The machine gun squad continued to move forward, hiding in the lava rocks where snipers could not find them. A marine mortar squad just below them attempted to lob mortar shells into a cave entrance located just ten yards ahead of their location. Firing three shells in rapid succession, one mortar shell went straight up and came down, exploding just a few feet

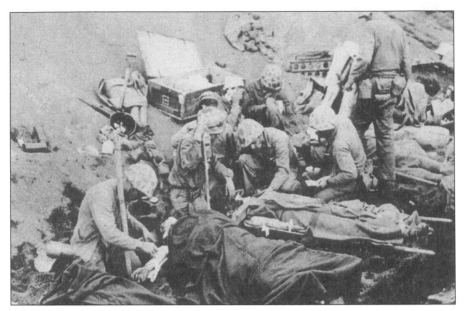

Medics were kept very busy attending to the wounded for all thirty-six days of the battle.
(Marine Photo i.e.)

from the mortar. One mortar man started screaming, "I'm hit! I'm hit!" The back of his uniform was in shreds, and when the mortar crew helped him take off his shirt, they found red marks all over his back. With shrapnel marks everywhere, the skin had not been penetrated and there was not one drop of blood to be seen.

DAY TWELVE: Moving to a new location above a cave, they set down the tripod, mounted the gun, and fed a ribbon of ammunition into the chamber. Suddenly a marine ran by shouting, **"FIRE IN THE HOLE! FIRE IN THE HOLE!"** Suddenly the ground beneath them erupted in an enormous explosion, knocking them down and covering them with dirt, rocks and debris. The ground trembled for several seconds as the explosion moved through the system of tunnels. The machine gun squad, emerged from the dirt, dusted themselves off, and cleaned out their eyes, ears, and nostrils, thankful to have survived the blast with no casualties. They cleaned their weapons, gathered their gear, and began looking for a new field of fire.

One of the replacement ammunition carriers assigned to the squad was a young man from Ohio named Hubbard. He was a particularly unlikable young soldier, distant, withdrawn, a loner, conniving, and always finding an alternative to suit his own purposes. He went through boot camp reporting to sickbay every single day. His conduct during training would predict his being undependable and unreliable, characteristics not appreciated or tolerated by marine conventions. On the fifth day of battle he was assigned to Rich's 2nd squad, 3rd group as an ammunition carrier. Upon his arrival, he threw away his lighter carbine rifle and acquired a Garand M-1 rifle, since it had more distance and accuracy. Slightly built, he wore a shoulder pad and cartridge belt with hooks for carrying the metal canisters of shells. He located a backpack and adapted it to carry machine gun canisters on his back, instead of conventionally by the metal handles. He scavenged for aluminum gear, canteens and mess kit, instead of the standard stainless steel issue. For some strange reason, Hubbard loved combat, excelled in Rich's squad always delivering belts of ammunition, and then wandering off to do some sniping. Though outwardly congenial, because of his quirky personality he was not well liked, but he was always smiling, enjoying his role in the squad. On the thirtieth day of combat Hubbard was hit by a bullet that went through his aluminum canteen, driving aluminum splinters into his hip. Taken to an aid station, he never returned to the squad. Once gone, squad members quietly admitted he was really missed.

DAY FIFTEEN: The Japanese hated "napalm," a jelly like substance that burned ferociously until it had consumed itself. Once ignited, there was no way to put it out, and if you got some on your body, it caused incredible burns. Using flamethrowers was grossly inhuman, but one of the few devices that would flush Japanese out of their intricate cave system. Strangely enough it was invented by President Conan of Harvard University, who found that combining two relatively simple compounds created a devastating weapon.

In one instance, an airplane dropped a several fifty-five gallon containers of napalm over a complex of caves on the side of Suribachi, and ignited it. When the fire finally subsided, marines looked into a cave and found forty or fifty Japanese soldiers in a state near death, unable to move. The intense fire had literally sucked oxygen out of that part of the cave system, and the men were essentially asphyxiated by oxygen deprivation.

DAY TWENTY: There was particularly rough terrain behind the airfields, and D Company spent several days trying to clean out pillboxes and caves, and were constantly taking and re-taking ground. The machinegun crew at one time occupied a Japanese sniper's location on a small rock outcropping, but was firing the opposite way. The terrain was a combination of sand and lava rock that had been blown apart several times, resulting in

The Japanese tank trap, a ten foot wide trench, became a refuge for Marines several times during the thirty six days of battle. (Marine Photo)

deep ravines and uneven landfall. Cave entrances and enclosures for snipers were everywhere, blending in with the terrain. Their occupancy or vacancy was always in question, requiring constant surveillance.

Second Lieutenant Goza was another sergeant who received a battle-field commission, and just happened to return from the command post wearing khaki clothing. The Lieutenant was perched on a rock outcropping with a machine gun, directing his platoon from above. He suddenly started shouting, **"I'M HIT! I'M HIT! I'M DYING! I'M DYING!"** Although he was actually hit in the elbow, he suffered extreme shock, totally panicked and just as suddenly, fell over dead. His khaki proved to have too high a visibility.

DAY TWENTY-ONE: A U.S. tank in the area hit a land mine and had one track blown off. The tank men left the tank for the night with the intent of returning the next day to repair it. That night several Japanese snuck into the tank, and waited for American tanks that were arriving the next day. As American tanks climbed over the horizon the next morning, they were fired upon from one of their own. A marine patrol worked their way behind the crippled machine and promptly dispatched its occupants. The tank was repaired and put back into action that day. One of the tank men was from Carroll, Iowa, and while Lewis was chatting with him, dynamite was thrown into a nearby cave. The explosion flushed out two men wearing nothing but loincloths, and both were killed. They turned out to be Korean miners, brought in to direct the cave excavations.

Some Marine tanks were outfitted with flame-throwing cannons. The Japanese feared napalm and would do anything to knock them out, exposing their men to great risk. As a result, all US tanks mounted a dummy napalm cannon that lured many Japanese soldiers out of their caves in an attempt to demolish them. It was one of the few times Japanese troops exposed themselves to direct fire.

DAYS TWENTY-THREE TO THIRTY-TWO: These days were spent cleaning out caves and sniper positions. The marines were so tired of fighting and so fatigued, most did not care if they survived or not. They were tired of being on constant guard from snipers, and tired of taking and retaking ground on the desolate landscape. Although the number of firefights were reduced, the medics were kept busy because the doggedly determined Japanese snipers knew their days were numbered and wanted to carry out General Kuribayashi's orders.

DAY THIRTY-THREE: This day something occurred that Rich still feels badly about. A squad of marines were engaged in a heavy firefight, and called for a machine gun squad to back them up. Rich's machinegun squad

The caves on Mt. Suribachi had a commanding view of the landing area.
Fire from the caves could reach every square inch on the island.

moved into position to add firepower in the skirmish. Bill Chapman, with the Rich's squad since they first landed on Iwo, assisted with setting up the machine gun and directed fire from an adjoining foxhole. As they commenced firing at a variety of targets, the gun suddenly stopped. Rich, who was firing the gun, raised the receiver on the air-cooled weapon and called to Chapman to pull the cartridge belt. As Chapman raised his head to look at the gun, he was hit just below his nose by a ricocheting bullet that literally tore off half of his head. As he stood there in shock, his rapidly beating heart was pumping blood out of his throat artery, and by the time he fell, he had lost most of his body's blood.

They carried the machine gun back to armament, and found a bullet in the receiver where the belt enters. The bullet was sticking out of a one-inch piece of steel in the receiver, in line with the sight Rich was looking through. A second bullet found lodged in the front leg of the tripod indicated how close they all were to being casualties.

With the loss of still another machine gun, Rich picked up a Browning Automatic Rifle (BAR) and continued using it for several days. He cleaned the weapon and picked up several BAR magazines from a container. Unknowingly, he had picked up armor-piercing shells, and when he test fired the BAR, it jammed after one round. He suspected that armor-piercing ammunition carried more gunpowder because of the bullet's weight, which expanded the shell casing, causing it not to eject. Better to find out in a test firing than a firefight.

When D Company moved off the line into reserve, of the original two hundred men and one hundred replacements, only thirteen men reported for muster. It was later confirmed all thirteen men received the Purple Heart.

At the command center, the men slept as they had not slept for four weeks. The command center's protection was a series of "trip wires" surrounding the area that would set off flares when moved or rearranged. Every night the Japanese would attempt to sneak into camp, not to kill, but to acquire food and water for their men. Once the invasion began, the Navy worked overtime making certain the Japanese garrison received no supplies of food, ammunition, or water. A few small craft were able to sneak by, but the total amount of supplies delivered was negligible. At 4:00 AM that morning the wire was tripped and a flare lit up the night. Only twenty feet away from their sleeping area a Japanese soldier was shot while running away with a five-gallon can of water.

The bizarre terrain rearranged by two hundred thousand tons of bombs and artillery shells, that did not dislodge the Japanese who were secure in their caves. (Marine photo)

DAY THIRTY-FOUR: The squad reorganized, cleaned up, repaired equipment and spent the day organizing for the final push. There was still sporadic fighting on the island as the thirsty, starving Japanese continued to make a last effort before dying for the Emperor. Lewis Rich counted his blessings having been nearly hit and dusted several times, he remained not only alive, but whole.

DAY THIRTY-FIVE: Clean-up operations continued, as the battle was essentially over. Rich and his squad were sent back to the northern part of the island as backup support for marines cleaning out caves. As the men advanced through a cleaned-out area, they were suddenly exposed to several rounds of sniper fire. Rich, carrying his BAR, dove in to a shallow depression on the ground. Before he could look up Rich was hit by a bullet that penetrated his side, traveling downward and exiting through his back. After the sniper was dispatched, medics arrived to take him to the aid station. The doctor prepared him, placed a swab on a long depressor, and ran it through the injury. It was a relatively clean wound, if there is such a thing as a relatively clean wound. The exhausted Doctor, who had spent many hours repairing young men, said, "You are a very lucky soldier. If that bullet entered two inches in any other direction, you would be paralyzed or dead!" Lewis Rich spent four days in bed, and then was up moving about.

Another friend named Bofort was also in the hospital. He was a 60mm mortar man, who had lost the base plate and was using his helmet as a base. He was sitting cross-legged, firing the mortar at a target only fifty feet in front of their squad. A Japanese threw a grenade that landed between his feet. Although protected by the helmet, he leapt up, taking a full load of shrapnel in his legs, and he was in terrible shape. Through the good work of the doctors and the miracle of medicine, he managed to keep his legs, and ultimately recovered.

A good friend from another company who was also in the hospital was shot from the side through his torso; the bullet entered his side and exited through the front, cutting off his nipple. The marine was not as concerned about his injury, as he was about being teased as a "one nipple marine."

DAY THIRTY-SIX: Iwo Jima was essentially secured, and hostilities ceased. It was March 26th, 1945. America had paid a fearful price.

CASUALTIES:
Killed in Action: Marines - 4,558. Navy - 363. Army - 7. Total - 4,928
Died of Wounds: Marines - 1,290. Navy -70. Army - 1. Total - 1,361
Missing In Action: Marines - 46. Navy - 448. Army - 1. Total - 495
Wounded In Action: Marines - 17,319. Navy - 1,917. Army - 28. Total - 19,264
Totals: Marines - 23,213. Navy - 2,798. Army - 24. Grand Total - 26,078
Of the Japanese 21,000 soldiers, only 216 survived to be taken prisoner.

As previously mentioned, the island of Iwo Jima contained three airstrips. On March 4th, while the battle was underway, a B-29 running low on gasoline made an emergency landing on one of the air strips. The crew of ten survived. However, the plane, damaged beyond repair, was pushed into the sea.

Before the war was over, 2,251 B-29 Superforts with 24,761 crewmembers were saved by making emergency landings on Iwo Jima.

RICH • CHAPTER 5

As the marines held in reserve assessed the cleanup job needed on the island, and repair of the airfields began by the engineers, the tired and wounded marines were loaded aboard ships for a return trip to Camp Tarawa, on the big island of Hawaii. Lewis was placed aboard an APA (Attack Personnel-Armor), along with other wounded. Unknown by the Navy, the ship had been sabotaged when someone placed iron filings in the transmission case and as a result, the ship could only make six knots, or about eight miles per hour. The trip to Hawaii was long and arduous. Lots of pinochle was played to pass the time.

Arriving at Camp Tarawa, replacements arrived to fill out the depleted ranks, and serious training began for action in the Philippine Islands. The men trained throughout the summer, and in early August the 5th Marine Division began packing it's gear for the long trip across the Pacific. On August 10th the Division was once again climbing the gangway to board ship when word was received that horrendous bombs had been dropped on Hiroshima and Nagasaki, Japan. Finally, the Japanese agreed to an unconditional surrender. It was a day Lewis would never forget; it was his birthday. Lewis Rich was now nineteen years old

The men returned to their camp and tents to await further orders. A week later the men boarded a transport for Sasbo, Japan, to assume occupation duties. Arriving at port, they boarded trucks that took them to dormitories formerly occupied by Japanese anti-aircraft personnel. Serving in the occupation forces was difficult for the veterans of Iwo Jima because of their experiences and intense feelings about the Japanese.

The Marines performed a number of duties. Since Lewis' regiment was the lead regiment on Iwo Jima, they were assigned reserve duty in Sasbo. Unfortunately, that meant they spent their time unloading transport vessels and freighters while the rest of the division were traveling the countryside on leave. Lewis did manage to take a leave to visit the religious city of Kyoto, and on route traveled through the city of Hiroshima. The total devastation and "emptiness" of the city made a lasting impression on Lewis. There were no buildings or trees to soften the landscape - "just a lot of nothing."

Rich observed that if the United States had invaded Japan, tanks and trucks could not have been used because of the nature of Japanese soils. Most of the islands are volcanic islands covered with a deep layer of fine ash, bound together by the root systems of vines and plant materials. The narrow roads could not support a concentrated wheel load, and leaving the road would be a disaster. With thirty-eight million men, women, and children trained and conditioned to fight to their death, it would have been impossible to succeed without a great loss of life. The military experiences in fighting on Okinawa served as a warning of the tragic consequences of attempting to conquer the Japanese mainland.

In May of 1946, the division received orders to return to the United States and boarded a transport bound for San Diego. Once in San Diego, they boarded a train for the Great Lakes Naval Training Center, where they were processed for discharge. In the big railway station in Chicago, they found a Chicago Northwestern train headed for Iowa, and Lewis finally returned to Carroll County. His parents met the train in Carroll and drove him to the family farm just in time for a freakish late May snowstorm that killed most of the early spring planting.

Lewis was happy to be home. The nineteen-year old marine had experienced conflict, battle deaths, and emotions that few others would experience in a lifetime.

Since Lewis had not finished high school, he enrolled in a special program at Drake University, in Des Moines, to acquire a GED (General Education Diploma). Lewis did not return to school without a few demons and nightmares from his Iwo experience. His cousin, Alice Hamilton Walters who lived in Des Moines, attempted to help his adjustment to civilian life. She would invite him to her home for dinner and keep him abreast of family news. She remembers one evening after his favorite dinner of waffles, sitting in her living room having a quiet conversation, when Lewis quietly offered, "If I had aimed better, I might have saved more lives!" With that, he bolted out of the door into the cold winter's night. He did not return to her home until she once again invited him over for waffles.

Lewis managed to complete his GED in the spring of 1948, and looked forward to attending Drake as a college student that fall. Just before the start of his second year at the University, he was involved in an auto accident that broke his back and his jaw, putting him in the hospital for several weeks. He never returned to college, but instead helped his father farm five hundred acres at three different sites in Carroll County.

During the summer, he would occasionally visit the Carroll swimming pool, where he casually met a young lady named Marion Underberg. Marion attended high school at St. Angela's Girls Academy in Carroll, graduating in 1944. Raised in a strict Catholic family, Marion continued her education enrolling in a nurses program at St. Anthony's Hospital. Lewis and Marion never really started dating until early 1949. The dating became more serious, and the two were married November 22, 1950. They headed west for their honeymoon, but with some trepidation.

When Lewis joined the Marines, it was for the duration of the war, but carried the caveat that he remain in the Marine Reserves for a period of ten years. A few weeks before the wedding Lewis received orders to report to a Marine Office in Omaha for a physical examination for induction into the Marines, due to the impending conflict in Korea. Returning from their honeymoon, they stopped in Omaha, where Lewis took his physical. Fortunately, he failed his examination.

He and Marion returned to Glidden to help farm the rich Rich farmland. They were blessed with five children; David, born August 25, 1952, Margaret, born October 17, 1953, Kevin, born March 15, 1955, Jeff, born April 13, 1960, and Tracy, born March 20, 1965 with Downs Syndrome. The active family life was severely stressed because Lewis continued to carry the "demons from Iwo," usually resulting in consuming too much alcohol. Lewis, from the time he returned from service, smoked three packs of cigarettes a day, and found solace in drinking. It was only through Marion's deep religious faith and courage that the family remained a single unit.

At the age of forty-one, Lewis finally realized his

Marion and Lewis wedding picture in St Lawrence Catholic Church, Carroll, Iowa.

After the ceremony, the trip to the reception was treated in the finest Carroll County style.

world was falling apart, and stopped drinking. A much more difficult task was stopping smoking; according to Lewis, much more difficult. He became active in community projects and the American Legion. He decided to run for the Carroll County Board of Supervisors. The Hamilton family tradition was basically neutrality in all politics. Lewis broke step, became active in Democratic politics, and was elected to the Board in 1970. He ran for re-election and was elected to another four-year term in 1974.

In 1978 a challenger vied for the position, and in the primary election that spring Lewis was defeated. So, Lewis set his square jaw, ran as an Independent candidate, and enjoyed re-election. He ran again in 1982, won, and finally retired from the Board of Supervisors in 1994. Because of his daughter Tracy, he became interested in providing for the mentally and physically handicapped, and served on the Iowa Human Services Board for twelve years.

He worked very hard with several other prominent citizens of Carroll County to start New Hope Village, to provide living/work opportunities for the handicapped. This very successful program has expanded to additional counties in western Iowa, providing countless educational and work opportunities for its constituency.

Lewis Rich's participation in the American Legion, providing military honors for service men and women buried in the Glidden Cemetery, is a responsibility he cherishes.

The Glidden Cemetery contains the remains of many heroes who served our country. Private Merle Hay, who as an eighteen year old went with the American Expeditionary Force to Europe in 1917, is buried here. He was one of the first three American soldiers killed in action the first day of battle. Captain Charles Bruning also fought in the Great War, now referred to World War I. He was a member of the famous Rainbow Division and was a survivor in the celebrated "Lost Battalion," which fought a pivotal battle during the war. He returned to serve as a rural mail carrier until his retirement. Sergeant Ralph Nepple, won the Congressional Medal of Honor for bravery in action in World War II, in Germany. His anti-tank gun, set up on a narrow street in a small town, took a direct hit that blew off both of his legs below the knees and killed the rest of his squad. That action so enraged him, he single-handedly repositioned the cannon, loaded it, and in successive firings knocked out four German tiger tanks. The medics finally were finally able to get to him to treat his wounds. He returned to Carroll County to farm until his death. Sergeant Fredrick Rudi Jr. fought in the Battle of the Bulge. When the Headquarters Company of the 9th Armored Division was decimated, he gathered twenty or so soldiers from other units and fought door-to-door in a small Luxembourg village until they managed to unite with American forces. Although his feet were frozen from the intense winter storm, he managed to continue fighting until relief columns arrived. Of the 110 men in his company, only nineteen survived.

There are a number of additional highly decorated Army, Navy and Marine servicemen from more recent conflicts who also lie in the Glidden Cemetery. It is not unique. It occurs in every cemetery in every small town, not only in Iowa, but throughout the land.

The many young, naïve boys who entered the Marines along with Lewis Rich could never anticipate the carnage they would experience, or anticipate the intensity and commitment of the opposing force. Even with all the pre-planning, intelligence assessment, modern military weapons, air and naval power, and the ability to deposit enormous firepower on a small rock in the middle of the Pacific Ocean, the success of battle rested upon the courage and determination of these "boys." In the annals of American history, there are few examples of bravery, courage, and honor that surpass the efforts of the young men who served on Iwo Jima.

BOOK 7

Frank Horn

Lieutenant - U. S. Navy
LST - 358

When we arranged our LCVPs in a line
and headed for the beach,
we were sitting ducks!

~Horn

HORN • CHAPTER 1

The pretty, young college girl unbuttoned her raincoat as she entered the university bookstore, emerging from the soft summer rain. Wiping her white saddle shoes on the floor mat, she entered the brightly lit bookstore, heading to the used books' section. Arriving at college a day early for summer school meant she could find used textbooks in the best condition, easily resold at the end of the summer session. Surveying the class list, she found the name of the required text for Education:Advanced Elementary, and began sorting through the pile of books. She found books for E:AE and two other classes, picked up some blue books for teat-writing, five Dixon #2 lead pencils and went to the checkout counter. She was pleased with the economy of her purchases.

Kansas State Teachers College in Pittsburg, Kansas, prepared young people for the teaching profession, drawing students from a three state area. Located in the lower southeast corner of Kansas close to the Missouri and Oklahoma borders, KSTC furnished educators for the small consolidated school districts in the area. Students liked the small town atmosphere and the small-school friendliness they shared. It had very competitive athletic teams in all sports, which eventually produced excellent, knowledgeable, competitive coaches.

Dorothy Dean Fee was born in jail. Her father was the county sheriff in Albany, Missouri, and lived in an apartment above the sheriff's office and jail. He later became the chief of police in St. Joseph, Missouri, a step up from responsibilities in Albany. Dorothy's mother passed away when she was only three years old, so Dorothy went to live with an aunt and uncle on a farm near Albany, Missouri. After graduating from Albany High School she attended Iola Junior College in Iola, Kansas, and earned a two-year degree in elementary education. She attended Iola JC because her sister, Frances, lived there, and after graduation from the two-year college, Dorothy was fortunate enough to get a job teaching second graders in Iola Elementary School. At the end of her first year of teaching, she began work on a four-year degree at KSTC during the summer session. It not only would improve her ability to teach, but assure her of better paying teaching positions once she earned the degree.

Dorothy walked back to the rooming house, holding the books close to her body so they would not get wet from the gentle sprinkle. Arriving at the rooming house, she climbed the stairs to the second floor, entered her room, and dropped her purchases on the bed. Removing her coat, she placed the books neatly on her study desk, placed the blue books in the second drawer and the pencils in the center drawer. With over an hour before dinner, she selected the advanced education book, stretched out on the bed, and started to thumb through it. As she flipped the pages checking the chapter headings, she found a loose wallet-sized picture. It was the picture of a young man, probably college age, almost handsome, but not quite. Well, maybe he was handsome! There was no marking, no name: just a picture.

She tossed the picture off to one side and continued to thumb through the book, reading the headings and chapter names, until several friends came by on their way to the dining room. With some giggling, she showed the girls the picture before they all left for dinner.

Returning to her room after dinner, she once again picked up the black and white picture. How did the picture get there? Was it his book? What color were his eyes and his hair? She decided he really was "kind of cute" and she had to meet this young man, if he was on campus. She carried the picture to the next meal and showed it around, informing the girls in the rooming house that if they ever saw him, to give her a call.

The summer session started and Dorothy focused on her studies, writing papers and taking examinations. The picture remained on her bulletin board, mostly forgotten. That is, until Shirley burst into her room a month later and shouted, "I think I found your picture guy!"

Dorothy looked at Shirley, then at the picture, then back at Shirley and asked, "Where did you see him?"

"He is over in the library, sitting at a table with Nancy Schereling."

Dorothy took down the picture, placed it on the desk, staring at it for a while. Slowly, she removed her pink sweater, pulled the beige one out of the drawer and pulled it on over her white blouse with the lace collar. The sweater would accentuate her brown eyes. She brushed her long brown hair from the underside so it turned just so, and added a beige ribbon. A dusting of powder, a short spray of lavender, and one more look in the mirror. She walked down the stairs, into the damp evening air toward Porter Library, wondering if the young man in the picture was worth all this excitement.

Dorothy glanced about the high ceilinged study room filled with dark oak tables and heavy oak chairs. Near the far wall next to rows of encyclopedias sat a boy and a girl, each engrossed in their reading. Dorothy slowly worked her way toward the wall stacks, glancing out of the corner of her eye as inconspicuously as possible, to make certain it was Nancy and the young man. She selected a large volume of the encyclopedia and approached the table. "Nancy! How is summer school going?"

"Hi Dorothy! It's going fine!" She hesitated, glancing awkwardly at her book. "By the way, have you met Frank? Frank, this is Dorothy Fee. Dorothy, this is Frank Horn." Frank lifted his six-foot-three frame, nodded, smiled, nodded, smiled, nodded and smiled. With a cheery "Pleased to meet you, Frank," Dorothy looked into his eyes, smiled, and went to an adjoining table two tables away, where she could look Frank straight in the eyes. Opening her book, she suddenly wondered why she had selected "Q" out of the encyclopedias.

A week or so later, Dorothy received a call from Frank, and he started seeing her regularly. Frank thought he really worked hard to get her attention when they had their first few dates.

Actually, the young man did not stand a chance of getting away!

Frank Horn and Dorothy Fee attending
Kansas State Teachers College.

HORN • CHAPTER 2

The twelve to four AM watch always seemed to be the loneliest. The night was very dark, sucking in light from any source and making it inconsequential. As they used to say in rural Kansas, "It was blacker than the inside of a cow." Water lapping against the sides of the rusty old tub was monotonous and mind-numbing, the rhythm encouraging sleep. The walk around the exterior steel deck of the control bridge was icy cold as the wind rolled in from the Canadian north through the Hudson River valley. Even though the old ship was anchored in the Hudson River upstream from Manhattan Island, on this dark night it gave the sensation it could just as well be moving slowly across the North Atlantic. To make matters worse, it was New Year's Eve, and while many families were enjoying each other's company in gala gatherings or the warmth of their homes, Ensign-to-be Frank Horn stood on the bridge-walk with binoculars, staring into the bleak, black night. Occasionally a small craft would motor by without running lights, and was noted in the watch log. Since it was wartime, all running lights had to be hooded. Frank was cold, lonely and homesick, no three ways about it.

Frank Horn was attending Columbia University in New York City as a "ninety day wonder." He was a midshipman, wearing Navy blues, attending class, and working hard all day to learn "the Navy Way" of doing things. Meals, study, marching, and more study went on from early morning until "lights out." Training consisted of intense courses Monday through Friday on all aspects of the Navy that could be taught on land. Many hours were spent marching, to and from meals, on the parade grounds, and around the neighborhoods near Columbia. Sunday mornings they marched in formation to churches of their respective faiths. Liberty was granted every three weeks from Saturday noon to Sunday noon, but the time was usually spent in the library or the dorm room catching up on the accelerated coursework assignments. Being a midshipman was certainly no picnic.

Frank joined the Navy's V-7 program while he was attending Kansas State Teachers College in Pittsburg, Kansas. He entered college in the fall of 1938, and scheduled to graduate in the spring of 1942. December 7th, 1941, changed all of that, and young men were called into service every day from every endeavor and state in the country. Frank was born in Moline, Kansas, southeast of Wichita. He stood a tall six foot three inches and enjoyed a modest high school career in athletics, particularly basketball.

His first year at KSTC found him trying to make the basketball team, but his skills were not polished enough to compete at the college level. Besides, he was working two jobs in order to earn money to remain in school.

After the bombing of Pearl Harbor, Frank enrolled in the V-7 program, because the Navy would permit you to finish your college studies before induction. After graduation, Frank enrolled in additional courses in summer school, taking mathematics and trigonometry in order to enter the midshipman's program. His first degree was in Business Education, with minors in Physical Education, Social Studies, and Coaching.

Frank began dating Dorothy Fee while in college, and they wanted to get married before Frank left for service, but the Navy had a rule that entering midshipmen could not be married. Frank and Dorothy waited to marry until after graduation from the V-7 program, but they later learned that a number of the trainees were married, just not reporting it.

Frank looked at his watch. Only two-thirty AM and he felt he had been on watch for six hours. Not only was he on watch New Year's Eve, but also stood watch on Christmas Eve and was even more homesick then. He wondered how Dorothy and her family were celebrating the entry into the New Year. He wondered how much time Dorothy had off from teaching her second grade class to spend with her family. She had not mentioned any of this in her frequent letters. He wondered what the New Year would hold, with the war and all. Frank was cold, lonesome and tired as he thought about home. Each cadet was required to spend time on night watch aboard the old hulk anchored in the Hudson River, to gain early experience in being alone on deck at night. It would prepare them for duty at sea, with the opportunity to lessen the homesickness and loneliness and attend to their assigned duty. The young ensigns were inexperienced enough, without their becoming blubbering idiots in front of the enlisted men. Frank took another turn about the catwalk, noting and logging a victory ship motoring in slow motion south past his vessel. In another hour, he could find a hot cup of coffee, and turn in.

The Midshipmen finally completed their ninety-day course with the men receiving commissions as Ensigns in the United States Navy. Frank had ten days to report to Little Creek, Virginia, his next assignment. He hurried home to find Dorothy and marry the person he had pursued so persistently in college until she caught him.

Dorothy was teaching second grade in Iola, Kansas. Frank arrived in Iola early in the morning, February 19th 1943, and during Dorothy's lunch break the two went to the courthouse to obtain a marriage license. That very evening, at 7:15 PM, in Dorothy's sister's apartment, they exchanged vows. Dorothy's sister, Frances, was married to a soldier in the army who could not make it back for the ceremony, so several of Frances' friends stood with the couple as witnesses. Frances also arranged for a local minister to be present to perform the simple ceremony.

Francis had a small dog, named Sport, who had the run of the house. Sport spent the entire, though brief, ceremony actively and aggressively sniffing Frank's pant leg. Fortunately, there were no accidents to make his untimely activity even more memorable.

The married couple drove to Moline, Kansas, to visit Frank's family, and then boarded a train for Little Creek, Virginia, to enter married life. After two days sitting upright in a crowded passenger car, they arrived in Norfolk, Virginia, and managed to find a furnished apartment for their brief stay in transition.

Reporting to the Naval Base at Little Creek, Frank entered a new level of training to prepare him to contribute to winning the war. The Navy would find an appropriate responsibility for Ensign Horn in it's determination to assure victory.

HORN • CHAPTER 3

Little Creek, Virginia, was the training location for amphibious land-ings, guiding small craft carrying tanks and personnel to the beaches dur-ing an invasion. Some of Frank Horn's comrades had remained at Columbia as cadre for incoming midshipmen; this appealed to Frank, but he was not aware of the possibility and had not applied for it. Amphibious operations required a good amount of coordination, since the landing boats carried only thirty to thirty-five men, and depositing a division of fif-teen thousand men required many boats, many trips and the necessity to make order out of possible chaos.

The Landing Craft-Vehicle-Personnel, or LCVP, was a wooden boat with a steel front face that lowered to serve as an exit ramp. Also called a Higgins Boat, the designer, Andrew Higgins of New Orleans, had manu-factured a shallow hulled boat for use in the Louisiana swamps for many years. A few days after the Japanese bombed Pearl Harbor, Higgins con-tacted the War Department, submitting a design for the landing craft. He recognized invasions would require a special carrier, and he had the resources and facilities to manufacture such a craft. A contract was imme-diately offered to the Higgins Boat Works of New Orleans, Louisiana, and later General Eisenhower credited the craft as a major reason for winning the war on both the Atlantic and the Pacific fronts. "Higgins is the man who won the war for us. If Higgins had not designed and built those LCVPs, we never could have landed over on an open beach. The whole strategy of the war would have been different."

He obviously did not intend to devalue the efforts of the fearless men who ran out of those boats into an uncertain future on the beach.

Designed with a deep V hull, the boat rear had a reverse-curve section that protected the propeller shaft from extending below the hull line. For use in the swamps, the V hull pushed debris to the side so only water reached the propeller, thus avoiding damage. It adapted perfectly for land-ing troops, then backing off for a return trip. A 225HP diesel engine pow-ered the boat, and it could achieve a speed of ten knots per hour or almost twelve miles per hour, when fully loaded. The boat was thirty-five feet six inches long and had an eleven-foot beam. Each boat carried a crew of two or three; a coxswain who steered the boat from the rear, an engineer locat-ed in the prow who lowered and raised the front steel ramp, and the officer in charge. The steel ramp had a small sliding panel that permitted the engineer to look ahead, with some protection from small-arms fire. The officer in charge also rode on one of the craft with the coxswain, directing one or two other boats. In the Pacific Theater, a twin machine gun stand was installed at the rear next to the coxswain, to counter any attacking Japanese fighter planes. The landing craft was designed to carry thirty to thirty-five armed troops in full battle gear, or a jeep and twelve men. Six of the boats would fit on the deck of a Landing Ship Transport, or LST, for transporting to the dispersal area.

Ensign Horn trained to be responsible for two landing craft, as well as perform duties aboard the support ship. He learned to supervise unloading the LST, setting the Higgins boats into the water, then dropping the cargo net for the invasion troops to crawl down to the landing craft. Once in the water and loaded with soldiers, the six boats would form a "V" and circle until the scheduled time to head for the beaches. Then rows of landing craft several miles wide would advance under the cover of big naval guns shelling the beach.

LSTs formed the backbone of the invasion forces. Designed to also run up on the beach, they carried rolling cargo as well as troops. The ships were three hundred fifteen feet long and fifty feet wide, almost the size of a football field. They could travel at fourteen knots or almost seventeen miles per hour. Built with two levels below deck, they could carry tanks as well as trucks loaded with ammunition and supplies. The second level also contained quarters for the crew and officers. A prominent feature was the prow made of two huge doors that swung open in order to discharge the equipment aboard. When heading for an invasion, the deck carried the six LCVPs as well as the soldiers to be delivered to the beach. LSTs were very adaptable, and there were probably no two ships alike. Some had three decks, some served as beach medical aid stations, and others hauled supplies only.

The living quarters of the LST were tight, with six officers sharing a small wardroom, but the officers slept between sheets. Each man had a small metal locker and they shared a hot seawater shower and stool with another wardroom.

The training at Little Creek continued for several weeks, and each morning when Frank said goodbye to Dorothy he was not certain he would be back, since they might ship out at a moments notice. Notice of overseas duty was finally received, and Ensign Horn boarded a train for Bayonne, New Jersey. Dorothy and Frank said their goodbyes, and Dorothy made arrangements to return by train to Kansas. Their brief honeymoon ended in a tearful farewell.

Ensign Horn was assigned to LST-358, and it joined a large convoy of ships headed for the Mediterranean Sea. Designed as relatively flat bottom boats to accommodate beach landings, the LSTs were, as a result, slow and unstable. Once the ship was fully loaded with trucks and tanks, they could only make eleven knots; that meant crossing the Atlantic was a thirty-day ordeal. Many of the crew were seasick for several weeks. Frank was sick the first three days, then adapted to the many motions of the LST as it bobbed along. After a brief stop at Bermuda, the convoy continued on.

Leading Higgins boats prior to the invasion of Sicily. Soldiers carrying full battle gear had to negotiate climbing down a cargo net to the tossing vessel. (Photo US Army)

The officers stood watch on a rotating basis, which meant the four-hour duty could occur during the day or night. The watch training on the rusty hulk on the Hudson River was nothing like being in the middle of the Atlantic Ocean in a convoy in the middle of the night.

The convoy finally reached the coast of Spain and proceeded through the Straits of Gibraltar, along the North African coast, finally making port at Bizerte, Tunisia. A natural, large, lagoon-like deep-water enclosure that formed the Bizerte port was big enough to house the entire convoy. It was also large enough that the LCVPs continued to train forming and landing. The North African campaign was essentially over, and military planners and operations were preparing for the next military undertaking.

On July 9th, 1943, LST-358 was loaded with tanks, trucks and soldiers ready for the invasion of the island of Sicily to take place early morning, July 10th. In preparation for the landing, heavy aircraft bombed beaches and installations close to the Sicilian shore. Navy cruisers and escorts fired their big guns at land targets for several days to "soften the enemy." Before dawn, the soldiers crawled down the cargo nets into the bobbing LCVPs, who circled at sea waiting for the command to proceed.

The invasion of Sicily happened on two broad fronts. The Americans were to land on a fifteen mile front extending from Licata, to Gela, to Scoglitti., on the southwest point of the island. The British forces landed on the southeastern tip at Pozzallo, Pachinp, Noto, and Avolia. Even with all of the preliminary bombing and shelling, the Germans managed to mount a stout defense protecting the landing sites. Naturally there was more resistance in some areas than others. For the Americans, the resistance at Scogletti was much worse than at Licata. During the British landing, the entire front met with stiff resistance.

Ensign Frank Horn climbed into his LCVP as it was lowered into the water, and the coxswain held it alongside the LST as the soldiers worked their way down the cargo net. This maneuver was difficult, not wanting to lose a soldier by crushing him between the two vessels as he descended. Once loaded, the landing craft continued to circle, until the flares were fired signaling the advance toward the shore. This landing was on a huge front extending almost fifteen miles along the coast of Sicily. Horn's destination was near Licata, and small arms fire from the shore was intermittent. Cruisers were firing shells overhead toward the beach, providing a rolling barrage to move the enemy back. They also fired smoke bombs to conceal the approaching LCVPs. Over the noise of the engines and the shelling, they could hear the slapping waves on the steel ramp of the flat-bottomed

Delivering soldiers as close to the beach as possible was the first task of the Higgins boats. The first day, several trips were made by the hundreds of boats to get twenty thousand or more troops in the invasion force to the beaches.

craft as it approached the beach. Finally, they felt the lurch and heard the rasp of wood on sand as the boat grounded. On command, the engineer released the winch and the steel door dropped to the ramp position. The soldiers rushed forward, some determined, some with hesitation, all of them scared to death. Leaping into the ankle- deep water, they rushed ashore to find their objective, dig foxholes, and set up defensive perimeters. There was shouting, exhorting, noise, and chaos as the men formed their squads and advanced inland.

Horn gave the orders to raise the ramps, and the engineers cranked the landing steel back into place, making certain the seals engaged. With a roar, the propellers churned the water as the craft, now a couple tons lighter, backed off the sand and returned to the LST. Pulling along side, a jeep appeared overhead, slung from a crane, and deposited on the bottom of the LCVP. Twelve men climbed down the cargo net, and squatted alongside the vehicle. Once both boats were loaded, Horn gave the order to proceed and the two boats returned to the beach. The steel ramp was lowered, and this time the men exited in knee-deep water.

The rest of the day, Horn and his two LCVPs made continuous trips to and from the beach. Once the beach was secure, the LST moved into the beach, opened its big doors and dispensed the tanks and trucks filled with supplies: ammunition, food, and medical supplies. Once it was empty, the lighter LST backed from the shore, and returned to Bizerte to again fill its bowels with the equipment of war.

The Sicilian campaign lasted for thirty-seven days. The LST hauled supplies around the clock to Licata and other beaches, then to Palermo once it was secure, and later to other locations on the island as new ports were captured by the advancing troops.

The sailors aboard the LSTs caught sleep whenever they could. The galley was open twenty-four hours a day and the men ate when time permitted. Coffee was always available, drunk out of heavy ceramic mugs without handles. You could wrap your hands completely around a ceramic mug that held the heat, to warm them up. It felt particularly good after coming off a cold night's watch.

Two more landings using LCVPs were made on the northern Sicilian coast in flanking actions around German defenders. Frank Horn was not involved in these two landings, but it indicated the versatility and mobility of naval support of the land forces as they leapfrogged behind enemy defenses.

After the island of Sicily was secure, the port of Palermo became the warehouse for the next big invasion, and stockpiling of equipment began. All available cargo ships and LSTs worked around the clock hauling material to Palermo from Bizerte. The LCVPs were again loaded on the deck of the LST, and calm seas aided in hauling and unloading cargo.

Early in September they were alerted that another large invasion would soon take place. The Italian Campaign had begun with British troops landing on the toe of southern Italy across the Straits of Messina. The landing was established, and Italian and German troops rushed to drive the Brits back into the Mediterranean.

On September 9th, American forces landed on the beaches of Salerno, south of Naples (Napoli). A large convoy left Palermo on September 8th, and by nightfall were in position. The LCVPs were lowered in the water, and before dawn troops were aboard and ready for the landing. Preliminary bombing was completed, and naval shelling was underway when the LCVPs aligned and started for the beach. There was a good deal of small arms fire directed at the invasion fleet, and everyone, except the coxswain and boat commander, kept their heads down for protection. Steel helmets worn by the coxswain and officer offered some protection from incoming fire. The steel ramp would deflect small arms bullets fired from some distance, but not the larger caliber guns. Horn made certain his launches were aligned as they neared the beach, and deposited the army soldiers in shallow water.

After the initial invasion, the LSTs spent several weeks delivering the material necessary to sustain the invasion. (Photo-US Navy)

The LCVPs withdrew, returned to the LST and were loaded once more with soldiers, and again turned toward the beach. Delivering troops, ammunition, and supplies, without stop occupied their time for five days. After several days of fighting, the Italian Army surrendered to the Allied troops. They were not interested in defending their homeland, dying for the Germans. Complete units threw down their arms and ran to the Allied lines. The Germans made a daring raid to rescue the Italian Dictator Benito Mussolini and return him behind defensive lines. The Germans fought with new vigor to repulse the Allies, but once the beachhead was established, the American soldiers pushed inland. The fighting was intense and continuous.

LST-358 and Ensign Horn's two boats continued to deliver supplies under intense small arms fire, without damage. For several months, the deliveries continued, and as the troops moved inland, deliveries were made without being fired upon. Occasionally a German fighter plane would appear out of nowhere and race down the beach strafing the soldiers, then turning to the mountains, trying to get away without being shot down. The Allies controlled the air, but there was always a daring run or two by members of the Luftwaffe.

As the Germans were fighting fiercely in Salerno, another invasion was already being planned as an end run further up the coast of Italy. On January 22nd, 1944, at 2:00AM, the Americans and British landed on the beaches of Anzio, Italy. Catching the Germans completely by surprise, the Allies quickly established a beachhead and dug in, a fatal mistake. Because of the surprise, they could have moved inland many miles, capturing high ground and forcing the German army to fight a defensive battle. Instead, the American troops dug in, giving the Germans an opportunity to occupy the mountains overlooking the Anzio beaches with an enormous quantity of artillery able to blanket the area. It was a costly error. For four months, the Allied soldiers were pounded by artillery until they advanced to knock the Germans out of the mountains and break out.

For Ensign Horn, middle of the night landings were difficult. With floating mines in the harbor, the engineer had to guide the launches into the shore, attempting to dodge objects that were difficult to identify at night. The first wave met little opposition, but subsequent landings on the beach were under intense fire from artillery and mortars, as well as small arms. This continued as long as materials were being deposited on the beach. The Navy delivered one hundred ten thousand troops to their respective areas. The next several weeks, jeeps, trucks and artillery were hauled to the beach, day and night. During those weeks, Germans stopped shelling the navy vessels and concentrated on the ground soldiers. Some of the bitterest fighting in the Italian campaign took place at Anzio, and losses in men and equipment were substantial.

LST-358 was fortunate to escape damage during time spent at Anzio. However, a nearby LST was damaged by German artillery. One sailor lost a leg, and flying shrapnel wounded several other sailors.

Once the Germans were pushed back into the mountains, Rome captured, and northern advances made up both coasts, members of the LST crew were given liberty. The men had access to the Ruins of Pompeii, the Isle of Capri, and tours of Naples and the Vatican. The men had been training and invading for over six months, and a few days liberty were a welcome relief.

The men began preparing and repairing their equipment for another invasion. This time the target was southern France. Using Palermo as the staging area, the task force assembled, and on August 15th, 1944, LCVPs once more circled off the coast of southern France. The Germans knew there would be an invasion, and concentrated their resistance where they anticipated the main landing would take place. Fortunately, they guessed wrong. When the Americans landed, resistance was light, with small arms fire the main concern. There were no mines to be concerned about, and the landing was successful. Again, the LST spent several weeks delivering trucks, jeeps and supplies to support the troops that were now attacking Germany from a different direction. The invasion of Normandy earlier on June 7th, 1944, committed the German forces to defend their homeland to the north. With the Allies slowly working their way up the east and west coasts of Italy, and the Russians bearing down from the east, the Germans now had an additional front to repel.

It was apparent that there would no longer be a need for landing craft in the Mediterranean, so the crews of the LSTs and LCVPs were scheduled to return to the States for re-assignment to the South Pacific. While preparing to leave Sicily by air for a return trip to the United States and a long-awaited leave, Frank was finishing up paper work for the Navy. While riding in the rear of a truck traveling back to the base, the truck was rear ended by another truck. Frank suffered multiple contusions and was taken to the hospital where he spent several days recuperating. As a result, Horn missed the airplane flight back to the U.S. He was re-assigned to board and return to the U.S. on an LST temporarily consigned to the British fleet. Once more, it took thirty long wave-rocked days to cross the Atlantic. The cramped quarters and Spartan accommodations made it even more tedious. Standing watch was a formality, and each officer took his turn searching the horizon for enemy vessels. The British Navy traditionally has a ration of whisky every day, served as regularly as teatime back home. However, on this trip they refused to share with the American officers on board. For thirty days, this one single episode severely strained the American's attitudes about Lend-Lease and Anglo-American relations.

As the LST approached the port of Norfolk, Horn began thinking about his plans once he was on U.S. soil. Where would he contact Dorothy? What sort of travel arrangements should he make to get home? How soon would he go to the Pacific?

When the LST finally tied up at the dock, there was Dorothy standing at the end of the gangway. He had no idea how she found out where they were landing or when they were landing. Nevertheless, it was a wonderful homecoming welcome!

Frank was given a brief leave, before reporting for his next assignment. He was at home when they received word that his older brother Joe, a radioman on an Air Corps bomber, was killed while on a training flight. Frank was there for the funeral, and it was a particularly sad time. Two days after the funeral, Joe's wife gave birth to a young son.

The thirty-day crossing of the Atlantic changed Frank's next assignment to his benefit. He learned that the officers who had flown home were given only a few days leave, then were immediately shipped to the South Pacific where they participated in some of the most difficult and bloody island landings of the Pacific war. The distances between the islands were far greater than in the Mediterranean Sea, and the Japanese were much more formidable opponents. The Allies did not always control the skies over the islands, and LCVPs suffered a lot of casualties.

Horn, now a Lieutenant Junior Grade, was sent to Rensselaer Polytechnic Institute in Troy, New York, to serve as a V-7 watch officer. After two weeks, he was sent to the Philadelphia Navy Yard, in Philadelphia, Pennsylvania. After two weeks in the Navy Yard, he proceeded to Ursinus College in Collegeville, Pennsylvania to oversee the V-12 program and Navy ROTC (the Reserve Officer Training Corps).

Dorothy, who was pregnant with their first child, traveled with him to Rensselaer. However, they decided she should return to Kansas to be with her family, since she was nearing her delivery date. Frank put her on a train for Kansas City, then reported to the Navy Yard in Philadelphia.

After two weeks at Ursinus College, Frank was re-assigned to the Navy ROTC program at the University of Kansas in Lawrence, Kansas. It was good duty, and he taught in the program until late July 1946, when he was due to be discharged. He reported to Great Lakes Naval Training Center and received his official active discharge on August 6th, 1946. He exercised his option to serve in the Navy Reserve for a limited time. The good news was he would no longer be ordered to form the LCVPs in a line and head for beach landing under fire.

HORN • CHAPTER 4

It was now time for the Horns to get on with their lives after serving in the military. Frank and Dorothy enjoyed their time spent in Lawrence, and Frank decided to continue his education while there. He enrolled in the University, and took a class from Coach Phog Allen in Sports Injuries. Of course, Coach Allen was a legend in Kansas, and Frank found him to be an inspiring teacher. Dorothy applied to teach in the Lawrence school system, but with all the returning veterans and wives, there was no position available. Frank applied to Clay Center Kansas High School to teach business education and coach, and worked there for one year. He next went to Chanute Junior College in Chanute, Kansas, where he taught business education and served as an assistant coach in football, basketball, and track.

Dorothy and Frank added to their family during this period. The oldest daughter, Elizabeth was born November 9th, 1945, while Frank was still in service. Daughter Frankee Dean was born while the couple lived in Chanute, on October 17, 1948.

For four years in Chanute, Frank taught full time and recruited in all sports, as well as coached. Since there were no scholarships, he spent what few waking hours that were left looking for jobs for the athletes he recruited. The job was time consuming and exhausting, and he decided there just might be an administrative position that would let him spend more time with his young family. While a Chanute, Frank completed his Masters Degree in Business Education at Kansas State Teachers College.

He went to Glenwood, Iowa, as a high school principal, and for three years enjoyed working with the students. When the superintendent left the school board offered the position to Frank, but he declined. He felt he was more effective as a principal.

Frank applied for an opening in the school system in Cedar Falls, Iowa, and became the Junior High Principal. For twenty-eight years, he worked with young students and Dorothy taught second grade for a comparable time. They thoroughly enjoyed the college town and the students. Frank finally decided to complete his career in the classroom, resigned his position and taught seventh grade social studies until his two girls graduated from college.

Daughter Frankee married a fellow music student at the University of Northern Iowa, (formerly Iowa State Teachers College), Jim Olesen. Jim returned to college to study Entomology, and now works at Iowa State University managing a corn-insect research project. After retirement, Dorothy and Frank moved to Ames to be near Frankee and Jim, and to enjoy Big XII athletics. It also moved them closer to their daughter Beth and three grandchildren (and five great-grand children) who live in Council Bluffs, Iowa, where Beth's husband, Frank Pechacek, is an attorney and a University of Iowa Hawkeye fan. Frank and Dorothy keep peace in the family when college competition gets out of hand by raising their voices in the Kansas State Teachers College fight song.

Frank Horn's service experience prepared him to see how important it was that each member of the military team performed and contributed to the big picture. He continued to serve in the Navy Reserve for several years after he left service, but resigned because frequent moves made it was difficult to meet his obligations. When he finally separated from the Reserve, his rank was a Lieutenant, comparable to a Captain in the Army.

For his service to our country he received the WWII Victory Ribbon, the American Theater Ribbon, and the European-African-Middle East Theater Ribbon with five stars.

BOOK 8

William Stucky

Captain
30th Regiment
3rd Division

Bill's *wife, Lorraine*

"War is the stupidest thing man ever does!"

~William Stucky

STUCKY • CHAPTER 1

Approaching the long table for the graduation procedure certainly lacked ceremony. Every college and university appears to attach a different degree of emphasis to this particular ritual that distinguishes this particular rite of passage. Universities steeped in long held traditions tend toward an almost religious observance; bedecked in robes, elaborate processions, symbolic staffs amusingly reminiscent of a shepherd leading the sheep, and the sobriety of receiving communion. Other institutions use variations of the above. And then there are the basics: less formal, simple gowns, here's your sheepskin, a firm handshake, and join the alumni association.

Montana State College used the long table approach. Their students arrived on campus from isolated ranches, small mining towns, and even more isolated ranches. In 1941 rural Montana sustained mining, pastureland, grain crops, and cattle. Montana State College in the 30's addressed mining, pastureland, grain crops and cattle. Also, agriculture economics. That is what attracted young William Stucky to MSC. Being born and raised on a ranch just outside Bozeman, Montana, home of Montana State, certainly influenced his decision.

Bill Stucky was born in the farmhouse. He was delivered on December 30, 1918, by a doctor who rode on horseback out to the farm, spent the night, and returned to his office the following day. The farm had no electricity, a hand- dug well, and a medium sized-trip to the outhouse. It was consistent with rural living in 1918. It helped to develop a character and demeanor of optimism and opportunity that was reflected in Bill Stucky's personality throughout his life.

When Bill finished high school in 1937 he took the opportunity to enroll at Montana State College. In addition to Agricultural Economics, he took ROTC, because it subsidized a portion of his tuition; in the 1930's, any help was welcome.

When graduation day arrived in June 1941, he proceeded in the graduation line to walk past the long table. At the front of the table Bill Stucky was handed his diploma. At the middle of the table he was handed his commission as a Second Lieutenant in the United States Army. At the end of the table, he was handed his orders to report to the Presidio in San Francisco, California, to join an infantry unit.

STUCKY • CHAPTER 2

Second Lieutenant Bill Stucky first reported to Fort Lewis, Washington, where he joined the 30th Regiment of the 3rd Division, considered to be one of the outstanding "spit and polish" regiments in the peacetime army. The young Second Lieutenant spent two weeks in a tank division, before finally joining F Company, 2nd Battalion, 30th Regiment of infantry soldiers. Since there was a large influx of men into service about this time, training methods were still being developed. As a result, Lt. Stucky and the regiment were assigned a number of tasks just to keep them busy. They marched, went on maneuvers, and performed other tasks for almost two months. The regiment then proceeded to San Francisco to the Presidio.

Considered the premier military base on the west coast, the Presidio was situated on the edge of the peninsula forming San Francisco, and benefited from its association with the sophisticated city. The post included many regular army officers, West Point graduates, who tended to look down on the ROTC graduates. There was a caste system that was not calculated, but certainly evident to the officers who studied agricultural economics instead of military history in great detail. The 30th Regiment returned to Fort Lewis, Washington, in November of 1941, and was continuing its training when the Japanese attacked Pearl Harbor.

Lorraine McBride was in her final year of nursing at Montana State College. Lorraine and Bill had attended high school together and been dating since Bill's senior year. Lorraine decided to visit Bill at Fort Lewis, since several friends were traveling there. Once at Fort Lewis, they learned several of the officers and soldiers were intending to get married, even though they soon might be going overseas. Lorraine and Bill gave it considerable thought, and decided their lives would have more meaning if they were wed. This might be the only opportunity to celebrate their vows, given the uncertainty of coming conflict. Their only problem: Washington had a three-day waiting period.

On Friday evening they contacted a local Judge at his home to determine if there was any possibility of a waiver being granted, since Lorraine had limited time from school, and Bill would soon be shipped out. The Judge invited them out to his home to discuss the matter. After some difficulty, the two managed to find the huge house hidden in the hills outside Fort Lewis. The young couple was awed by the opulence of the Judge's large, beautiful residence. Approaching the colonnaded entry, they rang the bell and were met by a butler. He escorted them into the library where a fire

Lorraine and Bill Stucky after their military wedding seven days after the bombing of Pearl Harbor. Special permission was received from a Judge to waive the three-day waiting period for the wedding.

in the huge fireplace warmed the room from the chilly December air. After the proper introductions, the Judge was very friendly and personable. Finally, the Judge, always suspicious of a last minute fling, critically surveyed the two and asked, "Is this a wartime wedding?" They assured him of their dating commitment since their senior year in high school and through their college years; they convinced him this was the "real thing." The Judge agreed to grant a waiver, and asked them to meet him at the courthouse a few hours later, at 11:00 PM, to take an oath and sign the documents.

After taking the oath, filling out the proper documents and signing them, the Judge scrutinized the two, and observed, " This deserves a drink." He reached into a nearby drawer and brought out a bottle of bourbon. At 1:00 AM Saturday morning in the Judge's chambers of the courthouse, the three raised their glasses and toasted the upcoming wedding.

Saturday was spent making the final arrangements. The next day, Sunday, December 14th, 1941, only one week after Pearl Harbor, Lorraine McBride and Bill Stucky were married in the post chapel by Chaplain Roy E Langford. As the two left the church, they passed through a column of soldiers of the 30th Regiment, wearing steel helmets and standing at present arms. The honeymoon was short lived, and a few days later it was time for Bill to return to duty.

Instead of returning to her studies, Lorraine joined seven other officer's wives who wanted to spend as much time with their spouses as they could. As the division moved from camp to camp, the eight women became "camp followers," moving with them until they shipped overseas.

The 3rd Division was assigned to become assault troops, and was transferred to Fort Ord, California, where they practiced amphibious landings until May of 1942. Moving further south to San Diego, California, the 3rd Division and 2nd Marine Division utilized LSTs and the newly-produced Higgins Boats. The men would board LSTs, and go to sea where they transferred to Higgins Boats that aligned for a landing. Wading ashore, the men would establish a beachhead, and then run through squad, company, and battalion tactics. The training was intense and thorough.

Finally, in September 1942, the men received new equipment and clothing for use in Antarctica. Packing their new gear, they boarded a train for Camp Pickett, Virginia, where they once again practiced beach landings. In October, the 3rd Division moved to Newport News, Virginia, their point of embarkation. A distinguishing feature of Newport News is a large metal arch over the highway that welcomes visitors to the city. Lorraine and Bill stood under the arch the night of October 22, 1942, to say their goodbyes. On October 23rd the division was loaded aboard several liberty ships, and in the middle of the night put out to sea.

STUCKY • CHAPTER 3

The convoy arrived off the shores of North Africa, on the Atlantic side, and soldiers would soon perform the first invasion to conquer Hitler's soldiers. The fifteen-day trip across the Atlantic in the huge convoy managed to avoid attack from German submarines. However, aboard the USS Hugh L. Scott, crewmen noticed the fire extinguishers were missing on the main deck and had presumably been thrown overboard. Later a young soldier with a German last name, slipped past guards, and was caught with a pocketful of matches in an area that stored gasoline. Still later, another soldier was apprehended while concealed under a tarp-covered lifeboat, signaling with a hooded flashlight. Whom he was signaling was never established.

When the 30th Regiment shipped out of Newport News, they consisted of two hundred twenty-four officers, five thousand twenty-one men and four hundred forty-three vehicles. The combat team included:
- 30th RLG (Regimental Landing Group)
- 41st Field Artillery
- Battery C, 9th Field Artillery
- Company C, 10th Engineers Battalion
- Company C, 756th Tank Battalion
- 2nd, 3rd, and 4th Platoons, 443rd Coast Artillery Battalion
- Detachments of 71st and 3rd Signal Company
- Naval Liaison Shore Fire Control and Beach Units

This formidable assemblage of troops was deemed necessary to effectively function as an attack force based on current military experiences. The planning and operations arm of the military attempted to anticipate battle needs and build a task force to cope with anticipated eventualities. These requirements changed with lessons learned from successive, successful invasions.

The fighting men transferred from the liberty ships to LSTs as they approached the coastal waters. Rough seas made disembarking from the LSTs into assembled Higgins boats extremely difficult. Landing craft coxswains made a special effort to keep the landing craft close to the ship's side, difficult with the turbulent seas. Unfortunately, the 30th Regiment's first casualty of the war was a young soldier who was climbing down the cargo net. He was crushed between the landing craft and the ship, falling into the water with a sixty-pound pack, unable to avoid drowning.

The invasion north of Casablanca, on the beaches between Fedala and

Rabat, caught the French and Italians defenders by complete surprise. The big guns of the USS Massachusetts and several heavy cruisers shelled the beach several hours before the landing, and firing on inland targets continued after the landing. It was D-Day, November 8, 1942, and as the landing craft approached the beaches, they were subjected to a pounding by huge waves that built up during the night. Once the landing craft had deposited their men and tried to return to their ship to reload, they were dashed against the beach and torn apart. The beach was in complete disarray with broken and battered craft, and many jeeps and tanks were lost in the landing. Without landing craft, supplies and additional men could not be delivered and the soldiers on land were required to carry out the mission tasks.

Troops of the 3rd Infantry Division waded ashore, ran up the beach, and pressed forward to establish a beachhead. The defender's large artillery responded to the navy gunfire and one shell bounced off a Massachusetts eighteen inch steel turret without exploding. The invading force easily dispatched small arms resistance from the protective forces near the beach. The American troops were two miles inland before stopping to establish a secure battle line.

Fort Blondin, a former enclosure for the French Foreign Legion, was a major obstacle in the path of advance. Before the invasion, the French had agreed that in the event of an invasion by the Allies, they would point their searchlight straight up, signifying surrender. Due to the air attacks, the searchlight was directed diagonally toward the suspect planes, and the attacking force misinterpreted the resulting light. The heavy artillery within the fort responded to the incoming barrage, and as a result, a concentrated assault on Fort Blondin became necessary. The Americans reacted, attacked the fort, and it was finally over-run. The invading forces moved forward so far, so fast, that a message was sent to the USS Massachusetts to stop firing as its shells were landing too close to the advancing Americans. By November 11th the resistance finally ended, and the success of the invasion was evident.

The 30th Regimental Combat Team had performed very well. Unfortunately, eleven men were killed and fifty-two were wounded. However, they had taken one hundred sixty prisoners, captured truckloads of armored equipment and an operating train. They were poised to move east.

Their first duty was to return to the beaches and unload supplies from the ships, since there were no constructed docks. Thousands of pounds of

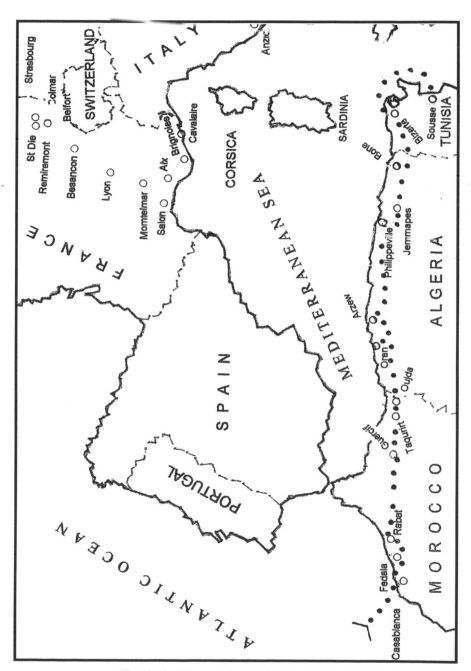

The North African route from Fedalia to Bizerte.

equipment necessary to sustain the invasion forces were delivered to the beaches of Rabat and were handled with military muscle.

Elements of the 3rd Division traveled by truck and train east to Oudja, then to Guercif, French Morocco, to an isolated French Foreign Legion Post, in the middle of the desert. They proceeded to patrol the area, sending squads out as far as two hundred fifty miles around the isolated fort.

On December 6th, they proceeded to Oran, where they guarded the airport, rail yards, and performed advance patrols in the area. In late January, Martha Raye, a popular comedienne, brought a group of entertainers to the isolated area, and treated the troops to a show. The pilot of the plane transporting the USO troop was Chuck Turner, a classmate and close friend of Bill's, who also graduated in ROTC from Montana State.

The 3rd Battalion of the 30th Regiment proceeded to Casablanca, where the leaders of the Allied forces were meeting to plan a strategy for the future of Europe. Winston Churchill, Joseph Stalin and Franklin Roosevelt as well as delegations from their countries, met for several days in what was to become a historic meeting. Serving as honor guard for the world leaders was fitting recognition for the reputation enjoyed by the 30th RCT.

Other Battalions of the regiment trained daily on house-to-house fighting and street fighting, anticipating the sort of battles the future would hold. They attended communication schools and continued to train in tactics and invasions, incorporating new equipment and replacements. The regiment finally moved several hundred miles east to Bizerte, where the training continued. Lieutenant Stucky was part of the proud tradition of the 30th RCT, and he entered the training with his leadership skills and characteristic enthusiasm. The next phase of the Mediterranean campaign was about to begin, and the 3rd Division would play a major part.

STUCKY • CHAPTER 4

One of the consistent complaints of the ordinary soldier was the "hurry up and wait" aspect of army life When many men are directed to perform a certain activity, the preparation, organization, and coordination of thousands of men sometimes appears chaotic, but is usually controlled by the activity beginning on time. There is a great deal of orchestration involved in coordinating the various components to be in the right place at the right time, and sometimes planners overestimate the time necessary to get things done. Other times, assembly occurs with great haste, and the difficult is accomplished. However, for the infantryman, the dogface, the grunt, it is usually "hurry up and wait."

To "hurry up and wait" at one AM, carrying a full field pack, with ammunition and rations for three days, often found a few soldiers asleep standing up.

The road to Germany next passed through Sicily, an island of mountainous terrain and rock. Most of the island's development was along the coast, while the interior was practically impassable, with few roads and a few towns scattered at the end of deep ravines. North Africa was defended by a combination of Italian, French, and German divisions. Sicily contained many well trained and dedicated members of the Third Reich, with considerable experience in mountain warfare. The Allied plan was for Americans to attack from the south, push over the mountains to Palermo, then work along the north coast to drive the Germans east. The English First Army would land along the southeast corner of the island, pushing north to catch the Germans in a pincer movement.

The Americans would land on twenty miles of beaches stretching from Licata to Gela. Preceding the landing, one thousand paratroopers from the 82nd Airborne would parachute inland to secure an airfield, disrupt communications, and engage the enemy, drawing them away from the beaches. The 3rd Division, and other divisions, after landing would secure the beachhead, then work inland to squeeze the Germans in a pincers movement.

Members of Lt. Stucky's company were finally loaded aboard the LSTs that would carry them to Sicily. Lt. Stucky's notes, in typical military jargon, were as follows:

"Company H was loaded into three LSTs. Capt. Nolle with _ of Co HQs, Lt.Way with the 1st platoon and a section of the mortar platoon were loaded into LST 318. Lt. Chinn with the 2nd section and the 2nd platoon,

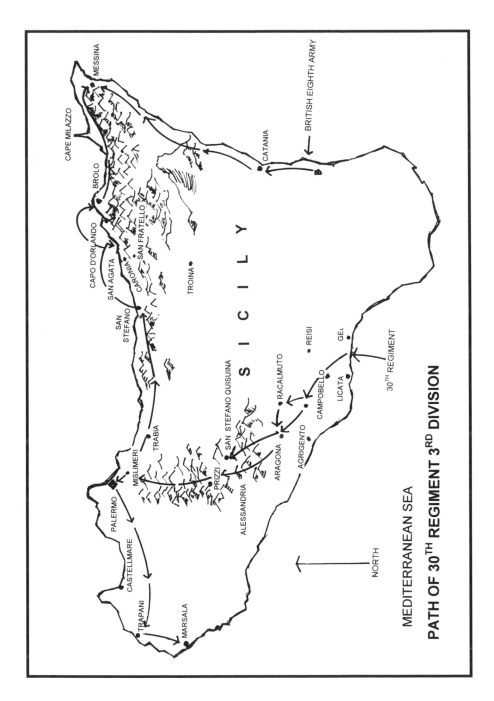

MEDITERRANEAN SEA

PATH OF 30TH REGIMENT 3RD DIVISION

The Sicilian Campaign over the rugged mountains from Licata to Palermo, two leapfrog invasions, and on to Messina.

Lt. Morse with the 3rd section of mortars were loaded into LST317. Lt. Stucky with _ Co HQ and the 1st section of 2nd platoon and 1st section of mortars were loaded into LST316. These three LSTs formed the first wave of the assault force to be landed at H+10.

"Lt. Morse with three mortar squads (2nd section and one squad from the 1st section) were formed into 3 LCUPs as the support wave of the first assault cover. The wave proceeded the 1st wave by two minutes and were to fire on the beach if fired upon. The wave was not to land but to stop 200 yards off shore and land with the 2nd wave. The support was not fired upon by the beach defenses, and consequently did not fire."

Although the regular infantryman seldom understood the organization and precision needed for deploying troops, the degree of planning needed to place the right combination of firepower in the right place was given considerable thought by military planners. The officers understood their role, and attempted to have their men in position to perform.

Before dawn the soldiers had climbed down the cargo nets from the LST into the LCUPs and were circling in preparation for alignment and heading for the beach. Lt. Stucky heard the drone of airplanes, and the C-47 transports carrying paratroopers were now overhead at about one thousand feet, heading for their inland target. Aboard one of the LSTs, a young sailor manning twin-forty mm cannon heard the planes. Suspecting the invasion force was about to be strafed by German aircraft he started firing at the slow moving targets. Other ships, suspecting something unexpected was occurring, joined in shooting at the American aircraft. In the ensuing chaos, before orders could be passed to cease fire, twenty-three planes loaded with thirty highly trained paratroopers each were shot down in flames, crashing into the water just ahead of the LCUPs. Six hundred ninety highly trained infantrymen who were to play a critical role in the invasion were killed, along with sixty-nine airmen who were given the task to drop them in the proper spot at the proper time. The remaining planes flew to their objective, attempting to carry out orders without two-thirds of their assault force.

Lt. Stucky and his men watched the tragedy in disbelief, with tears in their eyes. The sky was illuminated by the burning aircraft as they descended, and by the tracers showing the hits. As their assault boats approached the shore, they passed through downed airplanes and bodies floating in the water. This tragedy seared Bill Stucky's memory, and he could not mention the event without tears flowing. The unfortunate debacle was downplayed by the military, and not even reported in the Stars and

Stripes, the military newspaper. Subsequent historical accounts also avoided full disclosure, but several personal biographies recount the incident in graphic detail.

The 30th Regiment landed on the beach and moved toward its objectives over the flat Licata plain. They advanced into the low hills, then into the rugged mountains overlooking the plains. In the first thirty-three hours, they had moved inland fifty-four miles, and captured seven hundred fifty prisoners. As components of other divisions moved ashore, the 30th RCT moved into the mountains toward Aragona, Alessandria, San Stephano Quisquina, and Prizzi. The narrow roads and forbidding terrain aided the retreating Germans, who made every advance costly. In the major action at San Stephano Quisquina, German prisoners were taken during the fierce fighting. It opened the way over the mountains to Palermo.

With no roads, mules became the main method for transporting supplies and ammunition. As the men moved forward, it was impossible to deliver food to the troops, who were without food for three days. A field decision was made by the company commanders to kill, cook and eat one of the mules to provide the sustenance needed to continue the difficult passage over the rough terrain. As the men were about to dispatch one of their trusty transportation animals, a mule train arrived with canisters of hot food, which spared the mule "giving his life for freedom in his country."

The 30th RCT finally reached the outskirts of Palermo, where they raced to beat the 2nd Armored Division and the 45th Division into the main port, the final stepping off point to take the rest of the island. The prior intense training for Lt. Stucky and the men of Company H paid dividends in helping to defeat two Italian divisions in mountain combat. From the landings at Licata it had taken 12 days of intense fighting, with some losses, to reach Sicily's capitol city. Allied shipping now had adequate dock facilities to deliver the vast quantity of supplies needed to keep the several divisions moving forward.

The 30th RCT assembled outside the town of Trabia for some rest and replacements, as they prepared for the march west along the coast to Messina. It was a well-deserved rest. The soldiers needed to regain their energy and resolution for the next phase. The coastal terrain to the east consisted of a narrow slip of land with mountains abruptly rising to the south. It would be easily defended by the enemy, and require arduous mountain-scaling efforts to encircle the defenders. There were isolated pockets of resistance high in the mountains that would require great physical effort just to reach them, let alone defeat them in battle.

While the 3rd Division regrouped, the 45th Division continued their assault along the north coast driving the Germans and Italians back. It finally was stymied at San Stefano, where the terrain and the defense had the advantage. The 3rd Division replaced the 45th as the main force. A tactical decision was made to leapfrog the defenses, not by land but by sea. The 2nd Battalion, including H Company, boarded LSTs and put out to sea, only to return fifteen miles down the coast, where the assault troops once again ran ashore to attack the enemy.

The Germans suddenly caught in a pincer movement, hastily retreated, and established a new defensive perimeter. A new battle ensued, and again was a standoff. Companies E and H proceeded up the Rosamarino River and over mountainous terrain to attack San Marco D'Alunzio and rout the enemy. Patrols into the mountains attempted to locate additional enemy that might return to the coast to inflict damage. Along the coast, defenders again set up roadblocks and defenses to stop the advancement of Allied troops.

At San Agata, the 2nd Battalion once again boarded LSTs for an end-run twenty miles down the coast. They by-passed Capo D'Orlando, landing outside Brolo where they engaged the enemy. The battle was intense with both sides taking losses. The Americans finally prevailed, eventually capturing the high ground and forcing the Germans to regroup. The Germans and Italians were now totally disorganized, retreating along the coast, pursued by the 45th Division under command of General George Patton. The Americans finally entered the city of Messina.

To the south the British forces under the command of Field Marshall Bernard Montgomery waged a bitter fight as they moved north. It was Montgomery's desire to reach Messina and declare victory in Sicily as his own accomplishment. In one ironic confrontation, Montgomery assembled his troops and marched them down the streets of Messina, only to pass in review of the 3rd and 45th American Divisions who had arrived in Messina a few days earlier. The egos of Patton and Montgomery were often not in the best interest of harmonious Anglo-American relations, but it made delicious copy for the newspapers.

The end-run at Brolo inflicted heavy losses on the enemy, killing one hundred and capturing twelve German soldiers. The landing team destroyed two Mark IV tanks and disabled two more, destroyed one 77mm gun and six personnel carriers. The 2nd Battalion lost four officers and thirty-six men killed, three officers and sixty-seven men wounded and nine captured. In addition, they lost seven self-propelled 105mm guns, two half-track ammunition carriers and fourteen mules killed.

During the thirty-eight day whirlwind campaign from July 10 to August 18, the 30th RCT fought over two hundred ten miles of some of the most rugged terrain in European, African, Middle-Eastern Theater of operations. It sustained heavy casualties; a total of four hundred six men. Of these, one hundred fifteen men were killed in action including seven officers, two hundred fifty-one enlisted men were wounded and twenty-four men were missing in action. For their outstanding work in Sicily, the regiment received the British Distinguished Service Order. Individuals received six Distinguished Services Crosses, one hundred eight Silver Stars, two Legion of Merit Medals, thirty-eight Bronze Stars, sixty-three Regimental Commendations and the 2nd Battalion received a Presidential Unit Citation.

STUCKY • CHAPTER 5

After enjoying the sights and sounds of Messina for a few days as successful liberators of Sicily, the troops were trucked back to Palermo, where they proceeded to receive replacement troops, and to clean their equipment for the next assignment. There was mail from home, and many letters written to assure families at home the soldiers were healthy and well. Training continued, and Lt Stucky integrated the new men into the company, discussing tactics and responsibilities. His positive personality, effecting leadership discipline, prepared the men for the infantryman's role in winning the war, with as few casualties as possible. That discipline had its rewards.

The 30th RCT again practiced beach assaults, which meant once again they would spearhead the next invasion. The division was transferred to the Fifth Army under the command of General Mark Clark.

The British Army landed on Italy at the toe of the boot, indicatinmg military planners intended to fight the entire length of the Italian peninsula. The mountainous terrain of Italy meant fighting would be intense and difficult, similar to the mountain fighting in Sicily. It was not a pleasant thought, based on past experience. However, once the British had a "toe hold" there would be a series of leapfrog landings to entrap German and Italian defenders.

On September 16th the 30sth RCT once again walked up the stairs alongside LSTs in full battle gear in preparation for another assault. It was exactly one year after boarding trains at Fort Ord headed for the east coast and North Africa. This time the 1st and 3rd Battalions would be the main assault group, with the 2nd Battalion in reserve, scheduled to land a few hours later. On September 18th, the 30th RCT landed at Paestum, in the bay of Sorrento. Working its way inland to Battigalia, at the foot of the mountains, they began their advancement over the rocky terrain encountering strong resistance in the town of Acerno. The two-day battle was the first major engagement with the enemy.

Other Allied forces, the 34th Division and 45th Division, were delivered closer to Sorrento and fought their way around Mount Vesuvius toward Naples. The 34th Division finally secured the Bay of Naples, which would soon become the major supply port for Italy and future invasions.

The 30th RCT was given the difficult task of fighting through the mountains to circle the landing area and drive the Germans back toward

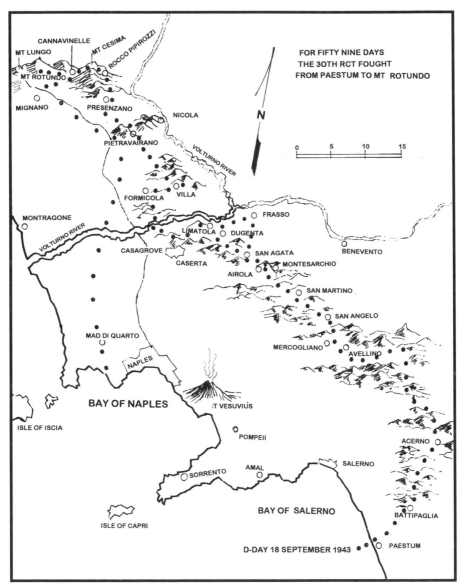

At Salerno, the 3rd Division, 30th RCT was again given the difficult task of fighting through the mountains. The fall rains made advancing difficult.

the north. The Apennine Mountains were much like the Rockies, with steep canyon walls. Roads winding through the canyons were visible from several vantage points, working to the defenders' advantage. The availability of American A-25s, medium attack bombers, kept the Herman Goering Panzer Division Recon Gruppe in continued retreat, with constant strafing and bombing. The Germans finally took a defensive stance in the village of Acerno, giving the high ground advantage to establish artillery control over the main road, Highway 7, and several canyons. The second battalion of the 30th RCT was given the task to circle behind Acerno, climb several peaks in the mountainous terrain, and attack from the rear. Lt. Stucky led his company through driving rain, over the steep slippery mountains, and initiated the intense two-day battle to drive the Germans off the mountain. There were many casualties on both sides but the Germans, with offensive pressure from several fronts of the Salerno Valley, were unable to reinforce their position and were forced to withdraw. The 30th RCT chased them north to the Volturno River, where the Germans once again established a strong defensive position.

On October 8th field kitchens caught up with the troops, and they received their first hot meal since landing on the Italian beaches September 22nd. Wet and cold, the men filed past the serving line to receive hot food, fresh bread, and coffee. While most of the soldiers enjoyed their meal and tried to dry out, patrols continued to probe to determine the strength and location of the enemy.

On October 12th, at the bridge over the Volturno, the Americans began intensive mortar fire and shelling towards the Germans on the other side. At 02:00 AM, Lt. Stucky led Company H in the attack, shrouded in smoke bombs set off to conceal the troop movement. The 2nd Battalion was ordered to cross at noon, but patrols were unsuccessful in establishing a foothold, due to intense mortar and machine gun fire. The battalion then marched two miles to a location where engineers had built a pontoon bridge; there the men crossed the Volturno with dry feet. By 01:00 PM, the 2nd Battalion was across the river in position to attack. Soon they were joined by another battalion, and at 02:30 PM began moving forward in another intense battle that lasted for two days. Again, the Germans were forced to retreat, taking a defensive position at San Nicola Ridge, and again, after intense fighting, the Germans were driven off.

The Americans suffered heavy casualties, but continued to keep pressure on the defending Germans. Heavy bombers were used to bomb the Germans off the mountaintops, and the pursuing Americans often engaged them in hand-to-hand combat. The Germans retreated to Mt. Rotundo, over three hundred fifty-seven meters high and densely covered with scrubby bushes, where they set up another defensive position. Allied bombers dropped over two hundred tons of bombs on the mountain, but the Germans remained dug in with tank traps, minefields, and machine gun positions. The Americans again executed a circling movement, attacking from the rear through the small town of Cannavinnelle. Without adequate maps showing the terrain, or local guides, the soldiers pushed ahead, frequently engaging enemy patrols in firefights. Running into the main body of the defense resulted in a two-hour exchange of hand grenades and hand-to-hand combat. This fierce engagement caused the Germans to withdraw after two days of battle, leaving many dead and soldiers who surrendered.

The pressure on the defending army continued until the end of December, with constant patrols and several skirmishes. For fifty-nine days the 30th RCT fought through the mountains, the cold, and the rain. From September 22nd to late December they pursued the enemy from Arcerno to the Volturno River to Mt. Rotundo, overcoming the delay tactics of a clever and determined enemy. They were now taken off the line, and trucked to Naples to prepare for their next challenge.

The reason the infantry is called "foot soldiers" is the fact they walk from battle to battle throughout the war. Walking through the Appenines was no exception. (Photo- US Army)

STUCKY • CHAPTER 6

Training on the beaches near Naples once again prepared the 30th Regiment and the 3rd Division for an invasion from the sea. Units received replacements who were trained to become a part of the combat team. Lt. Stucky was again in charge of assimilating infantrymen into their tactical units. Experience gained from previous invasions and mountain combat was passed on to incoming replacements not only in his own company, but throughout the battalion. The regiment was permitted a brief R & R, with the enlisted men in the Naples area and the officers at Sorrento. During the training several parades were held, medals were awarded, and some units received Presidential Unit Citations for their performance on the field of battle.

On January 21st, 1944, the 3rd Division boarded LSTs and sailed along the west Italian coast in the deep, blue Tyrrhenian Sea. The soldiers were tired of fighting enemy pillboxes, mud and hills. They recalled action in Sicily when the Germans were in retreat and did not have an opportunity to rest or set up major defensive positions. The end runs at San Agata and Brolo had the Germans in disarray, and Allied success was a result of their confusion. Perhaps this would be a similar battle. Unfortunately, it became four months of hell.

The 3rd Division landed at Anzio-Nettuno beach, south of Rome, with the 2nd Battalion leading the 30th RCT. Using lessons learned from previous assaults, they trained as teams to attack and destroy pillboxes, fortifications, coast defenses, wire beach obstacles, and minefields.

It was Bill Stucky's sixth invasion, wading through the water and racing up the beach. He was now the Company Commander of H Company and promoted to the rank of Captain. Again, the invasion caught the Germans off guard, since they had expected a landing nearer to Rome, where they had developed a thorough defense perimeter. Thus, the landing at Anzio was accomplished without much resistance.

The German troops stationed in the area were in full retreat, and instead of actively pursuing them, the American forces went to their assigned areas and set up their protective defense system. It was one of the major and costliest mistakes made during the Italian campaign. The Germans had several days to move soldiers defending Rome to the mountains surrounding the Anzio beachhead and entrench heavy artillery on the high ground. The Anzio area consisted of one hundred square miles of land, approximately two hundred feet above sea level, rising slowly to the mountains to the east.

The German control of the mountains had complete visual coverage of the plains area. In addition, German aircraft from airfields in northern Italy were available to fly intermittent sorties over the battlefield. The ensuing stalemate was devastating to the isolated American positions.

The 30th RCT landed on the "red beach" with the 2nd Battalion as the main landing unit, with the 1st and 3rd Battalions following hours later. The 30th RCT was reinforced with the 41st Field Artillery Battalion, elements of the 751st Tank Battalion, Part of the 601st Tank Destroyer Battalion, Company C of the 3rd Medical Battalion, the 10th Engineer Battalion, Company D 84th Chemical Battalion, and part of the 3rd Signal Company. They moved north to the Mussolini Canal, to help the Rangers capture Nettuno. The landing went so smoothly, with only a few casualties, the soldiers thought perhaps the war was over and they had not been informed. Once the Germans were established on the high ground, they could hurl artillery on the beach, where there were few objects to conceal the Americans; their only concealment was foxholes and small collections of buildings scattered about.

Once the Germans began shelling the beach, it was almost impossible to move forward. Tanks and vehicles took a terrible pounding. Soldiers moved forward yards, instead of miles. There were many individual examples of heroism in knocking out pillboxes and machine gun emplacements. These acts later resulted in subsequent awarding of several Congressional Medals of Honor, the highest recognition bestowed by the United States Government, for individual bravery and performance above and beyond the call of duty. Infantrymen continued to run patrols, probing the enemy line for soft spots. A number of units were distributed behind the front lines, prepared rush into battle when the Germans counter-attacked. The fighting and shelling was so furious, that in one company with eighteen replacements, six of the men were killed before their names could be placed on the company roster. Battalions were rotated every two or three days, so men could have a hot meal and a night's rest before moving back to the front lines.

The Germans made a concentrated effort to repel the Anzio beachhead, counterattacking at every opportunity. However, after two months the Americans were entrenched well enough to know they were going to stay. Two months of stalemate began, with both sides suffering from attrition, losing quality soldiers and equipment.

After several weeks pinned down on the beach, German artillery observers identified H Company's position, and shelled it continuously for three days. On February 24th, the third day of constant bombardment,

Captain Stucky was hit by artillery shrapnel in both the front and the back, while moving about checking company emplacements. Medics attended to him immediately, and he was taken to an Aid Station. Mobile X-ray units identified extensive shrapnel wounds, and medics placed him in an ambulance where he was evacuated to Naples to the General Hospital.

After immediate operations to remove the pieces of steel, Stucky was moved from the hospital to a hotel for rest and recreation (R & R) while he healed. He spent two months recuperating, and learned that, after recovery, he would be assigned to another division as a replacement officer. This did not please Stucky, who was a proud member of the 30th RCT, so he complained to the assignment officer, who was very sympathetic to Bill's desire to return to his old unit as company commander. As an interim duty during recuperation, Bill was put in command of the R & R Officer's Club. The assignment let Bill use his organizational skills; he was a chief rather than an Indian, and was in charge of staffing. The chef was from New York City, and many of the staff members were well schooled in catering and hostelry. The activity kept Bill occupied, and took his mind off his injuries. A surprise visit from Captain Chuck Turner and Captain Eric Anderson, both friends from Montana State, and ROTC graduates, certainly helped Bill's disposition.

The 3rd Division Commanding Officer, General "Iron Mike" O'Daniel, checked into the facility for a week of R & R. They spent some time together, and O'Daniel was well aware of Stucky's experience and competence during the previous six invasions. As the General was packing to return to duty, he summoned Captain Stucky and made a strong case for Bill's becoming his Aide-de-Camp and serve on his staff. Bill had a strong commitment to H Company as company commander, so he responded, "I'm not certain I want to be your Aide. I would like to return to my regiment and my company."

However, Bill contacted his Regimental Commander, Colonel Johnson to discuss the offer. Col. Johnson immediately responded, "Are you kidding? You say yes!" After mulling it around for a few hours, he contacted General O'Daniel and indicated, "OK General. I will try it as a temporary assignment."

When his wounds were healed so he could be released from the General Hospital, Bill joined General O'Daniel's staff as S-2, Planning and Operations. While the battle raged at Anzio, and the soldiers attacked the high ground, Capt. Bill Stucky began gathering data to assist in planning the invasion of southern France.

In the meantime, Allies made a landing on the north shores of France. This took the pressure off the Italian front, as the German General Command had to re-prioritize their commitment of resources to defend their homeland. After an intense pounding and struggle, the American Fifth Army finally broke out at Anzio, and moved east and north.

Fighting an additional front in the south of France would spread Germany's resources even thinner.

An LST fully loaded on the way to the invasion of Southern France. Coordinating the enormous quantity and variety of equipment is difficult to comprehend.
(Photo-Life-History of World War 2)

STUCKY • CHAPTER 7

It was impossible to keep the landing in southern France a secret. The Americans knew for a year it would ultimately happen. The Germans also knew it would happen, but not when or where. Because of this advance speculation, invasion planners decided to invade in the light of day, rather than trying to surprise the enemy in the middle of the night.

Captain Stucky observed the invasion from a Navy cruiser shelling the beaches between Cavalaire and St. Tropez on the southeastern beaches of France. The 30th RCT landed with the second wave and achieved its first day objectives. Four days later, the 30th fought an intense half-day battle, finally taking the city of Brignoles. Executing a brilliant flanking maneuver to capture the communication center in Aix, they continued to apply constant pressure to chase the Germans north. From August 29 to September 1st, Allied forces pushed the enemy well beyond the Lyons' area.

Moving into Aix, they met with heavy opposition. Reinforced with air support, the 30th RCT managed to keep the pressure on the Germans who set up roadblocks at every intersection and bend in the road. The Germans had artillery and tanks that were well-dispersed and difficult to attack. Fortunately, the Americans were able to approach Aix en Provence from several directions, forcing the Germans to retreat and abandon the town.

Briefing members of the 30th Infantry abard an LST bound for south France.
(Photo- US Army)

Each small town presented problems that required innovative assaults. Firing artillery into the streets drove the Germans indoors. That made it necessary for the Americans to form assault squads that went door to door, flushing out the enemy. As the Americans moved further north, they were joined by groups of the FFI (Forces Frenchise d'Interieur) who were part of seventeen or eighteen different local groups who obtained their weapons by ambushing German fighting units or from Allied parachute drops. They were valuable in fighting behind the German lines, blowing up bridges behind retreating Germans, and engaging reserve German troops in brief skirmishes to keep them from reinforcing their troops during battle.

Captain Stucky was directed by General O'Daniel to establish a rest and recreation area for enlisted men and officers in Lyon. His previous experience while recovering from wounds in Naples gave him the background to organize and develop a fine facility to serve the fighting men.

As the development of an R and R facility neared completion, General O'Daniel received a request from Colonel Mac Porter, the Commander of the 30th RCT. "General, I need Stucky up here at the front lines to help organize our attacks. Can you let me have him back?" General O'Daniel approached Stucky to see if he would like to return to his regiment. Stucky welcomed the opportunity to return to his old unit as a company commander, so the General released him. However, Colonel Porter had other plans. He made Captain Stucky 1st Battalion AS-3, in charge of planning and training.

Stucky chose to work in the field as a forward observer, organizing and coordinating the several companies and squads in attacking the enemy. The Allies managed to keep the Germans on the run, with the 30th RCT playing a major role. The tactical operations not only kept pressure on the German fighting units, but they managed to take over 600 prisoners with flanking actions.

The attacking force pressed on to St. Die, Nancy, and Colmar, for three months in constant battle. Fighting through the Vosges Mountains that rose from one thousand to four thousand feet in height in parallel ridges was a major obstacle for the attacking force. The Severne Gap that separates the Vosges from the north, and the Belfort Gap between the Vosges and Switzerland, provided the Germans an opportunity for a buildup of artillery, mines, roadblocks and booby traps.

On September 11th, the Germans attacked five times, with the American forces counterattacking, resisting with flanking movements, and catching the Germans off guard with a night attack. A furious battle ensued, with the Americans knocking out several German Tiger tanks and self-propelled cannon, forcing the Germans to withdraw.

Some of the attacks were so frenzied that American tanks fired on American tanks. Each road crossing and small village in the area was a hotly contested separate battleground. Every hill engaged twenty, thirty, or fifty men, under intense fire to eventually rout the enemy. Each confrontation produced a new hero, who stood firm in the face of overwhelming opposition.

The wet fall weather made fighting slippery and miserable, but the American soldiers pressed on. After routing the Germans from small communities, suddenly hundreds of French citizens would appear to cheer on the US soldiers. However, these celebrations were short lived, and the American soldiers soon moved out to keep the Germans on the run. The 3rd Division was only one of three divisions in the area applying pressure on the Germans. Captain Stucky remained at the front to direct and position the groups of personnel to keep forcing the Germans back.

As they moved out of the rocky terrain, they found better highways in central France. However, the terrain was wooded, and there were fewer road networks. The rainy, cold fall meant that the 30th Regiment would enter its third winter in battle. The regiment was diverted south to join forces fighting against a strong concentration of Germans near Colmar. Fighting in the "Colmar Pocket" was one of the most fiercely contested battles encountered during their move north. Small groups engaged in firefights every few minutes, and hand-to-hand combat happened frequently. The Germans were making one last strong stand, and they used every device available in an attempt to stop the American advance. It was close to the German border, with several rivers draining into the Rhine, and a location where the Americans would make several brave attempts to cross into Germany. Ferocious fighting lasted from January 22nd until the middle of February. The fighting would be constant and deadly until a final crossing into Germany at Strasbourg and Zweibrucken.

Before daybreak, December 23rd, 1944, Captain Stucky and another officer were forward observers on the second floor of a building in a small town in Germany. An American half-track vehicle was parked behind the building while the men studied the terrain, attempting to spot German troop movements. The Germans spotted the half-track, and sent in a 88mm artillery shell which demolished the half-track, with the ensuing explosion knocking down the building. Totally buried with building debris, the two officers were dug out by nearby infantrymen. Bill suffered from the concussion, and had bruises, scratches and lacerations on his body from the debris. He was taken to a nearby medical aid tent where he was stitched and treated. The medics wanted to send him to the rear, but he insisted on returning to his unit.

That night Stucky was again serving as a forward observer from a position where he could spot German troop movements. He was talking on a radio directing artillery fire, when several rounds of German mortar fire landed in the area, knocking everyone down. Captain Stucky jumped up, shouting, "I'm OK. Is anybody hit?" An artilleryman shouted back, "Like hell you're OK!" Bill looked down to find blood on the front of his jacket, spouting from a vein in his neck torn by shrapnel.

A medic appeared, stopped the blood flow and placed him in an ambulance, which took him to a hospital in St. Die. Several small shards of steel were removed from his neck and throat area. He was in the hospital for four days, before his release to return to his unit. Many years later, after being involved in a rear-end car collision, Bill was x-rayed for damage, only to discover there were still a few small slivers of steel in the muscle structure of his neck.

As the 30th RCT continued fighting in the Colmar pocket, they traversed a forest that ended at the Ill River. As the artillery pounded the opposite shore, a series of inflatable rubber boats were lashed together to span the sixty foot, steeped bank river. Several companies of the 1st

Captain Stucky was a part of General "Iron Mike" O'Daniels' staff in France. The 1st Battalion, of the 30th RCT kept intense pressure on the German army.

220

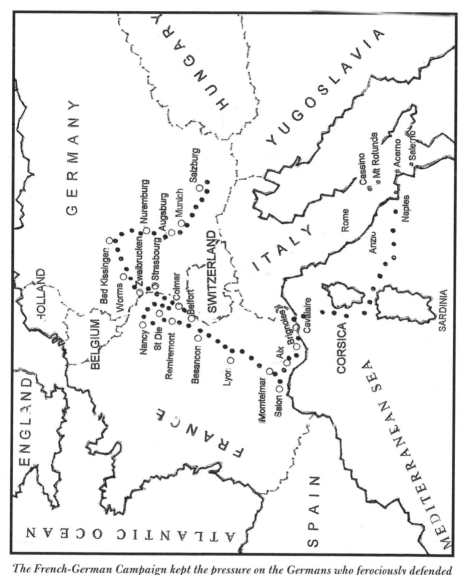

The French-German Campaign kept the pressure on the Germans who ferociously defended the path to their homeland. Colmar was the scene of intense German resistance.

Battalion struggled to get across, and found to continue to advance, it was necessary to wade several small streams. The soldiers proceeded through the waist-deep winter-cold water to establish a defensive perimeter, with room for reinforcement with additional troops. Lt. Col. Porter and Captain Stucky established a command post at the furthest point, in order to direct operations. That night, the Germans mounted a counterattack that would last for a day and a half. Immediately, Porter and Stucky began calling for artillery and mortar concentrated fire, to repel the attack. Throughout the night and the next day, the two officers gave a "play-by-play" of the counterattacking force, and continued to direct fire until the German's started their withdrawal. They immediately called for dry clothing, hot food and tents, so the soldiers could get some relief from wading the streams, and resisting the counterattack.

During the battle at Colmar on January 24th, Captain Bill Stucky's performance in the chaos of conflict and for outstanding bravery in action was awarded a Silver Star medal with Oak Leaf Cluster.

The division continued to fight through Worms, Bad Kissingen, Nuremberg, Augsberg, and Munich. The city of Nuremberg was devastated by Allied bombs, but the few standing buildings and parts of buildings were ideal locations for snipers to pick off the GIs as they took the city. Again, door to door fighting required extreme bravery on the part of the American soldiers in routing out the remaining enemy. Portions of the German Army continued to fight with great intensity, but many realized the war would soon be over, and military units began surrendering in large numbers. Unfortunately, the troops did not surrender without firm resistance, in spite of realizing they were out-numbered and out-gunned.

As the 1st Battalion, 30th RCT approached Bad Kissingen on March 30th, 1945, they met severe resistance, which subsided as they entered the city. Even though the town was an important road network city, they discovered the main commercial area was not severely damaged. The city contained twenty-eight hospitals, and was an excellent location for Corp and Army Headquarters.

As the soldiers exited the city, the Germans again counterattacked with ferocity, and once more Captain Stucky was directing operations to repulse the Germans. The numerous confrontations and firefights required coordination of tanks, artillery, and infantry, and once again Stucky directed operations from the front lines. For his actions in this conflict, he was awarded a Bronze Star.

However, it was apparent to his commander that Bill was taking far too many chances in his desire to end the war as soon as possible, and was putting his life in jeopardy. His commanding officer, directed him to march German prisoners to the rear, proceed to Marseilles, and from there return to the United States. Reaching Marseilles, Captain Bill Stucky boarded a Liberty ship, which joined a convoy for a twenty-seven day trip across the Atlantic Ocean. As the convoy neared the eastern shores of the U.S., his liberty ship veered to the south and made port in New Orleans. After a brief processing period, Bill boarded a train for Salt Lake City, where on the 26th of May, Lorraine met him with thankful, loving, open arms.

Lorraine and her seven friends lived in the same area, and shared letters and support while their husbands were overseas. Only two husbands returned from overseas alive. Lorraine's husband was one of the lucky two. The 3rd Division continued to push on into Germany reaching Berchtesgaden, Hitler's mountain hideout where he ultimately took his life. The division occupied several small towns in the area and resistance had essentially ended.

On the 5th of May, 1945, when the Germans finally capitulated, the division was in Salzberg. Two days later, two companies were put in trucks and taken to an area where it was reported a group of SS Troopers were refusing to accept the surrender conditions and were spoiling for a fight. The American soldiers were very upset and naturally reluctant to once again be placed in harm's way when hostilities were officially over. When the soldiers arrived in the area they learned the report was erroneous, and happily boarded the trucks to return to their quarters.

The 3rd Division carried out a number of responsible duties of occupation until they received orders to return to the United States.

The German Field Marshall Kesselring, who commanded troops on the Italian front and succeded General von Rundstedt on the western front, was asked a question by a war correspondent from the Chicago Tribune , "What was the best division faced by troops under your command in either the Italian or western fronts?" Without hesitation the Field Marshall named four divisions, two infantry and two armored. The 3rd Infantry Division was placed first on the list.

Substantiating the merit of the Field Marshall's observation, is the fact that the 3rd Infantry Division had more Congressional Medal of Honor winners than any other division. A total of thirty-nine men received the nation's highest honor "...who in action involving actual conflict with an enemy, distinguishes himself conspicuously by gallantry and intrepidity at the risk of his life above and beyond the call of duty."

Des Moines Sunday Re

THE NEWSPAPER IOWA DEPENDS UPON

DES MOINES, IOWA, SUNDAY, MAY 6, 1945.—SIXTY-TWO PAGES—SECTION THREE

Entered as second office at Des M

nday Register Now Has
375,000 Circulation

ARMY TO KEEP 6,968,000 FOR WAR ON JAPAN

Two Million Men to Be Released.

WASHINGTON, D. C. (*P*) —The army announced Saturday its V-E redeployment-demobilization plans, including provisions for the discharge of about 2,000,000 men during the next year.

The war department said these are the primary points in its plan:

1 "We believe that a program which gives us an army of 6,968,000 in 12 months from now will provide an adequate force to defeat Japan."

2 About 2,000,000 men will be returned to civilian life during the next 12 months. Of these, about 1,332,000 will be surplus troops and the remainder dischargees for physical and other reasons.

3 ABOUT TWO-THIRDS OF THE COMBAT UNITS will come through the United States en route to the Pacific and have furloughs. (Informally, it was said the furloughs would run not more than 30 days).

4 The larger proportion of service troops urgently needed in the Pacific will go there directly.

5 Transportation shortages, even with the 800 transport planes being used, will not get the last of the men who are to be discharged back to the United States before 12 months.

The army's detailed announcement said that the joint chiefs of staff, made up of the commanders of the army, navy and air forces, after consultation with Gen. Douglas MacArthur and Admiral Chester Nimitz, had arrived at a preliminary estimate of the troops and equipment needed to crush Japan in the shortest possible time and with the least cost in American lives.

Now 8.300.000.

Newspaper account of the buildup anticipated for the invasion of Japan, printed the day after the German surrender. European soldiers who fought so bravely defeating Germany were apprehensive about invading Japan.

STUCKY • CHAPTER 8

The 30th RCT had a proud tradition as a military unit, exhibited after every major battle. The troops would have a few days of rest and recreation, and then clean their equipment and uniforms to stand a full dress review. It was a time to present some of the many medals and citations they had earned, but more importantly, it established a strong sense of honor and military discipline. That discipline kept the men focused on defeating the enemy and pursuing them with constant pressure.

The 3rd Division returned to the United States to retrain for deployment against Japan. Replacements filled the ranks, and training began once again, since beach invasion forces would be needed for the assault on the many Japanese' islands. Fortunately, in the middle of their preparations, two large bombs dropped on Hiroshima and Nagasaki convinced Emperor Hirohito to end the war.

Now that the war was over, the unit celebrated with numerous parades, complete with "ruffles and flourishes." The 3rd Division was a "spit and polish" unit when young Bill Stucky joined it in San Francisco, and it returned to peacetime duty with the same "spit and polish."

On November 30th, 1945, Captain Bill Stucky was discharged in Fort Douglas, Utah. He immediately caught a train to Bozeman, Montana to meet Lorraine.

His first job was County Agent in Meager County, Montana. He enjoyed some success, as after one year he was invited to become County Agent Supervisor for Montana State University, and served in that position from 1948 until 1955. After his first year, he was offered a sabbatical to attend Cornell University to acquire a Masters Degree in Agricultural Economics. Completing his masters, Cornell University offered a healthy stipend to pursue a doctorate, but Bill felt he should return to his commitment at Montana State. In 1955, the State of Nevada approached him to serve as the state as Associate Director of Extension Services in Reno, Nevada, where he worked from 1955 to 1959. In 1959, Bill joined the faculty at Iowa State University at the Center for Agricultural Economic Adjustment, where he remained until his retirement in 1973.

Bill and Lorraine started their family when Susan was born April 7, 1946. Roger joined the family November 29, 1947 and David arrived January 28, 1950. Brian was born September 27, 1955. An active family kept Lorraine and Bill scrambling during their school years and beyond.

Bill finally rejoined Lorraine after thirty-three months overseas.

After retirement, Bill became more active in community affairs and ran for the Story County Iowa Board of Supervisors. His organizational abilities and agricultural background were an asset to the rapidly developing county, and he served two four-year terms, from 1978 to 1986. In addition, he served on several important city committees at the request of the Mayor. Bill was never one to avoid meeting a problem head-on, and usually managed to find a solution that met with almost everyone's approval.

When first out of college, Bill had the opportunity to return to his grandfather's homestead family farm outside Bozeman in the Gallatin

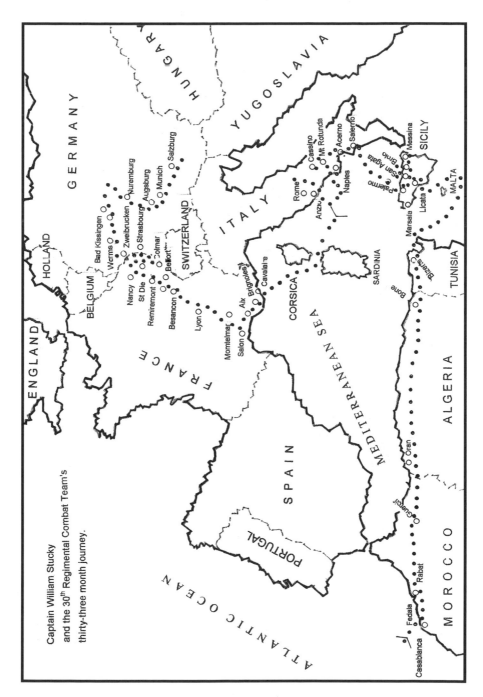

Captain William Stucky and the 30th Regimental Combat Team's thirty-three month journey.

The following place names appear on the map:

GERMANY · HUNGARY · YUGOSLAVIA · ITALY · SICILY · MALTA · SWITZERLAND · BELGIUM · HOLLAND · ENGLAND · FRANCE · SPAIN · PORTUGAL · CORSICA · SARDINIA · TUNISIA · ALGERIA · MOROCCO · ATLANTIC OCEAN · MEDITERRANEAN SEA

Salzburg · Nuremburg · Augsburg · Munich · Bad Kissingen · Worms · Zweibrucken · Strasbourg · Colmar · Belfort · Nancy · St Die · Remiremont · Besancon · Lyon · Montelimar · Salon · Aix · Brignoles · Cavalaire

Rome · Cassino · Mt Rotunda · Acerno · Salerno · Naples · Anzio · San Agata · Brolo · Messina · Palermo · Marsala · Licata · Bizerte · Bone · Oran · Djebel · Fedala · Rabat · Casablanca

The sojourn of thirty-three months that the 3rd Division and 30th Infantry (RCT) fought to defeat the Axis in Europe.

Valley. Lorraine's grandfather passed away while Bill was overseas, and the 160 acre farm was offered to Lorraine for $16,000, and they decided not to buy it. Bill decided he enjoyed working with farmers, but never wanted to be one. Four years later, the farm was sold to Montana State University for $56,000. Bill and Lorraine maintained a cabin on the Gallatin River in the Gallatin Range, and returned there every summer to fully enjoy the Montana mountains and their childhood roots.

Participating in the Reserve Officers Training Corps at Montana State prepared Bill Stucky with the proper attitude to serve in the Military for almost five years. Thirty-three months of overseas combat, several wounds, and a variety of responsibilities did not deter him from focusing on defeating the enemy. His military commendations were well deserved and include:

- The Silver Star with one Oak Leaf Cluster
  (the third highest medal in the US)
- The Purple Heart with two Oak Leaf Clusters
- The Bronze Star with one Oak Leaf Cluster
- The European-African-Middle Eastern Theater Ribbon
  (fighting in all three)
- Distinguished Unit Badge with Oak Leaf Cluster and Bronze Arrowhead and Nine Service Stars
- The American Defense Service Medal
- The World War II Victory Medal
- The French Croix de Guerre with Palm and
- The Combat Infantry Badge.

During the preparation of this biography, Bill Stucky suffered a stroke, and passed away on September 4, 2004. Bill Stucky, in his own modest way, was always grateful for the opportunity to serve his nation, whether in the military or the field of agricultural economics. The accolades our country bestowed upon Bill Stucky were far from modest, and appropriately celebrated his dedication, commitment and honor.

BOOK 9

Edwin Montgomery

Staff Sergeant
Medical Detachment
312th Field Artillery Battalion
79th Division

*"I have often wondered
why a nineteen year old kid from western Iowa
was asked to make decisions about life and death
as I was asked to do?"*

~Edwin Montgomery

MONTGOMERY • CHAPTER 1

"Do you have money?" the man asked in broken English.

The American sergeant fumbled through his pockets. "Here is one hundred ten dollars."

He handed it to the man dressed in dark clothes, and at close quarters, he still could not make out the man's facial features. Without lights from any source, the city of Pilsen, Czechoslovakia, was dark and foreboding. The sergeant was about to buy a friend's freedom, but had no idea what the outcome would be.

The war was recently over, but the Cold War was about to begin. Staff Sergeant Edwin Montgomery, a medic with the 312 Field Artillery Battalion of the 79th Division, reported to Battalion Headquarters at the request of the commander and given a new assignment. A nearby Russian prisoner of war camp was in dire need of a hospital. Most of the soldiers in the recently freed camp had been incarcerated for more than two years, without any medical supplies and barely enough food and water to keep them alive. The one thousand prisoners had not bathed, shaved or had a haircut during this period: disease, vermin, and tuberculosis were rampant. The Russians had four doctors, but no medicine or supplies to help the wounded and sick. Sergeant Montgomery's assignment: set up a hospital for one hundred patients and get it operational as fast as possible.

Visiting the site near Sturkod, Montgomery located an old barracks that housed tank troops early in the war. He immediately ordered beds, bedding, medical supplies and equipment, pharmaceuticals, clothing, cigarettes, candy, toothbrushes and toothpaste, razors, and scissors. Within days American trucks arrived with the requested equipment, and Montgomery and his staff rolled up their sleeves. Starting at 9:30 AM, the barracks was converted to a hospital and was ready for inspection by 4:30 PM that same day.

The Russians bathed, shaved, cut their hair, put on clean clothing, and suddenly became real soldiers once again. Sgt. Montgomery's trips through the camp were met with smiles and shouts of grateful approval. When a Russian Major arrived to assume military control of the camp, he immediately tried to kick Staff Sergeant Montgomery out of the compound. When Montgomery told this to his commander, the Battalion Executive officer, Major Savoris, confronted the Russian officer and told him to "shape up or suffer the consequences." Montgomery returned to run the hospital, but whenever he entered the building, the Russian Major would offer him a chair to sit on and always had a Russian woman nurse sit beside him. Montgomery never understood why the nurse attended, but observed it appeared she could "beat the crap out of any two men."

While there, Ed met a Russian Doctor whose name was A. J. Levitas, a Lt. Colonel who seemed to be a very reasonable person, was a good doctor, and claimed not to be a Communist. They worked well together, and when the doctor wanted to improve what little English he knew, Ed located a third grade English reading book to assist him in learning the language.

The doctor's wife and two children had been killed in Karkhov, Russia, and he was distressed that their graves had not been properly marked. His one goal was to return to Karkhov to properly mark their gravesites, but he feared the Russian Army would arrest him since he was not a member of the Communist Party. Montgomery was very sympathetic and indicated he would help if possible.

After thirty days in Sturkod, the 79th Division received orders to move to Cheb, Czechoslovakia. It became the opportunity for the doctor to escape from the prison camp. When the convoy assembled to leave, Ed told Dr. Levitas to wait for a signal, throw his clothing bag out of the dormitory window for the truck to retrieve, and when the convoy drove past the dormitory entrance, make a dash for the Medical Corps truck located at the rear of the column. Ed had a steel helmet and parka for him and, as usual for medical vehicles, they managed to pass through the gates without inspection.

Once the division arrived in Chub, Sergeant Montgomery was ordered by the executive officer to occupy a house of his choosing to set up the dispensary. Locating a house, Dr. Levitas and Montgomery set up shop. In a few days, they asked the right questions of local townspeople and made contact with partisans who might be able to assist the doctor to return to Russia. One evening a local citizen stopped by the facility and informed Ed he was to drive to Pilsen, and park at the intersection of two specific streets at 9:00 PM on a given date.

Driving the medical corps jeep in the early darkness, they followed the barely discernable highway into the city of Pilsen and, with some difficulty, finally found the particular intersection. As they sat in the dark, waiting, the doctor expressed his thanks to Ed for his friendship and assistance, but expressed his fear of reaching Krakhov to find his family's graves. Suddenly there was a tap on the window, and two men appeared, one on each side of the jeep.

The man accepted the money offered, and grunted, "Come!" Dr. Levitas slowly got out of the jeep, closed the canvas door and disappeared into the darkness.

Staff Sergeant Ed Montgomery waited for a few minutes, started the engine and returned to Cheb, down the same dark road. He never heard from Dr. Levitas again, and wonders to this day if his own money actually helped the doctor return to Russia, or paid to have his throat cut.

MONTGOMERY • CHAPTER 2

"In most battlefield injuries, the first thing you do is to try to stop the bleeding." The medical officer then proceeded to describe injuries to certain parts of the body and how best to deal with them. It was the beginning of instruction that would ultimately give the field medics background about inserting needles, cleansing wounds, splints, bandaging, sucking wounds, shock, plasma, survival evaluation and referrals. The Army prided itself on giving immediate support in the field to the wounded, and many lives were saved because of this fast response. Still, the training seemed incomplete and sketchy to Private Ed Montgomery who would soon have to apply what he had learned.

Montgomery had opportunities for other military tasks. When he completed basic training, he was offered an opportunity to remain at the base to train incoming draftees. When he turned that prospect down, he was offered a clerk's job in Headquarters Company at the base. Again, he indicated he would rather go to the next level of training with his buddies. When he checked the bulletin board for assignments, he discovered he was to join the 79th Division. When he inquired why they wanted him to remain in camp, he learned he had the second highest IQ in the battalion, and they wanted to utilize his skills.

Although born In Galva, Iowa, Ed spent most of his youth in Carroll, Iowa, graduating from the local public high school in May of 1941. His father, Lewis E. Montgomery, was of Scotch-Irish descent, while his mother, Caroline Welty, was from solid German stock. Lewis' father farmed in Johnson County, Iowa, and is buried there. Some how Lewis ended up owning a grocery store in Onawa. Lewis made his living establishing grocery stores, and when they were successful, selling them to other operators. He and Caroline raised six children, four boys and two girls, with Edwin being the second youngest. Unfortunately, Lewis passed away at the age of fifty-one when he became ill with flu like symptoms. It was determined he had an infection, and the doctors decided to extract all of his teeth, a practice common at that time, since they might be the basis of the infection. Two weeks later Lewis passed away. Edwin was only two years old. With his father gone, Caroline moved her family to Carroll, and Ed grew up in this tightly-knit family, under strict Catholic religious guidelines.

Graduating from high school in May of 1941, going to college was rarely considered an option, and getting married was not an immediate prospect unless there was an "accident." Full time employment and enjoying life were the goals for most of the graduating class.

Ed does not recall what he was doing December 7th, 1941, when he learned of Japan bombing Pearl Harbor, but he knew his life and the lives of all young men in Carroll County would soon change. Life in a small Iowa town in 1942-43 was good for an eighteen- year old boy. While in high school Ed Montgomery worked during the summers and after school painting churches for the Langenfeld Studios with his brothers Delbert and Everett. When not working, most likely Ed and his buddies spent a lot of time walking the fields and stream banks hunting ducks, pheasants and quail, as well as searching out the best fishing holes in the area. It was an idyllic life with few worries or cares for a young lad in Carroll. The painting job gave him a few dollars to spend on girls, hunting or maybe a little "Templeton Rye."

In the spring of 1943 Ed received his "Greetings and Salutations" from the draft board inviting him to join the war effort. With a birth date of October 3, 1923, he was five months into his nineteenth year when on April 8, 1943 he was inducted into the military at Camp Dodge, Des Moines, Iowa.

A group of young men from Carroll County gathered at the railroad station on a cool April evening to board the Chicago Northwestern train for Des Moines. All of the draftees stood talking to their dads except for Ed Montgomery, who never really knew his father since Ed was only two when his father died. One dad seeing his son off was a Carroll businessman, considered "shady" in some business circles, and of very modest means. The man approached Ed and chatted with him, reassured him about his new adventure, and pressed a twenty-dollar bill into Ed's hand. During basic training, every time the man's son received a letter from home, there was a ten or twenty dollar bill "for Ed." That father's concern for him was a thoughtful gesture that Ed Montgomery never forgot.

After physicals and a battery of tests, Ed was given the opportunity to choose the Navy, Marines, or Army; he chose the Army. A few hours later he was aboard a train bound for Camp Grand, Illinois, where he started his military/medical training.

For thirteen weeks, the men received their basic training of marching and military protocol. Instead of cleaning rifles and spending time at the firing range, a medical doctor gave lectures medical procedures and practices. It was basic information, and not too technical; in fact, Ed thought it was scarcely enough. A friend from Carroll, Roy Comes, was in the same training session. As basic training neared completion, the two managed to wrangle a weekend pass. The two soldiers went to Rockford, Illinois, rented a hotel room and spent most of their leave sleeping…on clean sheets!… and they did not have to make their beds!

After turning down the opportunity to remain at Camp Grand, Montgomery's next station was in Tellahoma, Tennessee, for additional medical training. He was assigned to the 312 Field Artillery Battalion, 79th Division as a First Aid man. The GI.'s referred to him as "Doc", a moniker he would carry throughout his army career. He worked very closely with Captain Edward G. Deming, an M.D., who would teach him the additional skills required for a medic in support of a combat infantry unit. The 79th Division insignia was the "Blue and White Cross of Lorraine", selected because of the unit's history and action in the Lorraine sector of the Allied front in France in the Great War.

The 312th Field Artillery Battalion of the 79th Division was sent to Camp Laguna near Yuma, Arizona, to test equipment. The troop train moved slowly, often stopping at small towns for coal and water. Since soldiers were not allowed to leave the train, they enticed the black porters to run shopping sorties for them. Armed with pockets full of cash, the porters returned with magazines, cigarettes, candy, whiskey, and other basic needs of the soldiers. They became very popular with the soldiers, and were amply rewarded for their efforts.

At Camp Laguna, the Battalion was to test vehicles in the desert environment. Private Ed Montgomery was assigned a three-quarter ton weapons carrier with large balloon tires for traction in sandy conditions. In a brand new Dodge truck, Ed joined the convoy on the long field exercise. Well into the desert his truck overheated, so he pulled out of line to cool it down, then retraced the path back to the camp. He was immediately upbraided and "caught seven shades of hell" for returning. The intent of the exercise was to continue driving until the engine overheated, "froze-up" and stopped. They were testing performance under harsh desert conditions. Private Montgomery wondered, "Why the hell didn't they tell me that? I did not want to ruin a perfectly good vehicle."

In December 1943, the Division moved from the heat of Arizona to frozen Camp Phillips in western Kansas, where the soldiers tested an "Aleutian suit" for use in Alaska and similar frigid climates. They remained "cold in Kansas" until March, 1944, when the Division boarded trains for their port of embarkation at Camp Myles Standish, Massachusetts. Once again, the railroad porters became the soldiers' closest friend, and trips for travel sustenance were numerous. For some reason, on this trip, the whiskey tasted better. For some soldiers, it would be their last taste of the common home variety.

On April 3, 1944, almost one year after leaving for Camp Dodge in Des Moines, the 79th Division walked up the gangplank of several "victory ships." These hastily built cargo ships were manned by English crews for the trip across the Atlantic, and leaving port, they joined a convoy that spent eleven days zigzagging to avoid German submarines. The Atlantic Ocean is never at rest: the change of direction horizontally was not as serious as the up and down, sideways, and rolling that caused the soldiers to become violently seasick. Montgomery was sick the entire trip, and after five days actually hoped the ship would sink to end his misery. Compounding the sickness was two meals a day of English food, consisting of boiled mutton and hardtack, and the terrible stench below deck caused by excessive vomiting and poor ventilation. The bunks were six high, from deck to ceiling, filled with moaning men. There were no showers, so the nauseous odor the last few days at sea was a mixture of body odor from the hot sticky woolen uniforms and stale cigarette smoke. Even the sturdiest of men were reduced to miserable, convulsive blathering.

At last, on April 18th, the ships berthed in the Firth of Forth, Scotland. Ed was still sick and weak, but dragged his sixty-pound duffle to the deck, where the men climbed over the rail to scramble down a cargo net to small ships that bobbed below. When they finally reached the docks and helped one another climb to the landing wharf, the men let out a cheer. Finally there was something stable to stand on. When the sergeant called for the men to form ranks, Ed threw his duffel over the shoulder of his six-foot three-inch frame and marched off like a new man. The soldiers discovered new energy in clean air and stable "terra firma."

MONTGOMERY • CHAPTER 3

The 312th Field Artillery Battalion to which Ed Montgomery was assigned was made up of four Artillery Batteries; A, B, C, D, plus a Service Battery and a Headquarters Battery. Each of the four batteries was comprised of eight 155mm artillery cannons. There were eight men to a gun crew and each battery had a 'medic" or first aid man assigned to it. Private Montgomery joined one of the artillery batteries. The cannon, mounted on a carriage with rubber wheels, were pulled by a special vehicle. In addition, the battery utilized several six-by-sixes (six wheels, with six wheels powered), jeeps, and several weapons carriers. Obviously, it was highly mechanized and required additional service vehicles for gasoline, oil, and repairs.

During the remainder of April and part of May, the 79th Division, along with many other U.S. Army units, trained in the field for the long awaited invasion of Hitler's "Fortress Europa." Artillery practice, cleaning equipment, and troop maneuvers were repeated and reinforced day after day. In late May, 1944, the 79th Division boarded trucks, joining thousands of other American, British and Canadian soldiers destined for Plymouth, Falmouth, and Southampton, embarkation ports in southern England.

The Division was ready to embark on the 6th of June (D-Day) in the largest armada in history, to back up the first waves of American troops that landed on the beaches of Normandy. Major General I. T. Wyche, the Commanding Officer of the 79th Division, wrote a message to be read to all men in his Division on that day..

"This division is now headed for the battlefield. After two years of training, I consider this division adequately trained for battle and feel perfectly confident it will accomplish it's mission with distinction

"In order to add to your effectiveness, I desire each of you to get yourself in a state of hatred against the Hun so that you will approach the battlefield mad as hell. Your state of mind should be that of the hunter who is bent on exterminating vermin and predators. There is one resolution that I want each of you to make and that is, to so conduct yourself in the first fight that the Boche and all of our allies will be impressed with the veteran performance of the 79th Division.

"May all of you have good crossing. I shall be on the beach to welcome you."

On June 10th, 1944, D-Day+4, the 79th Division boarded several LSTs to cross the English Channel to land on Omaha Beach of Normandy,

Ed Montgomery was assigned to an artillery unit, which often fought long distance engagements. This meant he treated more shrapnel wounds than bullet wounds. (Photo-U S Army)

a beach that was bathed in blood just a few short days previously. Private Ed Montgomery rode ashore with first aid kit in hand, praying he would never have to open it. However, he knew his compatriots intended to hunt down and kill the enemy, and that the enemy had absolutely the same intent.

The men moved inland about one mile, dispersed their equipment, and dug foxholes for their first night in France. After dark, planes of the German Luftwaffe attacked Allied ships off Utah Beach. With tracer bullets flying in all direction, it resembled a spectacular Fourth of July celebration. The men crawled out to sit on the edge of their foxholes to watch the extraordinary display; that is, until spent .50 caliber shells from Allied ships started falling around their position. The men scrambled back to their foxholes and hunkered down for the rest of the night.

The hedgerows of Normandy stood fifteen to twenty feet above the nearby dirt farm roads, which made it difficult to advance against the enemy. Each hedgerow was a battle unto itself, and some of the major casualties resulted from infantry skirmishes a few hundred feet apart. In the battery's first engagement, two infantry companies from the 79th Division were advancing through the battery for night patrol and to establish a new

Medics had to make instant decisions, under less than ideal circumstances, how to treat wounds or worse yet, who would be treated. (Photo-U S Army)

skirmish line. As they passed through the battery encampment, several enemy artillery shells suddenly landed in the middle of the troops. Immediately men began screaming, some calling for "medic," others groaning or crying. In the pitch-black darkness, Montgomery inserted a small pocket flashlight between his teeth and began looking for the men. The first soldier he came across had a large chunk of his skull missing, and his head was bleeding profusely. Ed immediately made the decision the man was beyond help and continued searching the area. He found men in various states of injury. He remembered the admonition "to first stop the bleeding!" and cut open the clothing of one soldier to expose the wounds. Applying pressure to stop the blood flow, he taped compresses in place and checked for other injuries on each soldier he found. As he moved among the screaming men, a soldier joined him who helped clean the wounds, giving Ed a chance to sprinkle sulfa and apply bandages. After tending to the men, they discovered three men were dead and eleven wounded. The wounded who could not walk were placed on litters and moved back to ambulances that would take them to an aid station.

When Pvt. Montgomery turned to thank his helper, he discovered it was Captain Frost, the Artillery Battery Commander. Although not a medic, the Captain gave valuable assistance and seemed to anticipate what treatment would be necessary. After this first terrifying night, Montgomery had a new respect for Captain Frost, and they became good friends for the duration of the war.

Ed finally turned in about 3:30 AM, and was sound asleep at dawn's first light. A soldier approached Captain Frost looking for the medic, as he had cut his hand on sharp metal while opening a C-ration. The Captain was not particularly sympathetic since his medic was up half of the night tending to seriously wounded men, and said, "You go suck on the cut for a couple of hours and I'll send the medic around when he wakes up!"

It should be noted that in many standing professional armies of the day, there existed a very strict no-fraternization policy between the officers and men. However, in the American Army, a wartime army made up of men from every social class and state in the union, the separation between the two groups was often blurred in combat conditions, with close friendships developing between some of the officers and the men.

While the hedgerows made for difficult fighting, they also created problems in recognizing the enemy. One of the more frightening experiences for Pvt. Montgomery happened when an American P-38 fighter plane failed to recognize the American soldiers and strafed the 79th

Fighting in the hedgerows was extra difficult, since one never knew what was on the other side of the foliage. (Photo-U S Army)

Division. As Montgomery crouched behind a hedgerow, the plane made a pass firing his six 50 caliber machineguns, cutting off hedgerow branches only a few inches above his head. Ed was afraid to lie down on the ground, because at six foot four, he made an even bigger target. Fortunately, the pilot found a better target down the road, and ripped into the hedgerows about a half-mile away.

The 79th Division worked its way east toward the vital port of Cherbourg, along with the 4th Division and the 9th Infantry Division. Ed's job as Battery Aid Man expanded to not only first stop the bleeding, but to patch them up and call for a jeep to transport the injured back to an aid station. Most of the wounded were from snipers, artillery, or strafing from German aircraft. Unfortunately, Ed kept very busy.

After the capture of Cherbourg, the 79th turned south toward the French town of Avranches. Ed was assigned a new job as a litter jeep driver. He designed and built a litter carrier with strap steel he found in Cherbourg, providing support for one litter across the back of the jeep and providing for two litter carriers over the engine. This design also enabled him to administer plasma while he was delivering wounded to the rear. The arrangement worked so well it was assigned to another jeep driver, so Ed had to improvise another one for his own use. Late one evening Ed was scouting for wounded near Avranches, and got lost. Without realizing it, he drove through a section of the town occupied by the Germans, finally managing to find his way back to American lines. He is not certain the Germans saw him, or if they honored the large white cross on his helmet and jeep. Needless to say it scared the hell out of him, and he was thankful not to be taken prisoner or shot.

The 79th Division left Avaranches, turned east toward Paris and fought it's way to the city limits, only to have their advance officially delayed, so General Le Claire and the French Army could have the glory and pleasure to free their capitol city.

The 79th Division was the first to get to the Seine River and establish a bridgehead. Once the engineers had built a bridge, most of the division got across before the German aircraft destroyed it. Fortunately, one of the units that crossed was an anti-aircraft battery (called the triple A's) that had a field day shooting down approximately sixty Messerschmitt-109s in a ten-day period. Many of the wounds Ed treated resulted from spent anti-aircraft shells falling on the troops. Eight or nine German aircraft crashed close to their position, with their pilots parachuting into the area. Ed rushed to provide first aid to the German pilots, as many had burned hands and faces that they received before they bailed out. They received the best American medical attention.

The Americans who crossed the Seine were now isolated in an area of two or so square miles, and for seven days were under constant attack. The Seine River made a large loop in this part of France, and the 79th Division was cut off, contained in the bottom of the loop. German Panzer units were located on the high ground, and three German tiger tanks were firing their 88mm guns into the troops dug into a forest area below. In a small clearing at the edge of the trees, a battery of the 155mm artillery was returning fire. Close by, a six by six truck loaded with artillery shells was being unloaded by Private Black. Suddenly, Pvt. Black was blown off the truck by a blast of shrapnel from a nearby explosion and seriously wounded. Another soldier raced to the truck and drove it back into the shelter of the trees, leaving Private Black exposed to further shelling.

Ed Montgomery responded by driving his litter jeep up a narrow tree-lined road, into the clearing, driving across the front of the American artillery for several hundred yards to park in front of the wounded soldier. As he leapt out of the opposite side of the jeep to begin first aid, an explosion rocked the jeep, spraying it with shrapnel and blowing out one tire. Fortunately, the jeep protected the medic, who discovered Black's leg was shattered and his main leg artery severed. Stopping the bleeding, Ed fashioned a splint to immobilize the leg and was able to roll him over onto a litter. Somehow he managed to lift the wounded man and litter to a front litter support, strapped him in place, and jumped behind the wheel. Starting the jeep, he drove through the falling shells, across the front of the American battery that continued to fire, and turn down the road to safety. Fighting the steering wheel while driving with the flat front tire, he delivered Private Black to a first aid tent where he received immediate aid. Black could not be taken out by ambulance, since Germans surrounded the division.

For his bravery in the face of intense enemy fire, Captain Frost, the Artillery Battery Commander, recommended Private Ed Montgomery for the Silver Star, the third highest honor the Army can bestow, after the Medal of Honor and the Distinguished Service Medal. However, Captain Deming, the Medical Commander, downgraded the as the recommendation to a Bronze Star. Deming did not feel the unarmed and non-combatant medics should be awarded such high medals; they were only doing their job. A heated argument took place, overheard by men standing outside the tent, and finally, in a fit of rage, Captain Frost shouted, " Captain Deming, you are a cheap-assed son of a bitch!" However, Captain Deming won out, recommending Private Montgomery for the Bronze Star.

The 79th Division remained trapped in the Seine loop for seven more days, finally fighting their way out of entrapment, aided by a British division that somehow arrived one week later than expected. Joining with other American divisions, they established a new frontal assault and proceeded to push the defending Germans back.

Two weeks later, Private Montgomery was told to put on his Class A uniform; he would be part of an award ceremony presided over by General George Marshall, Army Chief of Staff, who was visiting the front. Unfortunately, General Marshall could not make the presentation, so French General Le Claire, in front of an assembled group of field soldiers in dirty battle uniforms, pinned the Bronze Star on Private Montgomery's blouse.

Captain Deming, aware of the leadership role Private Montgomery displayed, determined he had been a private long enough and decided to submit his name for promotion. However, the Captain felt he should be promoted to a higher rank that one or two of the other medics in his charge. Since an advancement in rank could not be made on one leap, he promoted Montgomery one rank per day: first Corporal; the next day buck Sergeant; and finally on the third day, Staff Sergeant. Ed received the new stripes each day and was told to display them, so he used a safety pin to attach them to his uniform, until he could sew the Staff Sergeant stripes on permanently.

Located east of Paris, the 79th Division was now on the move into the Alsace-Lorraine area, passing through the champagne capital of France. They would remain in the area of Luneville in the northeastern part of France from mid-September through mid-October of 1944. The medics slept on the ground like the soldiers, rolled up in blankets along the hedgerows or in foxholes. The medics had an advantage, however; they always had a three-quarter ton truck to haul medical supplies, blankets, sleeping bags, and personal gear, including clean dry stockings. The soldiers lived on K-rations, dry food in a paper carton, C-rations in metal cans containing some pre-prepared food, or D-rations, consisting of a large chocolate bar. Once a week, when a mess company could be moved up to the front lines, they were served a hot meal of meat, potatoes, gravy, vegetable and maybe some type of cake dessert. Every three weeks a portable shower was set up so the men could have a cold shower, and a new change of clothing provided, much needed since those worn were getting "ripe."

Fortunately, the artillery units were not in constant combat, face to face with the enemy as infantrymen were. Usually a few hundred yards from the front, the battery was always in danger from artillery skirmishes, but not subjected to the constant daily/hourly pressure to attack and push back the Germans. These kids from Iowa, and New Jersey, and Alabama serving in the infantry, became mean, tough fighting men, who pulled their helmets down over unshaven, dirty faces to assault and defeat a combat-hardened, experienced German Wermacht. Their life was far more difficult.

As a medic, Montgomery learned quickly to deal with death and seriously wounded men. Badly wounded men would shake violently, easily slipping into shock, their fingernails and lips turning snow-white as blood flowed down to the stomach and away from their extremities. He learned to immediately stop the bleeding; elevating legs and feet to be certain blood flowed back to the head. He was nineteen years old, making on-the-spot decisions as to which wounded man had a marginal chance to survive, and which would receive medical aid. He did not have time to moralize or reflect about the situation in which he had to perform. He knew the battery was counting on him to be as effective as he could in taking care of them. He was given a job to do, and he carried it out to the best of his abilities, hoping it would soon end, and he could once again walk the fields and streams of peaceful Carroll County.

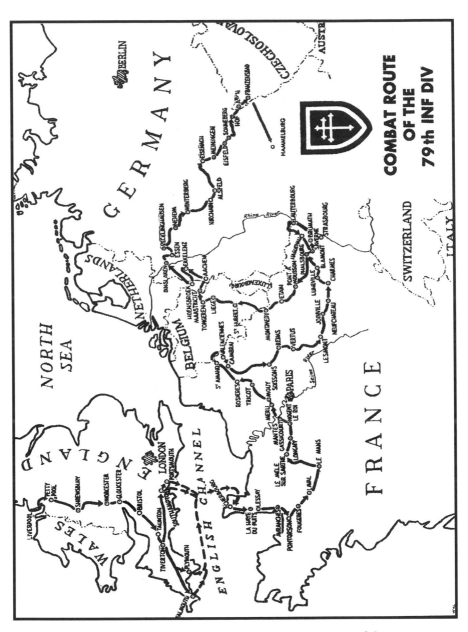

The combat trek of the 79th Infantry Division across France and Germany.
(Map-History of the 79th Division)

MONTGOMERY • CHAPTER 4

One of the toughest jobs for Sergeant Montgomery, and the one he dreaded the most, was "tagging the dead," which he did hundreds of times during the war. The dead were usually left in the field or hauled into clearings, as combat units fought and moved ahead. After a few hours the dead would turn black, always a very sobering sight. The task of the medic was to identify and tag the bodies. Information would include the man's name and rank, date of death, vicinity or locale, and the cause of death. While it was a tough job, Montgomery felt that if he did not take the time to properly record everything, a family would have no record of how and where their loved one died on the battlefields of Europe.

Another task was driving wounded back to the Division Clearing Station where surgical teams determined if the wounded would be immediately treated or sent back to the rear where hospitals were available. On one occasion Ed had to drive his jeep, with a wounded man on a litter, down a deserted dirt road to the Clearing Station. Since some areas were not fully secured from the Germans, an armed Military Policeman was assigned to accompany him. The young MP was so scared he was crying as they drove along with the wounded man. Once at the Clearing Station, Colonel Charles, the Battalion Chief Surgeon, asked Montgomery when was the last time he had hot food. Ed said it had been several days, but he could not stay since had to get back to his unit. The Colonel replied, "Hell, you can't go back the way you came, because the road is closed and controlled by the Germans. Get some hot chow and grab some sleep on that pile of blankets over there." Ed replied he did not want to get into trouble with Captain Deming back at the front. The Colonel stated, "I'll take care of Captain Deming. You go to sleep!"

Occasionally, Montgomery was called upon to treat members of a tank corps or tank destroyer group who were hit during battle. Infantrymen called tanks "coffins on wheels," as they were difficult to exit when hit by artillery. Any surviving men generally suffered severe burns that had to be treated with great care. Tank destroyers did not have the thick armament that tanks had, and often men were wounded from a single penetrating bullet that rattled around in the interior until its energy was spent. One tank soldier was burned so badly he lost his eyelids and ears, and had to have reconstructive surgery after he returned to the states.

In December of 1944, the Germans launched a surprising, massive attack on the thinly stretched American troops in the Ardennes Forest in Belgium. The ensuing battle, known as the "Battle of the Bulge," took place from mid-December through Christmas, when the skies finally cleared and American airpower was able to drop supplies to the surrounded GIs and resume attacking the Germans from the air. The 79th Division was ordered to move into the Bulge area to relieve the 101st Airborne Division, desperately hanging on against the invaders. The 79th Division was a part of General Patton's Third Army that rushed to aid the surrounded soldiers. When they arrived, the breakthrough was repelled, and the main thrust was now in retreat, with bitter fighting every inch of the way. The Americans had stopped Hitler's last serious offensive of the war. The Germans would now present a vicious defense protecting their homeland from advancing Allied troops.

The Commanding Officer did not tolerate the consumption of any alcohol during combat operations and anyone caught doing so was court-martialed. Officers had access to a liquor ration, but observed the admonitions of the Commanding Officer, since they were the leaders to set the example. One night after a particularly bad day in the field, Montgomery worked late assisting wounded to the rear, and when he returned to the base area, he was told to see the C.O. As the medic entered the C.O.'s tent, he was offered a shot of whiskey "for medicinal purposes" so he could sleep better during the night. It became a ritual after major engagements where there were excessive casualties.

While in Eindhoven, Holland, about twenty miles from the German border, some of the soldiers were invited into residents' homes. The residents were not particularly fond of the French and Germans, but were very friendly towards the American soldiers. Montgomery met a young man who had trained for the diplomatic corps, and earned two University degrees. The young man located a motorcycle with a sidecar, bought gas on the black market, and invited Ed to tour some of the surrounding villages. The local residents were very low on food, and when Ed and the young man discovered a basement with food stored for future use, they returned to Eindhoven loaded down with canned goods, which they distributed among the citizens. After the war, Ed got a three-day pass and returned to Eindhoven where citizens turned out in great numbers to thank him for supplying the food. Ed responded in kind by filling his steel helmet with cigarettes, passing them out though the crowd. He thought they were very nice, gracious, people.

Crossing the Rhine River was the last major obstacle before entering

Germany's heartland. The 79th Division had practiced its strategy for crossing the river many times, and would now attempt the major undertaking. Building a bridge across the wide, swift Rhine would be difficult at best. The Americans lined up sixty batteries along the riverbank, representing over four hundred eighty 155mm cannon, as well as numerous tanks. Setting up a "rolling barrage," the artillery fired in unison, then clicked the sights up one notch and fired again, and again, and again. The subsequent continuous firing literally cleared the area of all matter, living and dead, and permitted the installation of several bridges across the fast-flowing Rhine by the Engineer Corps. When the 79th Division and other divisions crossed to the other side, there was little opposition, and any surviving defenders were in a complete state of shock from the rolling barrage. The entry into Germany was successfully accomplished with a minimum of casualties due to the intense concentration of artillery fire.

The 313th Regiment of the 79th Division had the honor to capture Alfred Krupp, head of Germany's largest munitions industry. The collapse of the German army was imminent, and soldiers began surrendering in large numbers, due to lack of food and ammunition. The Air Force successfully eliminated Germany's ability to distribute food, goods and supplies, by dominating the railroads and road system. The end of the war was in sight as resistance to Allied advances disintegrated. On one occasion, Ed and another medic were in the Ruhr Valley, when they observed German soldiers on the bluffs overlooking the valley. Montgomery called to them to come down, and suddenly two hundred very hungry soldiers walked toward them. Montgomery told the German officer to stack arms, and they would have food and water delivered. Over one hundred thousand German soldiers were reported to be surrounded in the Ruhr Valley, and they soon surrendered to the Allied forces.

On May 8th, 1944, word was received that Germany had formally surrendered and the bloody war in Europe was finally over. There was some celebrating, with wine, beer, and schnapps generously liberated.

The 79th Division occupied an area known as Lower Franconia, formerly known as Bavaria, with population centers in Aschaffenburg, Wurzburg, and Schweinfurt. The Division patrolled the countryside, looking for stray pockets of resisters, usually fanatic SS or Gestapo troops. They also helped set up military government in the local communities.

Sergeant Montgomery and his crew moved into a nice Bavarian Hotel and set up a non-commissioned officers' club. American whiskey was readily available, but good German beer was nowhere to be found. The local brewer was a belligerent Nazi, who refused to cooperate with the Americans. Sgt. Montgomery paid him a visit, and arrested the man's brother, placing him in jail. A few days later the beer maker made a special plea for his brother to be released, so Ed struck a deal to free the brother if the manufacturer would deliver a barrel of beer on Thursday morning at 10:00 AM. The beermaker reluctantly agreed. This made Ed a local hero with the soldiers, until the Commanding Officer heard about it. Ed put the beer on a cart and covered it with a canvas tarp. When the C.O. arrived, he asked what was under the tarp. Montgomery replied, "Sir! There is a barrel of beer under the tarp!" The C.O. said, "Sergeant, you have forty-eight hours to get rid of that beer!" The soldiers did their best to comply.

Sergeant Montgomery and his crew were also given the task of rounding up members of the Hitler Youth Movement. Given the names of the young people, they visited their homes to make arrests. The hatred that had been instilled in the twelve and thirteen year old boys was terrifying; they would kill the Americans if given the chance. As a result, the youth were placed in underground bunkers under guard until a Youth Camp staff could be organized together to deal with them.

As part of the medical service, the doctors and Ed also had the responsibility of ensuring that POWs and thousands of Displaced Persons (DPs), Russians, Poles, Czechs, and others, were given adequate medical care. As a result, they visited Leisenbonn Hospitals in Bavaria. It was in these hospitals that pure Aryan German girls went to have babies fathered by SS troops, those deemed by the Third Reich to be of pure Germanic blood, worthy fathers of the next generation of the "super race." These attractive young girls were honored to have babies for Hitler and the "Thousand Year Reich."

During this period Staff Sergeant Montgomery was offered a Battlefield Commission as a Second Lieutenant in the Medical Administrative Corps by Captain Deming who had become a close friend. Staff Sergeant Montgomery now had nineteen men working under him, and was not certain he wished to remain in the service. Also, the 79th Division would soon be transferred to the Pacific to fight the Japanese. He noticed Medical Administrative Officers had a high rate of attrition. Ed felt very comfortable with his staff, giving these men orders and ins turn being responsible for their duties and actions. He later proved his capabilities in Sturkod, Germany, establishing a hospital to process Russian soldiers.

Near their area was a prisoner-of-war camp for die-hard Nazi SS soldiers awaiting trial for war crimes. Each week, Sgt. Montgomery would visit the camp to determine if they needed medical supplies. Part of the procedure was for a SS officer to come out of the hospital and stand outside when Ed went inside. The message given was that if any harm came to Montgomery while inside, the SS officer would be shot on the spot. As a small measure to ensure the Nazis understood they lost the war, whenever Sgt. Montgomery entered the hospital, the wounded were to get out of their beds and stand at attention. It was standard procedure when an officer entered the room, but to do it for an American non-commissioned officer added further insult to injury for the fanatical Nazi and SS soldiers.

Ed came across an alleged SS soldier who was fluent in several languages, who pleaded he was forced to serve the SS as an interpreter, and was not a Nazi or a part of the SS. Checking the man's records, Ed found out he was telling the truth, and pulled him out of the hospital to make him his own personal interpreter.

When Sergeant Montgomery attempted to help Dr. Levitas return to Russia, it was a single, isolated incident that typified the kindness, generosity, and decency of the average American soldier. It explains why, when the American soldiers entered a liberated or vanquished village, the civilian population was not in fear of being assaulted, robbed, or raped as exemplified by the armies of Japan, Russia, or Germany. The intrinsic goodness and values of the Americans were demonstrated repeatedly. The soldiers were not interested in the spoils of war or wanton retribution through destruction of enemy civilian property. To the contrary; when soldiers moved into a town, they gave the children candy bars, chewing gum, and Christmas parties. Occupation of a country did not include murder, terror, and destruction. The average GI was only interested in ending the war as soon as possible, and going home.

While stationed in Czechoslovakia, the 79th Division Artillery Units were given the task of processing and releasing German Prisoners of War. Artillery personnel established a large camp at the local airport outside Cheb. Approximately forty thousand enemy soldiers were in the camp, and the problems associated with feeding, housing and guarding them was a monumental task for the artillerymen and medics. However, as usual, the Army got the job done and gradually the POWs were processed, released and told to find their way home. The Nazis, SS Officers, and others accused of war crimes were detained, and ultimately put on trial at Nuremberg, Germany.

A new First Lieutenant reported to the Medical Detachment. To acquaint him with the operation, Sgt. Montgomery showed him around the medical area and reviewed the reports on supplies and number of treated patients. After an hour of touring the facility, the Lieutenant said, "Sergeant, I am not a doctor. I am a motor pool officer. They are filling out the roster for shipping us back to the United States."

One day the new Lieutenant approached Ed with a request. "Sergeant, I want to go into town and get drunk. However, as an officer I can not do that. We are about the same size. Let's exchange uniforms for a day. You can go to the Officers club in town, and I can have a good time." Ed agreed to the arrangement, so they traded uniforms, and Ed provided a jeep that the Lieutenant/Sergeant drove to town. The Lieutenant/Sergeant dropped Ed off at the officers Club, gave a snappy salute, and drove away. Ed checked into the Officer's Club, had a good night's sleep, and the next morning went into the dining room, found a table, and ordered breakfast. Two officers sat down at the next table, and Ed discovered one was Major Savonis, from the Artillery Battery. The Major glanced at Ed but never acknowledged him. Later in the day, Ed received word that the frisky Lieutenant/Sergeant had gotten into a fight in a tavern, broken furniture, and was in jail. Montgomery went to the jail and arranged for the Lieutenant/Sergeant to be signed into his custody. When offered the clipboard, Ed signed his name as Lt. John Doe, 999th Mess Kit Repair Shop. They found the jeep and the Lieutenant/Sergeant drove back to their quarters, with a monstrous headache. A few days later, Ed went to Major Savonis and told him the whole story. The Major, keeping the event in perspective, got a big laugh out of it.

Medics were not line soldiers, so they were not included in the reveille report. One evening, some of Ed's contingent used the jeep to pick up some girls, and drove into the ditch on the way back. Returning to their quarters, they woke up Ed in the middle of the night to explain what had happened. Ed called a friend at the motor pool, who immediately went to the outskirts of town to tow the jeep back with a wrecker, and started work on it. The motor pool replaced the engine, straightened the fenders, repaired the bumper, touch painted it, and had it ready for 10:00 AM inspection. They did an outstanding job, and as Ed observed, it helps to know who your friends are.

While the Division was training to transfer to the South Pacific, Ed did not feel particularly well, and one day, with some difficulty, passed a kidney stone. The next morning he had difficulty getting dressed, and was helped to the hospital where he described his symptoms to a young doctor. The doctor stepped behind him and tapped him on the kidney. Ed woke up in the hospital two days later, and remained there for some time, recuperating. It was ironic that he might complete his own tour of duty in a hospital, where he had sent so many young men.

When word was received in late August that Japan had surrendered, there was tremendous relief felt by every soldier in Europe and around the world. It ended the prospect of shipping out to the Pacific where casualties would have dwarfed those in Europe. The experiences at Iwo Jima and Okinawa forecast a long and bloody campaign in the Japanese Islands' homeland. The atomic bombs dropped at Hiroshima and Nagasaki not only saved millions of American casualties, but also saved the Japanese as a people and a nation.

When it came time to return to the United States, Sergeant Montgomery realized that he was a unique member of the "five percent club." Of the original division of over twelve thousand men, only five percent had survived. The statistics were appalling:

- Killed in action: 2,475
- Wounded in Action: 10,971
- Later died of wounds: 476
- Captured or missing in action: 1700
- Disease and non-battle injuries: 14,875
- Prisoners of war captured: 35,466

Traveling to the Port of Marseilles, France, in late November 1945, Staff Sergeant Ed Montgomery finally boarded a Victory ship headed back to the United States. For some reason, seasickness on the way home was almost welcome. When they arrived at Newport News, Virginia, the men stowed their gear and were marched to a theater where a Major started to give a "welcome home speech." However, he made the mistake of mentioning that after the presentation, t-bone steaks would be served at the mess hall down the street. Slowly the men began to filter out, and before long, the Major was talking to an empty house.

After initial processing, Ed boarded a train for Camp Grant, Illinois, where his Army duty had started, and final processing would be carried out. By now it was December, and the soldiers were told not to go to Chicago to catch a train because there are twenty-five thousand soldiers, sailors and marines all trying to get home for Christmas. As Ed was leaving the camp, a First Lieutenant sitting in a car motioned him over. Ed thought, "What the hell have I done wrong now?" The Lieutenant asked where he was headed, and Ed replied, "Carroll, Iowa!" The Lieutenant said, "I'm going that way. If you know any others, grab 'em and let's go!"

Ed called to two other soldiers, and the three piled into the car and headed west. One man got off at Savannah, Illinois, and the other in Des Moines. When they reached Carroll, it was raging blizzard. But on Christmas Eve, 1945, Ed stepped out of the car in front of his mother's home, after having been gone twenty-one months. It was a wonderful homecoming for the Montgomery family.

The Lieutenant intended to drive on to Sioux City, but the storm forced him to stay in Carroll. He called a distant relative who lived there, and spent his first night in Iowa as a guest in Sharp's Funeral Home.

Mary Rita and Edwin Montgomery on their wedding day, January 5th, 1946.

MONTGOMERY • CHAPTER 5

The Lincoln Club was a favorite hangout for the young people in Carroll who wanted a quiet place to have a drink in the late afternoon, or to jitterbug on Tuesday, Thursday and Saturday nights to local bands. The young folks visited the club every afternoon about five PM to see who had returned from service with wild and crazy stories, or who talked about some of the crazy people they had served with. Checking out the Carroll girls was also a full-time activity, and lining someone up for the next "wedding dance" kept them busy. Every German Catholic wedding in Carroll County always included a wedding dance and lots of beer. Carroll County never dried up during prohibition, and in most families the drinking age was twelve, but done under very watchful eyes.

Ed Montgomery was back working for Langenfeld Studios painting churches. The opportunity to mix subtle tones of paint, the steady routine of stenciling, adding embellishing colors and gold leaf, all were once more exciting.

It was time for happy hour, and as he pulled his brother's Packard sedan into a parking stall in front of the Lincoln Club, he saw a high school acquaintance. He had not seen or thought about Mary Rita Schapman since he graduated from Carroll High. However, she was always special because she was the first girl he ever asked to dance. It took place in the basement of a private home made into a "Teen Club," where young folks could hangout after school before they went home to do chores. Ed was a gangly freshman or sophomore, and it took a lot of nerve to dance, let alone ask a girl to dance.

Ed bounced out of the Packard and asked Mary Rita if he could buy her a cocktail, but she replied she had an appointment and could not join him. Ed then said, "Tex Beneke and the Glen Miller Orchestra is playing at the Cobblestone Inn in Storm Lake tonight. Do you want to go?" Mary Rita could certainly not turn down an opportunity to hear Tex Beneke. He picked her up at 7:00 PM for the hour's drive north.

Ed Montgomery and Mary Rita Schapman were married January 5th, 1945, in St. Lawrence Catholic Church in Carroll. Once again, half of Carroll County turned out for the wedding dance.

Ed continued working for Langenfeld Studios until Langenfeld retired; then in 1979 he started Montgomery Specialty Company, carrying on the tradition. He kept very busy, painting church interiors in a four state area, until he retired in 2004.

Mary Rita and Ed had three children; Deborah born August 9th, 1947, Marla Ann born October 19th, 1953, and Mark L. born October 12th, 1957. One boy died in childbirth.

In later years, Ed looked back on his family and realized that while working sixty hours a week, usually out of town, he did not get to see his family grow up as he would have liked. Running his own business with several employees certainly demanded much of his time. He knew what had to be done, and he did it, just as he had assumed responsibility in the service. One day he looked at his son who had just turned twenty. He reflected on the things he had done by the age of twenty, and asked the age old question: "Could my son do what I did in service?" There is no answer, of course, but every generation appears able to respond to our nation's demands. Ed was in charge of many men and ordered them to do things that were not safe. But he never asked a soldier to do what he had not done, or would not do.

Ed Montgomery served in campaigns in Normandy and Northern France, the Rhineland, and Central Europe. His awards include:
- Three Overseas Service Bars,
- American Campaign Medal,
- European-African-Middle Eastern with four Bronze Battle Stars,
- Good Conduct Medal,
- The World War II Victory Medal,
- And The Bronze Star.

The awards or rewards not listed are the "thank yous," not expressed by the young men who met Ed Montgomery only briefly: by touch and tourniquet, gauze and syringe, comforting words and compassion, and occasionally a wild jeep ride to an Aid Station. Ed Montgomery never fired a shot in anger, but was most certainly angered by those who tried to steal life from his comrades and friends. Those friends were rewarded with Ed's dedication, courage, and intense sense of personal responsibility.

POSTLUDE

After completing three books of biographies of World War II veterans, a number of calls were received by the author asking, "Have you ever met…?" or "Have you talked to…?" These names were dutifully recorded in a notebook, with some uncertainty as to whether or not they would be contacted about their military experiences.

One day a friend called indicating he kept his fishing boat in storage in the small town of Fernald, IA, where he met a fellow who was stationed at Pearl Harbor when it was bombed. A visit to Fernald to meet Ralph Corbin determined he was not only at Pearl Harbor, but was sitting on the fantail of the USS Arizona when it was bombed. This interview was the impetuous prompting a follow-up interview on several of the other names and potential stories recorded in the notebook.

Some amazing correlations emerged. Ralph Corbin was in a gun turret aboard the USS Massachusetts hurling shells over Lt. Bill Stucky who landed on the North African beach with the 3rd Division. When Bill Stucky was involved in seven invasions, Lt. Frank Horn drove Higgins boats toward the beaches in four of them. Lt. John Phillips was in the same prison camp in Germany as Hartley Westbrook (An Iowa Pilot Named Hap) and William Singer (A Neighborhood of Eagles). Bombardier Lt. Melvin Harms bombed Iwo Jima and nearby islands twenty-three times before Corporal Lewis Rich crawled ashore to discover the terrain had been rearranged, but with Japanese defenses substantially undamaged.

The Isle of Capri was the scenic area visited by thousands of soldiers and sailors serving in the Mediterranean as their chief locale for Rest and Recreation (R&R), as were Naples and Pompeii. Years later, these historically scenic locations were remembered almost as much as the combat areas where men fought.

The world travels of sixteen or seventeen million young men and women who left home to move from training areas to fields of operations to battlefields and back again, whether exposed to intense conflict or servicing those in conflict, produced many chance parallels that reflect symbiotic relationships in organizing and carrying out military operations. Each near chance experience, in its own way, exposed each participant to "a full measure" of service in assuring an Allied victory.

ACKNOWLEDGEMENTS

Max Olsen, who served in the 13th Air Force in the South Pacific, generously shared several names of persons included in this book. Max is too modest to have his story told, but acquainted the author with the little recognized 13th "Jungle" Air Force that wallowed about on small isolated islands in the South Pacific for more than three years.

Architect Jeff Fenimore's casual comment, "Yesterday I met this guy who was at Pearl Harbor when it was bombed," rekindled an effort to record WWII experiences.

Donald Mangel's constant, cheery, "How's the book coming?" kept the pressure on the author to diligently pursue the work. His friendship is truly valued.

Richard Lees, (Col. USAF Retired) interviewed and wrote articles about Edwin Montgomery and several other WWII veterans. He was not only kind enough to introduce the author to Mr. Montgomery, but allowed the incorporation of some of his material in relating Edwin Montgomery's unique story.

Conversations with Al Weber of McMillen Publishing are informative, encouraging, and relevant. The newspaper editor, turned publishing executive, heads a list of positive positives. Just don't get him started telling fishing stories.

Once again, Ann Andrews Rudi applied her University of Iowa Commerce Degree in editing the manuscript. Once again, her value is irrefragable, and after four writing efforts, she remains my lovely wife.

BIBLIOGRAPHY

Flags of our Fathers
James Bradley / Ron Powers
Bantam Books May 2004

Fly Boys
James Bradley
Anchor Books 2002

Citizen Soldier
Stephen B. Ambrose
Simon & Schuster - Touchstone
1997

The Last 100 Days
John Toland
Random House New York 1965
(Pg 285 Chapter 17, Task Force Baum)

History of the 30th Infantry Division-WWII
Rupert Prohme
Washington - Infantry Journal Press 1947

History of the 3rd Infantry Division-WWII
Donald G Taggert
Washington - Infantry Journal Press 1947

The New Yorker Magazine
January 6, 1945

Semper Fidelis
English 305 - Essay No. 2
Charles Dekovic 1994

Autobahn to Berchtesgaden
A View of WWII from the Bottom Up
Lt. Col. Sherman W. Pratt
Gateway Press Inc. Baltimore 1992

The Timetables of History
A Horizontal Linkage of People and Events
Bernard Grun
Based on Werner Stein's KULTURFAHRPLAN
Touchstone Book-Simon & Schuster
New York 1963

Reader's Digest Illustrated History of WWII
Pleasantville New York
The Reader's Digest Association 1969

Ghost Soldiers
Hampton Sides
Anchor Books 2002

Spearhead No. 2 - Iwo Jima Edition
Fifth Marine Division
Public Relations Section G-2
1945
(Mailed to the families of those killed or wounded on Iwo Jima)

Somewhere In Italy
Lt. Randall Matson AUS Ret
Privately Published 1986

MLH
(6")